Get the eBooks FREE!

(PDF, ePub, and Kindle all included)

We believe that once you buy a book from us, you should be able to read it in any format we have available. To get electronic versions of this book at no additional cost to you, purchase and then register this book at the Manning website following the instructions inside this insert.

That's it!
Thanks from Manning!

tch!

Gabriel Ford
Sadie Ford
Melissa Ford

ANNING
SHELTER ISLAND

Fountaindale Public Library
Bolingbrook, IL
(630) 759-2102

For online information and ordering of this and other Manning books, please visit www.manning.com. The publisher offers discounts on this book when ordered in quantity. For more information, please contact:

> Special Sales Department
> Manning Publications Co.
> 20 Baldwin Road
> PO Box 761
> Shelter Island, NY 11964
> Email: orders@manning.com

©2018 by Manning Publications Co. All rights reserved.

No part of this publication may be reproduced, stored in a retrieval system, or transmitted, in any form or by means electronic, mechanical, photocopying, or otherwise, without prior written permission of the publisher.

Many of the designations used by manufacturers and sellers to distinguish their products are claimed as trademarks. Where those designations appear in the book, and Manning Publications was aware of a trademark claim, the designations have been printed in initial caps or all caps.

⊗ Recognizing the importance of preserving what has been written, it is Manning's policy to have the books we publish printed on acid-free paper, and we exert our best efforts to that end. Recognizing also our responsibility to conserve the resources of our planet, Manning books are printed on paper that is at least 15 percent recycled and processed without elemental chlorine.

Manning Publications Co.
20 Baldwin Road
PO Box 761
Shelter Island, NY 11964

Development editor: Helen Stergius
Review editor: Aleksandar Dragosavljević
Technical development editor: Robin Dewson
Copyeditor: Corbin Collins
Proofreader: Alyson Brener
Technical proofreader: Gonzalo Fernando Huerta Cánepa
Graphics: Richard Sheppard
Typesetter and graphics: Marija Tudor
Cover designer: Leslie Haimes

ISBN: 9781617294259
Printed in Canada
1 2 3 4 5 6 7 8 9 10 – TC – 22 21 20 19 18 17

To Daddy for showing us a *New York Times*
article about Scratch many years ago and saying,
"This looks cool!"

And to Truman, our Wonder Pig.

Contents

Preface

When we were in first grade, our mother picked us up early from school and told us that our arcade game education started that afternoon. We played *Pac-Man* at Chuck E. Cheese's on a large arcade cabinet while she told us about the games from her childhood. It was hard for us to see because the arcade cabinet was so tall, and we were so short.

Fast forward to fifth grade. We got an Intellivision Flashback machine, and our mother sat us down to play a round of *Astrosmash*. It's a game where colorful asteroids fall down the screen and you shoot them with little white line "bullets." It was her favorite game from childhood, the one that she wanted so badly but had to go over to her friend's house to play.

Although it wasn't complicated compared to the games we play now, it was still a lot of fun to blast the rocks apart and avoid being crushed by the falling debris. Plus it was cool to see what our mother played when she was our age.

And these games played a huge role in the games we have today. All the games we know and love, like *Asphalt 8* and *Candy Crush* and *Monument Valley,* wouldn't be possible without these arcade predecessors paving the way.

We realized we could recreate these games together in Scratch, an open source programming platform maintained by Massachusetts Institute of Technology (MIT), which made our mother happy. But we also realized that we could teach you, too, and you could make your own versions, either with your parents (so they have a reason to drone on and on about video games from when they were your age) or on your own.

In this book, you'll learn how to program your own video games as well as draw your own unique characters. By doing the exercises in this book, you'll also walk away with general programming concepts that will help you even outside of the Scratch environment—concepts like XY coordinates, variables, and conditional statements.

Don't worry if math isn't your strong suit or if you've never written a line of code in your life. This book will give you all the tools you need to get started.

That's what this book is all about. Get ready to dive into game design, pixel art, and programming.

Acknowledgments

We are very grateful to all the people who helped make this book possible. First and foremost, the whole Manning team, especially our fearless development editor, Helen Stergius, and Brian Sawyer and Marjan Bace, for giving two kids a chance. Thanks to all the reviewers whose comments helped make this a better book: Gonzalo Fernando Huerta Cánepa, Jan Vinterberg, Karim Alkama, Khaled Tannir, Larissa Kun, Manjula Iyer, Martin Beer, Meredith Godar, Michael Jensen, Michal Konrad Owsiak, Peter Lawrence, Pavol Kral, Philip Coates, Rebecca Jones, Rocio Chongtay, and Rodney Weis. Thank you to Aleksandar Dragosavljević, Robin Dewson, Gonzalo Fernando Huerta Cánepa, and Matko Hrvatin in development, Corbin Collins, Alyson Brener, Kevin Sullivan, David Novak, Janet Vail, Marija Tudor, Richard Sheppard, Leslie Haimes, and Mary Piergies in production, and Candace Gillhoolley and Susan Harkins in post-production for helping us publish our first book!

Thank you Rick Kughen for being the first person to embrace this book. This book wouldn't be here without you.

Our friends who cheered us on include Emma, who asked how the book was going almost every day, and James for the *Overwatch* breaks. Also all our friends at Coderdojo, including Alex, Megan, Ben, and Finn (plus their awesome parents who run the group—Frank and Josh), for brainstorming ideas and giving us coding advice.

We've had really great teachers over the years, but we especially want to thank Mrs. Siska for teaching us how to read and Ms. Letina for making us love writing.

Thank you to our family! Grandma, who always lets us use her computer, and Grandpa, who gave us his laptop so we could continue the book. To Saba and Safta for all the love and support, plus Olivia, Penelope, Wendy, Jonathan, Randall, Morgan, and all the other people who sent their cheers along the way.

Thank you to Truman for wheeking through every chapter recording (and being the best piggie) and Linus, who joined our family near the end of the book.

Thank you to Daddy, our Peggy, who was the hidden member of our team. You may not see his words in these pages, but his love feeds our creativity and energy. He gives hugs when we're frustrated, knows the right words to say when we're overwhelmed, and makes us laugh with his questions. (Plus he watches *Buffy* with us after a long day's work.)

Thank you to Mommy. If you hadn't decided to be an author, we wouldn't have gotten a chance to become authors, too. You helped us get this book deal *and* you typed up all of this. You are the coolest mother. Thank you for helping us organize our thoughts, turn in pages on time, and for turning an after-school thought into a reality. You taught us how to handle a time-sensitive, high-pressure work environment.

And now to switch gears, this is Gabriel, and I want to thank Sadie for giving me amazing artwork to turn into games and for being a comforting sister throughout the book. I loved working with you on this.

But wait! This is Sadie, and I want to thank my very smart twin brother, Gabriel. It has been fantastic to work with you. Thank you for making fun games for the book. I'm grateful you're my brother.

And finally, this is Melissa. Thank you to Sadie and Gabriel for teaching me Scratch through your wonderful book. Your dad and I are so honored that we get a front row seat to watch you grow up, and you constantly amaze us with your ideas and energy. You are the coolest kids I ever met—from the time when you plucked a loose tooth out of your mouth and kept on interviewing, to teaching people how to make a browser in Java, to being the best travel partners in the world. Here's to many more work meetings at Carmen's. I love you and can't wait to see what you do next.

About this book

Before you dive into learning how to make your own games, we need to tell you a little about the site you'll be using — Scratch.

What is Scratch?

Scratch is a drag-and-drop programming language. *Drag-and-drop* means that there are blocks that are assigned pieces of code, and you stick them together like LEGOs to create a program. It's visual, so you don't have to type lots of brackets and semicolons and weird coding words like "bool." Instead you snap together a brown Events block to a blue Motion block to make things happen.

Although that may sound odd right now, it will make total sense after you read chapter 1 and get familiar with the Scratch workspace.

Scratch is a friendly community with millions of users, and the biggest issue you'll have is to not be distracted by playing other people's projects when you should be making your own. People upload their finished games to the Scratch website where they can be viewed and played by other Scratchers. We'll teach you how to upload your creations, too.

Joining Scratch is free, and you should go over right now (to scratch.mit.edu) and make an account so you'll be ready to make your first project. But wait — first grab a parent so they know the information you're entering online as you sign up.

Navigate to the top right corner of the screen and click the Join Scratch link. This will open a pop-up box that will include the ability to choose a user name and password. Once you sign up, Scratch will send a confirmation email to your parent's email address. Ask them to check it and confirm your account and you'll be on your way.

And what are retro games?

When we use the term *retro games* in this book, what we're talking about is games played on Intellivision, Atari, ColecoVision, and Nintendo, or in arcade cabinets—the sort of games your parents probably played when they were your age.

These games were mostly made in the 1970s and 1980s. Because computers were just getting started at that time, they had blocky, pixelated graphics. The shapes were simple but colorful. The storylines were basic; they mostly involved shooting at asteroids, dodging barrels, or sinking penguins. Usually one task was done at a time, unlike today's games, which make you juggle a lot of things at once.

There are plenty of ways to play retro video games today if you want to play the original games that inspired the ones in this book. The easiest way to access retro games is at an arcade. There are plenty of websites online that you can find with a little Googling that will tell you if there are arcades in your area. Visiting arcades wherever we go is one of our favorite pastimes.

Many old console makers are releasing their games on Flashback-like systems. These small boxes are preloaded with many of the classic Intellivision, Atari, ColecoVision, or Nintendo games. Additionally, app stores sell a lot of these old games for Apple or Android devices. The Midway Arcade app, Atari app, and Activision app have hundreds of games bundled together.

Our favorite games are *Astrosmash*, *Snafu*, *Crown of Kings*, *Utopia*, and *Adventure*.

What types of games will you learn how to make?

There is a reason why we chose retro games. Not only are these early games visually simple with straightforward goals, making them easy to create and easy to play, but they're also the building blocks for all modern games.

What types of games will you learn how to make with this book? You'll start with a two-player ball-and-paddle game, which is one of the oldest types of video game out there. There are two ball-and-paddle games in the book. In these types of games, there is a "ball" that you need to hit against a target. In our first case, you're hitting an egg between two frying pans.

You'll move through the ever-popular shoot-'em-up genre, which includes reflex-testing games and fixed shooters. These games are where enemies are constantly attacking you and you need to defend yourself by shooting them. These enemies may be space ships, asteroids, or even falling ghosts.

There are two platformers, which are games where you move from platform to platform, trying to reach the end of the level.

We'll walk you through the steps of building these games, but once you learn the skills necessary for creating these games, we hope you'll leave our instructions and use your creativity to design your own Scratch projects.

How to use this book

This book is divided into three parts. The first part, "Setting up the arcade," includes the first three chapters. You'll learn your way around the Scratch workspace, how to use the Art Editor, and how to pull together a simple program.

But the most important piece of our book is chapter 3, which introduces you to eight core coding concepts. Starting your program, XY coordinates, conditional statements, loops, variables, Booleans, cloning, and broadcasting: these are elements of all programming languages (including Scratch programming) that will pop up over and over again. In fact, you'll use most of these coding concepts in each of the games you'll make in this book. Chapter 3 gives you a taste of each before you dive deeper into them in later chapters.

Which takes us to the second part of the book: "Turning on the machines." In the next two chapters, you'll make a fun retro-inspired game with a lot of handholding. You'll get step-by-step instructions and reminders on the location of each Scratch tool as you make your game characters, plus you'll read where to find each block as you make your first programs.

Each game is broken down into a two-chapter set. The first chapter teaches you how to make the pixel art necessary for the game, and the second chapter walks you through the code for the game. In each chapter, you'll encounter a few recurring helpful boxes titled Fix It, Learn It, and Answer This. Make sure you don't skip over these sections because they include important facts and tricks that will help you make your games. Don't worry—you don't really need to answer our questions in the Answer This boxes. The questions and answers are provided together and are meant to teach, not quiz, you.

Then there is the third part of the book: "Coding and playing games." The remaining game chapters follow the same format as the ones in part two, with an important distinction: the training wheels are off, because at this point, you'll be familiar enough with Scratch that you can make design decisions and easily find the blocks for your code. By the time you're done with this book, you won't just know how to make five games. You'll also be able to go on and make your own games because you'll understand the basics of computer programming and game design.

Before you jump into making games, you should know that your games won't be playable until you write your final script for each program. But that doesn't mean you have to cross your fingers and hope for the best. The way you check your work is to compare the scripts you create on your screen to the scripts in the book. If they match, you're good to go, and we'll help you make any tweaks in the troubleshooting sections.

You may be inclined to skip over the "Setting up the arcade" chapters. Who doesn't want to jump straight into the game making? But these chapters are super important if you want to understand the rest of the book and become a game programmer. Plus we promise that they're fun and hands-on. You'll play inside Scratch, creating mini programs that will help you understand how all the pieces of your games fit together.

We've also included copies of our sprites on the Manning site that you can download (though we hope you'll make your own!), and you can find all of our code under our Retromakers Scratch account (scratch.mit.edu/users/Retromakers/).

The offline editor

Scratch works best as online software, but that requires an internet connection. If you're in a space where you have trouble connecting to the internet, you can always download the offline editor, which is a Scratch application. If you go this route, your work will only be on your computer, but you can upload it when you get back online. One thing to know is that the offline editor is missing the autosave feature, so save your work early and often.

Using the offline editor requires Adobe Air. Download it from the official Adobe website (get.adobe.com/air). Next, download the offline editor from the Scratch website (scratch.mit.edu/download) for your appropriate operating system (Mac, Windows, or Linux). Finally, run the installer, which will download the application to your computer, and then launch the program called Scratch 2.0.

If you always have an internet connection, the offline editor isn't necessary. But it's a great option if you ever want to work on a project when you don't have access to the internet.

Words you need to know

There are words we toss around in this book that you need to know in order to make your own games.

Sprites are any programmable object in a game. This could be the main character, but it may also be the enemy or a tree or sparks coming out of a wand. Any pixel art you make for your game falls under the category of sprite.

Which brings us to the term *pixel art*. Pixel art is a digital image. It's usually blocky in nature and cartoonish instead of realistic. You will learn the basics of constructing pixel art in this book as well as how to make each of the individual sprites for each game.

Backdrops are the backgrounds for your games. You may have a single, static backdrop, or you may alternate between several backdrops for a platformer. You'll use the Art Editor in Scratch to make your backdrops in the same way that you make your sprites.

Online help

What if you have a question about using Scratch that isn't covered in the book? Manning Publications has provided a free web forum where you can make comments about the book and ask questions. The forum is online here: https://forums.manning.com/forums/hello-scratch. We might be able to answer the question for you, or you might get help from another user. Who knows, you might see a question from a fellow Scratcher that you can answer! We can't guarantee that we will have the time to answer all your questions, but we'll be interested to see the challenges you encounter as you begin creating with Scratch. You can learn more about Manning's forums and the rules of conduct at https://forums.manning.com/forums/about.

Are you ready to start programming?

The most important thing to know about Scratch is that you can't break it. Sure, you may mess up a sprite you're making or forget how you tweaked your code, but you can always go back to the beginning of the chapter and start with a clean slate. What we mean is that Scratch is resilient. Try every single button and block on the site. Exploration is how you learn new things.

We'll walk you through the code step-by-step, but we've also provided plenty of challenges at the end of the game chapters so you can play with what you've learned and make your games uniquely your own. Don't be afraid to leave the well-worn path and see what else you can get Scratch to do after each game is done.

By the way, a word of warning: these games have the power to make your parents talk nonstop about when they were your age. But on the flipside, these projects are educational, so your parents may forget to nag you to do homework while you make your games. If they give you any grief for spending a lot of time on Scratch, remind them that making video games is a great, hands-on way of learning programming skills.

Whether your first exposure to old arcade and console games comes from your parents reminiscing about their Atari and making you watch YouTube videos, encountering sticky arcade games at your local pizza place, or playing the Midway Arcade level in the new game *LEGO Dimensions*, we're glad that you're diving into retro game programming with Scratch.

Let's jump into making your own games.

About the authors

This is where it gets a little confusing, because there are three people writing this book. Let us introduce ourselves so you will get a sense of who is speaking in each section.

I'm Gabriel, and I'm the Code Editor. That means that I programmed the games and wrote the chapters that present the code in the book. I am Happyland440 if you want to find me on Scratch.

I'm Sadie, and I'm the Art Editor. I made all the sprites and backdrops for the games and wrote the chapters that teach you how to make the pixel art in the book. I am Cat1234567 on Scratch.

And I'm Melissa, and I'm their mother, the provider of games and arcade field trips. I shaped the chapters, edited the writing, and served as the chief typist for the book because I have quick fingers from all the video game playing in my youth. All three of us also use the Retromakers account on Scratch.

Part 1

Setting up the arcade

This part covers the first three chapters, which are meant to get you familiar with Scratch. You'll take a virtual tour of the workspace, learning how to use the Art Editor and how to snap together a simple program.

Make sure you don't skip chapter 3, which teaches the eight core coding concepts. This is where you'll learn about starting your program, XY coordinates, conditional statements, loops, variables, Booleans, cloning, and broadcasting. These ideas will repeat in every game chapter, so make sure you set aside time to dive deep into chapter 3, and don't move on until you think you have a basic understanding of these concepts.

Along the way, you'll encounter a few recurring helpful boxes titled Fix It, Learn It, and Answer This. These boxes are meant to teach, not quiz you, so don't feel stressed out about trying to answer questions. Use these boxes to learn important facts and tricks that will help you make your games.

Okay, so you may be thinking right now, "All of this is fine, but I want to get to the game making!" You will, but these first chapters are super important so you don't get lost in the rest of the book. Plus they're hands-on: you'll learn by doing, making mini programs that help you understand how the pieces of games fit together.

1

Getting to know your way around Scratch

Scratch is a drag-and-drop programming language made by the Massachusetts Institute of Technology (MIT). Each *block* (piece of code) is written in ActionScript, Adobe's programming language, which means your game will need Adobe Flash to run. That's important to know because Scratch won't work on any device that doesn't have Flash, such as iPads, so you'll need to work on a computer.

To make a game, you snap the virtual blocks together like LEGOs, and Scratch implements the code behind the scenes to run your program. That's what makes Scratch a visual, drag-and-drop language. MIT programmers assigned pieces of code to each block, and now you can snap those blocks together to create a program.

What can you make with Scratch? The short answer is *anything*. With this book, you'll learn how to make multilevel platformers, fast-paced shoot-em-ups, and reflex-testing games worthy of an arcade. Rather than wait for companies to make the next hot game, *you'll* be the designer making the games everyone wants to play.

Before you begin making games, you need to learn about the various sections of the Scratch workspace. In this chapter, you will learn

- How to navigate the five main areas of the Scratch workspace
- How to locate the tools you'll use when making your games
- How to snap together blocks to build a program
- How to manage your sprites

Think of this chapter as a tour. By taking a moment now to poke around in every nook and cranny of the workspace, you'll be able to quickly dive into coding your games in the following chapters.

Building your first program

Years ago, when I started with Scratch, I had no clue what I was doing. I was teaching myself, which meant spending a lot of time confused, snapping random blocks together. Let me save you a lot of time by showing you around the space so you can jump right into the game making and skip over the stumbling-around-the-workspace part.

Open Scratch by going to https://scratch.mit.edu in your web browser. To be able to save your work, you will need to create a free Scratch account by clicking Join Scratch in the top right corner.

Once you have set up your account and logged in, click the Create button in the top left corner of the homepage. This will take you to the Project Editor screen.

Figure 1.1 shows the five main areas of Scratch: the Block Menu runs down the middle of the screen. The Script Area is the big, grey box on the right side of the screen. The Sprite Zone is the area in the bottom left corner of the screen. The Stage is the big, white box containing the cat. And the Grey Toolbar runs along the top of the screen.

As you read this chapter, look back at this figure if you don't know where to go. Now let's get started moving some blocks from the Block Menu to the Script Area.

Grey Toolbar   Stage   Block Menu

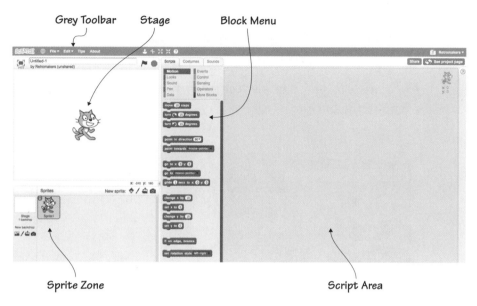

Sprite Zone   Script Area

Figure 1.1   The Scratch workspace is made up of five areas.

Getting started

Look on your Stage, the big, white box on the left side of the screen. You currently have one sprite on the Stage, which is the default cat that appears every time you open a new project. Let's make it move across the Stage, as the cat is doing in figure 1.2.

Figure 1.2   You're going to write a program that will make the cat move in the direction of that arrow.

The way you do this is by writing a program that tells the computer to make the cat move, and the way you write a program in Scratch is by clicking and dragging blocks from the Block Menu to the Script Area.

Navigate to the Block Menu to begin:

1   Click the word Events to switch to the Events block menu.
2   Click the When Flag Clicked block.

3 Hold down the mouse button and drag the block to any space in the Script Area.

4 Release the mouse button.

In figure 1.3, you can see the path the block makes from the Block Menu to the Script Area.

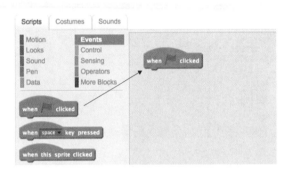

Figure 1.3   To start programming, drag and drop the blocks from the Block Menu to the Script Area.

You've told your program to start when the green flag above the Stage is clicked. Now you need to tell it what you want it to do after the green flag is clicked.

Moving the cat

The cat is standing there on the Stage, which is kind of boring. Let's make the cat move. Navigate back to the Block Menu to write the next step in your program:

1 Click the word Motion to switch to the Motion block menu.

2 Click the Move 10 Steps block.

3 Hold down the mouse button and drag the block underneath the When Flag Clicked block in the Script Area.

4 Move the Move 10 Steps block close to the When Flag Clicked block to see a white strip form on the bottom of the When Flag Clicked block. You can see this white strip in figure 1.4.

Figure 1.4   When the white space appears between the two blocks, you know that they're ready to snap together when you release the mouse button.

5 Release the mouse button so the new block snaps against the existing block. You can see the two blocks together in figure 1.5.

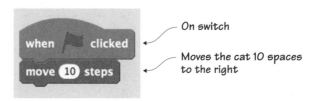

On switch

Moves the cat 10 spaces
to the right

Figure 1.5   The two blocks
work together to make a
small program that moves
the cat 10 steps.

To check your program now that it is finished, click the green flag above the Stage. You should see the cat move slightly to the right. The Green Flag block tells the program to run. The blue Motion block tells Scratch what the sprite should do: move 10 steps.

FIX IT   MY CAT DOESN'T MOVE   What happens if you click the green flag above the Stage, but your cat doesn't move? It means the two blocks in the program aren't snapped together. If the Move 10 Steps block is in the Script Area but isn't touching the When Flag Clicked block, click the Move 10 Steps block again and drag it toward the When Flag Clicked block until you see the white strip appear. Release the mouse button to have the two blocks snap into place.

Each time you click the green flag above the Stage, you should see the cat move 10 steps.

Changing a block

Some blocks are dragged and dropped as is, but other blocks have spaces where you can add other blocks, choose an item from a drop-down menu, or type in a new value. You can change the number *10* inside the Move 10 Steps block by typing in a new value.

FIX IT   HELP! I CAN'T FIND THAT BLOCK!   This is a common situation with Scratch: you're searching the Block Menu for a certain block, and although you see one that's very close to the one I'm talking about here in the book, it has a different number listed in the number bubble or a different name in the drop-down menu area. For example, maybe the block in the Block Menu says Move 10 Steps but here in the book I say it's called Move

100 Steps. Calm down, they're the same block. If I talk about a block and you can't find that exact block in the Block Menu, check if there is a similarly named block. The permanent words on the block will always be the same (such as *Move* and *Steps*), but the changeable words or numbers on the block (such as 10) may be different.

Change the value from 10 to 100 steps:

1   Click inside the white bubble on the Move 10 Steps block.

2   Erase the 10.

3   Type in *100.*

In figure 1.6, you can see the new value in the middle of the Move 10 Steps block.

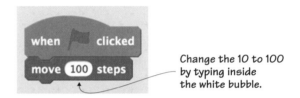

Change the 10 to 100 by typing inside the white bubble.

When you click the green flag above the Stage, you should see the cat take a much bigger

Figure 1.6   **There are plenty of blocks in Scratch that can be changed by typing new information or choosing from a drop-down menu.**

step across the screen because it's now moving 100 spaces at a time instead of 10.

FIX IT   RUNAWAY SPRITES   Click that green flag enough times and your cat will disappear off the right side of the Stage with only a leg and tail showing. Don't worry: you can get the cat back to the left side of the Stage so it can walk across again. You can move any sprite on the Stage in order to position it wherever you want it to begin. Click the cat on the Stage and drag it toward the left side of the Stage while holding down the mouse button. Release the mouse button when your cat is where you want it to begin.

Right now, each time you want the cat to move, you need to click the green flag. You can also set up your program to keep doing the same step over and over again until the program stops.

Continuing a step

You're going to need a lot of room if you're going to program your cat to keep walking until the program ends, so move the cat on the Stage to the far left by clicking and dragging it to a new place on the Stage. (See the *Fix It: Runaway Sprites* box for more information.)

To make the cat continue moving with a single click of the green flag

1 Change the value in the Move 10 Steps block (or, now, the Move 100 Steps block) back from 100 to 10.

2 Move to the Block Menu and click the word Control to switch to the Control blocks.

3 Click the Forever block. It looks like an alligator head, which is appropriate because you're going to make it swallow the Move 10 Steps block.

4 Hold down the mouse button and drag the block underneath the When Flag Clicked block in the Script Area.

5 Move the Forever block close to the When Flag Clicked block to see a white strip form on the bottom of the When Flag Clicked block. The Move 10 Steps block will be underneath the Forever block so you may not see it for a moment.

6 Release the mouse button so the Forever block snaps against the When Flag Clicked block and the Move 10 Steps block is inside the Forever block.

Look at your script. Are your three blocks in the same order as figure 1.7?

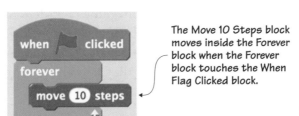

The Move 10 Steps block moves inside the Forever block when the Forever block touches the When Flag Clicked block.

Figure 1.7 Sometimes blocks go inside other blocks in Scratch.

Click the green flag above the Stage to test your program and watch the cat slide smoothly across the screen.

FIX IT   OH NO! THE BLOCKS ARE OUT OF ORDER   If you're having trouble sliding the blocks in the correct order, get rid of the Move 10 Steps block for a moment by dropping it back into the general Block Menu area, and get the Forever block snapped into place. Then reopen the Motion block menu, grab a new Move 10 Steps block, and slide it inside the Forever block.

The Forever block causes the program inside the block to run indefinitely. In this case, it makes the cat keep moving 10 steps until you stop the program by clicking the red stop sign next to the green flag.

ANSWER THIS   WHAT DOES THE STOP SIGN DO?

Question: what happens if you click the stop sign above the Stage while the cat is moving across?

Answer: the cat stops! Reset the cat by dragging it back to the left side of the Stage. Click the green flag to watch the cat start moving. Before it reaches the right side of the Stage, click the red stop sign. Does your cat stop? Try it again, watching the program in the Script Area once the cat starts moving. Do you notice the yellow glow around the program? That means the script is in use. What happens to the yellow glow when you click the stop sign?

You can have more than one sprite on the Stage. Let's add a second sprite so you can see what happens when you start adding multiple sprites to your projects.

Adding a new sprite

Look at the bottom left corner of your screen: your Sprite Zone. This is where all the sprites and backdrops for your games will live once you create them. It's also the space where you'll switch between sprites so you can program each one. Right now, the Sprite Zone only contains that default cat sprite shown in figure 1.8 that launches with all new Scratch projects.

Figure 1.8   All your sprites will live in the Sprite Zone.

You'll fill this area with your own creations that you'll draw in the Art Editor, but right now let's borrow a new sprite from Scratch's built-in sprite menu.

To add a new sprite

1 Click the head icon near the top of the Sprite Zone, to the right of the words New Sprite, as in figure 1.9.

2 Choose the bunch of bananas sprite by double-clicking the picture.

3 Look at the new banana sprite in the Sprite Zone.

Access the premade sprite library by clicking the head icon.

Figure 1.9 The head icon will take you to the premade sprite library.

You should see two sprites in your Sprite Zone, like in figure 1.10. Both sprites will also appear on the Stage.

The blue box is currently around your new sprite, the bananas. When you write a script in Scratch, you're programming a sprite. If you wrote a script right now, you would be programming the bananas because the blue box is around the bananas in the Sprite Zone. Click the cat to make sure you continue to program the cat and not the bananas. The blue box should be around the cat, as in figure 1.11.

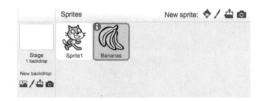

Figure 1.10 You now have two sprites in the Sprite Zone.

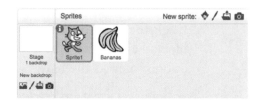

Figure 1.11 The blue box is around the cat sprite in the Sprite Zone, which means the cat will be programmed and not the bananas.

FIX IT THE BANANAS MOVED INSTEAD OF THE CAT! Programming the wrong sprite is the number one mistake Scratchers make. It is super frustrating to put together a program and realize once you click the green flag that you programmed the bananas to walk to the cat instead of the cat to walk to the bananas. Avoid this common mistake by always making sure the blue box is around the correct sprite in the Sprite Zone before you begin programming.

You're now ready to write one last script. Clear the Script Area by dragging the existing script back into the Block Menu and releasing the mouse button. You can do this by clicking the When Flag Clicked block and sliding over all the blocks attached to it at the same time.

Trying unknown blocks

The best part about Scratch is that it's impossible to break. The worst that can happen is that you mess up the program you're working on. (Don't worry: once your programs start getting complicated, you can create a duplicate of your project so you can experiment without messing up your work.) You should try each block to see what happens when you snap it into place, and you should also play around with drop-down menus and values.

To get started, use a different Events block to kick off your project:

1 Click the word Events to switch to the Events block menu.

2 Click the When Space Key Pressed block.

3 Hold down the mouse button and drag the block to any space in the Script Area.

4 Release the mouse button.

5 Click the drop-down menu on the block and choose a different option, such as the letter *a*.

Any time you see a little triangle on a block, it signals that there is a drop-down menu, as you can see in figure 1.12.

Now continue the script by choosing a new block. Do you want your cat to spin around? Go to the Motion menu

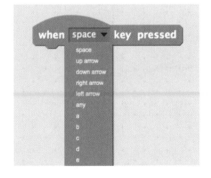

Figure 1.12   A drop-down menu gives the programmer multiple options.

and choose the Turn 15 Degrees block. Want your cat to meow? Go to the Sound menu and choose the Play Sound Meow block.

What program can *you* design by clicking and dragging blocks into place? Try making your own script, setting an option in the When Space Key Pressed block drop-down menu and snapping one or two other blocks to it. To start the program, press the key you designated in the drop-down menu. For instance, if you set it to the space key, press the spacebar on the keyboard to start the program.

Congratulations, you just created your first scripts. Using Scratch is that simple. Although your programs will grow longer as you create complex games, you will still create them all by dragging and dropping blocks into the Script Area.

Let me show you a few more options you need to know in each of the sections of the workspace.

Navigating your way around the screen

You already know everything there is to know about the Script Area and the Stage, but click around the Grey Toolbar, Block Menu, and Sprite Zone to check out a few extra options.

Meeting the Grey Toolbar

There are a few drop-down menus and icon-based tools that you'll use to duplicate, delete, grow, and shrink the sprites in your games. You can see the Grey Toolbar at the top of your screen and in figure 1.13. Let's explore all the menus and icons, beginning on the far left.

Figure 1.13   The Grey Toolbar runs across the top of the workspace and contains a few helpful tools you'll use while making your games.

- **SCRATCH** *Scratch logo*—Click this button and you'll find yourself on the homepage of the Scratch website. When you're finished looking at the homepage, click Create or the back button in your browser to get back to the workspace screen.

- **⊕** *Globe*—Click the globe and you'll see a list of languages; pick one if you want to change the language inside the Editor.

- **File ▼** *File*—You can make a new project, save your project, or save your project as a copy if you want to experiment with the duplicate version. You can also see all your projects by choosing Go to My Stuff, download any projects to your computer (which will be saved as a .sb2 file), record a project video if you want to record 60 seconds of your game in action, and remove all changes made since opening a project by clicking Revert.

- You can skip the Edit, Tips, and About menus, unless you're looking for more information about Scratch, and head over to the icons in the center of the toolbar.

- **⬩** *Duplicator*—This tool allows you to make a copy of your sprite. Click the stamp icon and then click the cat on the Stage. You now have two cats, but because the first cat is directly over the other cat, you won't see that at first. Click the top cat and drag it somewhere else to peel the two cats apart. See, now you have two cats.

- **✂** *Delete*—What if you want to get rid of a sprite? Click the scissor icon and then click one of the cats. It disappears, which means you're back to one cat.

- **⤬** *Grow*—This tool makes your sprite larger. Click the icon of the four arrows pointing outward and then click the cat a few times. The sprite enlarges with each click.

- **⤨** *Shrink*—This the opposite of the Grow tool—it makes your sprites smaller. Click the icon of the four arrows pointing inward and then click the cat a few times to watch it grow smaller.

- **❓** *Help*—The question mark gives you information about the various blocks in case you forget. Click it and then click any of the blue blocks in the center Block Menu. For instance, after you click the question mark, click the blue block that says Move 10 Steps, and you'll see an information box pop up on the right side of the screen.

Feel free to click around the Grey Toolbar.

 THE WORKSPACE IS A MESS   Do you remember what to do if you need to reset the workspace? Click the Scratch logo in the top left corner and then click Create on the main screen, or click File > New, and you'll be back to a fresh workspace.

Meeting the Block Menu

You've already used a bunch of blocks from the Block Menu, so you know that the space stores all the blocks you need to make your sprites run, jump, squawk, or disappear.

Three tabs are at the top of the Block Menu: Scripts, Costumes, and Sounds. Make sure you're on the Scripts tab. You've probably already noticed that each set of blocks is color-coordinated. For instance, all the Motion blocks are blue and all the Looks blocks are purple.

Let's click a block in each section so you can see what each type of block can do. You don't need to drag the block to the Script Area — clicking it while it's still in the Block Menu will also cause the cat on the Stage to move or meow.

USING MOTION BLOCKS

The Block Menu defaults to the Motion block menu. Figure 1.14 shows the first three blocks, but all these Motion blocks will get your sprites from one place to another. Any time you want your sprite to move on the screen, you use the Motion blocks.

Try clicking the top Move 10 Steps block. The cat on the Stage shifts over 10 spaces to the right. Click the block again and the cat will again move 10 spaces to the right.

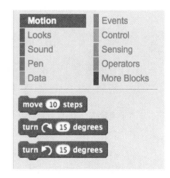

Figure 1.14   *The Motion block menu*

ANSWER THIS   CAN YOU MAKE THE CAT GO TO THE LEFT?
Question: how do you get the cat to move to the left?
Answer: change the 10 inside the block to read –10 and click the block again. Now the cat is moonwalking back toward the left side of the screen.

USING LOOKS BLOCKS

Now click the Looks block menu and you'll see the blocks are purple (figure 1.15). Again, this image only shows the first few blocks in the menu.

Looks blocks affect how your sprites appear on the screen. If you make a game using Scratch's premade sprites, you'll be able to tweak the way those sprites appear. But because you're making your own sprites for your games, you'll mostly be using the

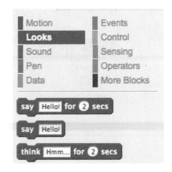

Figure 1.15   *The Looks block menu*

Looks blocks to switch between backdrops on your platformer games, or to show or hide a sprite in the game.

Click the Say Hello for 2 Secs block. Notice your cat now has a speech bubble that says "Hello." It disappears after two seconds.

 CAN YOU CHANGE THE SPEECH BUBBLE?

Question: how do you make the cat say something other than "Hello"?

Answer: erase the word *Hello* inside the block and replace it with another word. Click the block again, and you'll see your cat say the new word.

USING SOUND BLOCKS

Change to the Sound block menu and the blocks will turn magenta, as in figure 1.16.

You can import music to use with your games by adding it with the Sound blocks. Additionally, you can use the Scratch sound library to add sound effects—such as having a boing sound ring out when the egg hits the pan in the game you'll make in chapter 5, called Breakfast Wars.

Figure 1.16   *The Sound block menu*

Try out a Sound block by clicking the first block, Play Sound Meow. You should hear a small meow. If you don't, check the volume on your computer's speakers and click the block again.

USING PEN BLOCKS

Switch to the Pen block menu and the blocks change to dark green, as shown in figure 1.17.

These blocks let you program your sprites to draw as they move on the Stage or create non-programmable images of sprites. Click the Stamp block. It may seem like nothing has happened, but once again, there are two cats on the Stage, one on top of the other. Click the top one and drag it so you can see both cats.

Figure 1.17   The Pen block menu

 IS THERE MORE THAN ONE WAY TO COPY A SPRITE?

Question: how is the Stamp block different from the Duplicator tool in the Grey Toolbar?

Answer: Stamp produces a non-permanent, non-programmable clone of a sprite. You can't even move the copy of the cat you made on the screen. It's as if the real cat left a stamp of itself on the screen. Go ahead and click the cat that was on the bottom. (It should still be in the center of your Stage.) See, you can't even move it, whereas the Duplicator tool allows you to make a second, programmable version of a sprite. Which one do you think you'll use more to program in Scratch? You're correct if you guessed the Duplicator tool.

Let's get that cat stamp off the Stage. Click the Clear block in the Pen block menu, and the extra cat will disappear.

USING DATA BLOCKS

The last option on the left side of the menu is the orange Data blocks, shown in figure 1.18.

This is where you'll find variables and lists, two elements of programming that you'll find in every coding language. You'll learn more about variables and lists in chapter 3.

Figure 1.18   The Data block menu

USING EVENTS BLOCKS

Move over to the right side of the menu and switch to the Events block menu. Events are the brown blocks seen in figure 1.19.

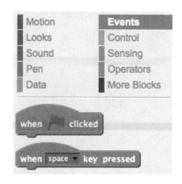

Figure 1.19   The Events block menu

Events blocks are the most important set of blocks you'll use in Scratch. If you don't have an Events block, your script can't run. Events blocks tell Scratch when to start running the program by setting a triggering moment, such as clicking the green flag. The Scratch team calls these *hat* blocks because they always top off the program.

Feel free to click any of these blocks. You'll notice that, for the first time, nothing happens, because these blocks only work together with other blocks. They can't do anything on their own because their purpose is to start a script.

USING CONTROL BLOCKS

Now click the Control block menu and you'll see the blocks are golden yellow, as shown in figure 1.20.

Figure 1.20   The Control block menu

The Control blocks tell the program what to do with the sprites as long as certain conditions are met. Like Events blocks, Control blocks don't do anything until you use them as part of a script, but click the Create Clone of Myself block. Similar to what happened when you clicked the Stamp block under the Pen block menu, the two copies of the cat are on top of one another on the Stage. Click the top one and drag it so you can see both cats.

ANSWER THIS   IS THERE REALLY A THIRD WAY TO CLONE A SPRITE?

Question: what is the best way to clone a sprite in Scratch?

Answer: you've now seen a third way to clone a sprite. This one is most commonly used to generate sprite copies *during* the game rather than create those copies before the game begins. For instance, you may want a game with two crabs in it. You can draw one crab and use the Duplicator tool to make a second, programmable copy of that crab before the game begins, for a total of two crabs. The Duplicator tool can save you a lot of time and work. But the Create Clone of Myself block generates clones *while* the game is running. Later, you will make a shoot-em-up game in this book called Wizards vs. Ghosts. As the ghosts fall and the wizard blasts them away with his wand, you'll need the Create Clone of Myself block to generate new copies of the ghost sprite so there will always be ghosts to shoot on the screen.

How can you get rid of the extra cat you made? Do you remember the correct tool from the Grey Toolbar? Click the scissor icon and click one of the cats to make the extra sprite disappear from the screen. You can also click the red stop sign above the Stage. This stops any blocks from running.

USING SENSING BLOCKS

Change to the Sensing block menu and the blocks will be light blue, as seen in figure 1.21.

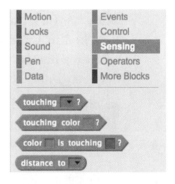

The Sensing blocks let Scratch detect what is happening within the game. For instance, it will be able to tell if two elements in the game are touching or if a button is pressed.

Figure 1.21   The Sensing block menu

Click the Touching Color block. The word *color* will be on the block, but you should also see a square filled with a color. In figure 1.21, the square is green.

When you click the block, you see a pop-up bubble that says *false*. That's because your sprite is not touching anything green (or whatever color is in your block's box) on the screen, because the background is white.

You can also click the Timer block and you will see a number appear in a pop-up bubble.

ANSWER THIS   WHAT IS THE TIMER COUNTING?

Question: what does the number on the timer block mean?

Answer: it's the number of seconds that has passed since you opened your Scratch workspace. Each time you click the block, the number will go up. You can place timers in your games to limit the number of seconds the player has to complete the level, or to let the player know how long it took to solve a board.

USING OPERATORS BLOCKS

Switch to the Operators block menu and the blocks are light green, as in figure 1.22.

Operators blocks solve math problems within Scratch, making quick calculations as the game unfolds. Math is what makes the program run because numbers are a constant in the computer world.

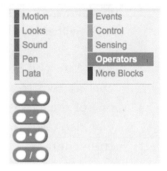

Figure 1.22   The Operators block menu

Click the Pick Random 1 to 10 block. When I clicked it, I got 3. When you click it, you will see a number between 1 and 10. Click it again to see a new number between 1 and 10.

ANSWER THIS   DOES CHANGING NUMBERS CHANGE WHAT HAPPENS?

Question: what happens if you change the numbers inside those two bubbles in the Pick Random 1 to 10 block?

Answer: change them to any two numbers and see if Scratch returns a number inside the new range. Also try putting the larger number in the left bubble and the smaller number in the right bubble. Even though the order of the numbers is mixed up, Scratch will still return a number within the range.

USING MORE BLOCKS

The last option on the right side of the menu is the More Blocks menu, shown in figure 1.23. These blocks are violet.

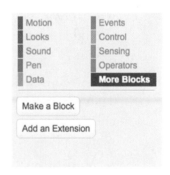

Figure 1.23   The More Blocks block menu

The More Blocks block menu allows you to make your own Scratch blocks. Maybe you have a long script that you need to reuse multiple times. Instead of having to continuously reconstruct it when you want to use it again and again, you can turn the script into a single block that you can use to run the script as if it was written out in full.

Meeting the Sprite Zone

You've already learned how to add a new sprite, but there are a few other options in the top toolbar in the Sprite Zone. Look next to the words New Sprite:

- The paintbrush icon lets you make your own sprites in the Art Editor (which Sadie will teach you how to do in the next chapter).
- The open folder icon will allow you to upload an image you made with another art program on your computer. Click the open folder icon, and your computer will bring up your local disk drive menu. You can now navigate to any image file you have on your computer to add it to your Scratch workspace.
- The camera icon opens your computer's webcam. You can now take a photo of yourself to use in your project. Say cheese!

Lastly, as you make each new sprite, they'll be labeled Sprite1, Sprite2, and Sprite3. But click the little blue *i* in the corner of the blue box that appears around the sprite and you'll open the menu shown in figure 1.24.

Figure 1.24   The Sprite menu appears when you click the blue *i* in the corner of the sprite.

You can rename the sprite and change other aspects of the sprite, including the way it moves or the direction it faces. Try erasing the name Sprite1 inside the box and typing a new name for the cat. To save this new name, click the blue circle to the left of the sprite to

The new name appears under the sprite after you type it in the box.

Figure 1.25   Name the sprites you make so it's easier to use them in your programs.

get back to the normal Sprite Zone. You should see the new name under the cat, as shown in figure 1.25, rather than the default, Sprite1.

Wrapping up the tour

You now know your way around the Scratch workspace. If you ever get lost while making a game, return to this chapter to be reminded of where all the tools are located.

Play in the workspace

In the rest of the chapters, this section will give you challenges so you can take your game in new directions. Think of it like extra credit—things you can try that build on the new information you learned in the chapter.

CHALLENGE Your only challenge at the moment is to continue to try out the various blocks in the Block Menu. Knowing what Scratch is capable of doing will help you plot out future games. So get busy dragging and dropping blocks into the Script Area and seeing what they do.

What did you learn?

In other chapters, this section helps you review what was covered before you move on. If you see something unfamiliar on the list, back up and reread the chapter.

Pause for a moment and think about everything you learned in this chapter. You learned

- How to navigate the five main areas of the Scratch workspace
- How to put together a simple program by snapping together blocks
- How to clear the Script Area so you can make a new program
- How to add a new sprite to your game
- How to rename your sprites for an easier time coding
- How to make sure you are programming the correct sprite
- How to use all the tools you will need to program your game

Now that you know your way around your workspace, chapter 2 walks you through Scratch's Art Editor.

2

Becoming familiar
with the Art Editor

You may think that game making is all about writing code, but think again. You've probably heard the acronym STEAM in school—it stands for science, technology, engineering, *art*, and math. These subjects all share similar thinking skills, which means learning how to draw can make you better at science and math.

Drawing is about angles and ratios and fractions. It's about creative problem solving and figuring out how to take an idea from your mind and get it onto the screen. Thinking like an artist means understanding which colors go together, how to break down objects into smaller parts, and how to create depth with shading. These are all things you'll learn with this book.

Pixel art is a lot more forgiving than paint and canvas; remember, you're not creating Picassos, you're creating Pac-Mans. Take a deep breath if you're worried that you don't have the talent to design your own sprites. I promise, you do.

You'll practice recreating shapes using the shortcuts Scratch provides in its art workspace, such as the Line tool, Square tool, and Circle tool. This will get you comfortable with drawing on the screen with your mouse, which is different from drawing on paper. You'll also learn how to build sprites pixel by pixel to give your images a retro feel like *Dig Dug* or *Super Mario Bros.*

Like the last chapter, this chapter is a tour, which means you'll get to try out every tool in the Art Editor so you can get a feel for drawing your own sprites. In this chapter, you will learn

- How to navigate the Art Editor
- How to locate the tools you'll use to draw your sprites
- Two ways to build a cat sprite
- How to add color to your sprites and backdrops

Let's get started trying your hand at making art.

Making your first drawing

There are two separate but similar-looking Art Editors in Scratch: one for sprites and one for backdrops. You'll use these to create your own, unique pixel art for your retro-style games.

To start making a new sprite

1   Clear the Stage by clicking the scissor icon on the Grey Toolbar and clicking the default cat sprite.
2   Navigate to the Sprite Zone and click the paintbrush icon to the right of the words New Sprite, as shown in figure 2.1.

Figure 2.1   To make your own sprite instead of using a premade sprite from the Scratch library, click the paintbrush icon in the Sprite Zone.

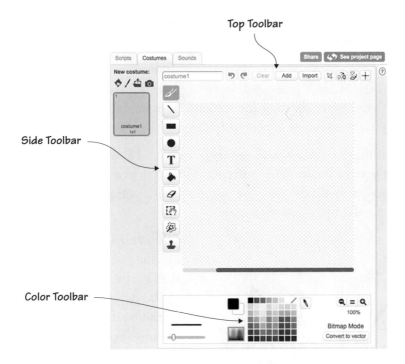

Figure 2.2   **The blank canvas is surrounded by the three tool areas.**

You should see the workspace that's in figure 2.2 open on the right side of the screen where the Script Area used to be.

The grey and white checked canvas is surrounded by three tool spaces: the Top Toolbar, the Side Toolbar, and the Color Toolbar. Before you dive into trying out all the tools in the Art Editor, it helps to understand the base measurement unit of arcade art: the pixel.

> **FIX IT**   THE ART EDITOR IS MISSING!   What if you're not looking at a grey and white pixelated canvas? Navigate to the Block Menu and make sure the Costumes tab is chosen.

Learning about pixels

A *pixel* is a unit of measurement. One pixel equals a single dot or miniature square of light on the screen. As your body is constructed out of billions of tiny cells, digital images are constructed out of tiny picture cells, or pixels. Those mini squares combine together to form an image on the computer screen. The smaller the squares and the more there are on the screen, the smoother the picture will appear.

To give you a sense of a pixel's size, an iPhone screen has about 326 pixels per inch. Take a ruler and draw a square measuring one inch on each side. Now divide up that square into 326 smaller squares, if you even can—your pencil line is probably thicker than a pixel on the screen!

What if there were only 25 pixels per inch? Take your ruler and divide up the square again. The individual squares are still tiny, but you can see each individual one. The fewer pixels per inch, the larger those squares will appear on the screen.

Old video games have a low number of pixels per inch, and that's why the graphics look a little boxy, or *pixelated*. Take, for instance, the Scratch cat in its default form and the Scratch cat in a pixelated form, shown in figure 2.3. The image on the right is the look you're ultimately working toward in this book.

Default Scratch Cat   Pixelated Scratch Cat

Figure 2.3   Two Scratch cats! The one on the left has a smooth, modern look. The one on the right has a pixelated, retro-style look.

Let's take a tour of the Side Toolbar so you can try out the tools and draw your first sprite.

Using art tools to make a sprite

Let's make the first of two sprites. You can use the grey and white pixelated background as a guide for creating your sprite's shape, almost like a ruler. In honor of Scratch's default cat, you're going to make your own, unique cat as your first sprite, like the one shown in figure 2.4.

Figure 2.4   A simple cat sprite using basic shapes drawn with the Art Editor tools

You'll start by choosing a color from the Color Toolbar and then use every tool on the Side Toolbar in order, moving from top (the icon that looks like a paintbrush) to bottom (the icon that looks like a stamp). This will not only help you create a cat, but you'll get to try out all of the tools along the way.

CHOOSING A COLOR

Let's begin by choosing a color for your cat. I went with a simple orange, but you can choose any color you like from the Color Toolbar.

> **FIX IT**   I'M WORRIED I DIDN'T CHOOSE THE RIGHT COLOR!   This book contains color instructions whenever you're making a sprite in order to help you focus on the skill you're learning rather than worrying about picking a color. I'll let you in on a little secret: you can always choose a different color if you want. Even when a color is used as part of the code, such as telling a sprite to stop moving when it touches something red, you can set those instructions to the colors you used on your sprites. When I tell you to choose a dark blue, don't worry about whether I mean this blue or that blue. Just pick the one you like best.

To choose a new color using the paint sample squares

1   Navigate to the Color Toolbar under the pixelated canvas.
2   Click any of the paint sample squares.

Scratch gives you the 56 little color swatches seen in figure 2.5 to choose from, with the lightest shades at the top and darker shades at the bottom.

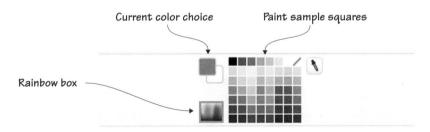

Figure 2.5   The 56 paint sample squares in the Color Toolbar, plus the current color box and the rainbow box

You can also change the color using the rainbow box:

1 Click the small rainbow-colored box to the left of the paint sample squares. Note that it will switch places with the paint sample squares.

2 Move the black bubble (seen in figure 2.6) around the rainbow until you find the color you want.

Bubble to set the color

Slider to make the color darker and lighter

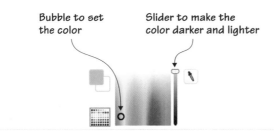

Figure 2.6   Choose a color from the rainbow box by moving around the black bubble. You can see the current color choice in the little square outside the top left corner of the rainbow box.

3 Check the current color by looking at the top square to the left of the rainbow box. You don't need to click anything to set the color. Instead, leave the bubble over the color you want.

4 Use the slider on the right side of the rainbow box to make the shade of the color darker or lighter.

You can use either method to choose a color for your cat.

DRAWING WITH THE PAINTBRUSH

Begin by giving your cat a head by drawing a square with the Paintbrush tool, as in figure 2.7, the top icon on the Side Toolbar.

By default, the Art Editor always begins with the Paintbrush tool ready to go. Use the Paintbrush tool to draw images, using the mouse as you would a pen or pencil. You need to have a steady hand to use this tool to make a straight line.

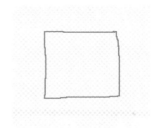

Figure 2.7   A freehand square drawn using the Paintbrush tool

To use the Paintbrush tool

1 Make sure the paintbrush icon on the Side Toolbar is chosen.

2 Move the mouse pointer onto the canvas where you want your cat's head to begin.

3 Click and hold the mouse button to start the line.

4 Move the mouse wherever you want the line to go.

5 Release the mouse button and you will see the square both on the canvas and on the Stage.

As you can see, it's hard to draw an even square with this tool.

> **ANSWER THIS**   HOW TO DRAW A SMOOTHER LINE?
> Question: it's hard to free draw with a mouse—is there something you can do to make it easier?

Answer: how about drawing your shape larger than you want and then using the Shrink tool on the Grey Toolbar to bring it down to the right size? Try drawing the cat's head a second time. Does it look better? Sometimes drawing something large is a little easier than drawing something small.

There's a second way you can draw a square for the cat's head. Erase your wobbly square by clicking the Undo tool, the counterclockwise curved arrow above the canvas. Now get ready to try the Line tool.

> **FIX IT**   ERASING LINES WHEN YOU'VE MESSED UP   Don't worry if you draw a line and don't like it. Two buttons directly above the canvas on the Top Toolbar are super helpful in erasing (or putting back) your last action. The counterclockwise curved arrow on the left (the Undo tool) removes the last line you made on the canvas. The clockwise curved arrow on the right (the Redo tool) brings back the last action, returning the last thing you removed from the canvas.

DRAWING WITH THE LINE TOOL

Use the Line tool to make straight lines. They can be vertical lines, horizontal lines, or diagonal lines, and they can be long or short. You can connect lines to form any shape—for instance a square, like the one in figure 2.8.

To draw your own square with the Line tool

1 Click the line icon on the Side Toolbar.

2 Move the mouse pointer onto the canvas where you want your square to begin.

Figure 2.8   A slightly neater square, this time made using the Line tool

3 Click and hold the mouse button to start the first line and drag it until the line is a few centimeters long.

4 Release the mouse button and you'll see a line show up on the canvas and on the Stage.

5 Continue your square by drawing another line leading off of the first line.

6 Repeat until the four lines connect.

This time your square is a little neater than the one made using the Paintbrush tool. But wait! There's a third way you can draw a square in Scratch, and this is the one you're going to use for the cat's head. Erase the square you made by clicking undo several times until your workspace is clear, or use the Clear button from the Top Toolbar, which will get rid of all lines in the Art Editor in one fell swoop.

DRAWING WITH THE SQUARE TOOL

The third option from the top is the Square tool. You can use it to draw perfect rectangles and squares, like the one in figure 2.9.

To make the cat's head with the Square tool

1 Click the square icon on the Side Toolbar.

2 Navigate to the two rectangles on the far left side of the Color Toolbar. One rectangle is an outline and the other is solid. Click the solid rectangle so it is surrounded by a blue box, like the one in figure 2.10.

Figure 2.9   This square will become the cat's head.

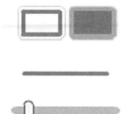

Figure 2.10   The blue square is around the filled square icon, which means the square will be a solid shape instead of an outline.

3   Click and hold the mouse on the canvas, and then drag the mouse pointer to form a square. The farther you drag your mouse, the larger the shape.

4   Release the mouse button when your square is a good size.

This tool helps you form a quick and perfect square. The Line tool is great for other shapes, such as triangles, but the Square tool is what you use when you need four even sides.

ANSWER THIS   SHOULD YOU USE OUTLINES OR SOLID SHAPES?

Question: do you want to use a single color for the cat's head, or outline the head in a slightly darker shade and then fill in the face in a lighter orange?

Answer: the choice is up to you because the Square tool and Circle tool both come with outline or solid options. In the previous example, you set your square to be one solid color, but you can experiment and try making an outline that you'll fill later in this exercise. Set whether the square (or circle) is an outline or solid shape by clicking the correct box on the left side of the Color Toolbar. Which look do you like better: solid, continuous color or a darker outline with a lighter center?

DRAWING WITH THE CIRCLE TOOL

If you thought squares were hard, try your hand at drawing tiny circle eyes for your cat with the Paintbrush. Mine looked like shriveled up raisins. Which brings us to the next tool down the Side Toolbar (fourth from the top): the Circle tool. This is used to draw easy ovals or circles, like the eye on the cat in figure 2.11.

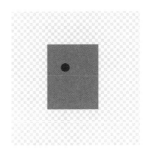

Figure 2.11   You can make any size circle—from tiny eyes to large heads—with the Circle tool.

To make the cat's eyes with the Circle tool

1   Navigate to the Color Toolbar and switch from orange to dark brown by clicking the appropriate paint sample square.

2   Click the circle icon on the Side Toolbar.

3   Navigate to the two ovals on the far left side of the Color Toolbar (exactly as you did when drawing a solid square). One oval is an

outline and the other is solid. Click the solid oval so it is surrounded by a blue box if the blue box is not currently around the solid oval.

4 Click and hold the mouse pointer about a third of the way down the orange square (about where a cat's eyes would be set) and then drag to form a tiny circle. The farther you drag your mouse, the larger the shape.

5 Release the mouse button when your circle is a good size.

Your cat currently has a single eye. You'll create the second, matching one in a moment using a different tool. But before you finish building your cat, let's make it say something.

DRAWING WITH THE TEXT TOOL

What if you want your cat to be saying "Meow," like the cat in figure 2.12?

You can add words to any image by using the Text tool. This will allow you to make a Game Over icon to flash on the screen at the end of a game or write a name across a sprite's shirt.

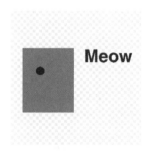

Figure 2.12   Any text added to your sprite with the Text tool will move with the sprite once you program it.

To make your cat say, "Meow"

1 Click the Text tool, which is a T icon (which stands for text box) on the Side Toolbar.

2 Click next to the cat's head to bring up an empty text box.

3 Use your keyboard to type the word *Meow.*

4 Change the font by navigating to the bottom of the screen where you see the word Helvetica with a tiny triangle. That triangle is a drop-down menu, as seen in figure 2.13.

Figure 2.13   Use the drop-down menu at the bottom of the screen to change the font.

The word *Meow* is technically attached to the sprite, and if you move the sprite on the Stage, the word will travel with it.

DRAWING WITH THE PAINT BUCKET TOOL

Sometimes you don't feel like coloring in your shape pixel by pixel. If you want every inch of your shape to be the exact same shade, use the Paint Bucket tool to fill the space with virtual paint. This is exactly how the cat's ears were drawn in figure 2.14.

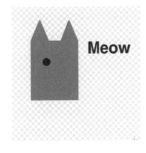

Figure 2.14   Two solid triangles are used for the cat's ears, and these triangles were filled using the Paint Bucket tool.

Return to your cat and use the Line tool to draw two sets of diagonal lines on the top of the cat's head for the ears, as shown in figure 2.15.

Now it's time to fill in those ears with paint. Choose the same (or a similar) shade of orange you used for the cat's body:

1 Click the paint bucket icon in the Side Toolbar.

2 Move your mouse pointer inside the first triangle.

3 Click once inside the first triangle to spill the orange paint.

4 Navigate to the second triangle and click again.

Figure 2.15   To use the Paint Bucket tool, first define the space you want to fill by creating an outline.

The ears are now solidly filled orange.

FIX IT   THE PAINT FILLED THE WHOLE SCREEN!   What if you click inside the ear and the paint fills the entire screen, blotting out the cat? Don't panic—just use the Undo button to remove the paint and start over. Usually, the paint stays inside the boundaries of the shape. But if even one pixel is open, the paint will spill out of the shape and into the rest of the canvas. Close off the shape using the Paintbrush or Line tool, and then switch back to the Paint Bucket tool to try again.

DRAWING WITH THE ERASER TOOL

If you make a mistake, you can immediately erase it with the Undo button in the Top Toolbar. But if you later change your mind about something you added to your picture and don't want to rewind all the work that has occurred since the mistake, you can use the Eraser tool. For example, if you decide you don't want the word *Meow* attached to your cat anymore, you can use the Eraser tool to remove it, which is what is happening in figure 2.16.

Figure 2.16   The clear bubble is an eraser. Slide it over any pixels you want to remove.

To remove an element of your drawing

1   Click the eraser icon.

2   Move your mouse over the word *Meow* inside the editor.

3   Click and hold down the mouse button as you rub the mouse pointer over the word, removing it from the canvas.

The word *Meow* is now removed from your picture. In the future, you can use this tool either to remove sections of your sprite or shave a few pixels off an edge.

ANSWER THIS   CAN YOU MAKE THE ERASER BIGGER?

Question: the eraser is pretty small. Can you make it bigger?
Answer: sometimes you will want a small eraser for doing tiny detail work. Other times you want your eraser much larger to make the job faster. Look around the Art Editor; can you guess how to make the eraser bigger? Navigate down to the slider at the bottom of the screen in the Color Toolbar and move the slider toward the right in order to make the eraser bigger. Sliding it to the left makes the eraser smaller.

DRAWING WITH THE SELECT TOOL

The Select tool allows you to move a segment of your drawing. It will draw a box around the chunk of the image that you want to move, and then you can drag with your mouse to move that segment wherever you need it on the screen, which is how the body got under the head in figure 2.17.

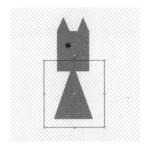

Figure 2.17   *The green circle in the center of the Select tool outline lets you know that the shape is ready to be moved.*

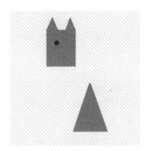

Figure 2.18   *You can draw the body anywhere in the Art Editor, because you can move the triangle using the Select tool.*

Try out this tool by drawing the cat's body somewhere else on the screen. The body is going to be a simple triangle made with the Line tool and then filled with the Paint Bucket tool, as seen in figure 2.18.

Now you need to move that triangle body into place under the head:

1 Click the Select tool in the Side Toolbar.
2 Outline the body using your mouse in the same way you would draw a square. Try to get the rectangle around the body as closely as possible.
3 Notice the small, green circle in the center of the box, seen back in figure 2.17. That green circle is what indicates that the shape (and everything inside it) is moveable.
4 Move your mouse pointer inside the Select outline.
5 Click and hold the mouse button while dragging the body underneath the head. Release the mouse button when the body now touches the head.

Your sprite is beginning to look more and more like a cat.

LEARN IT   LAYERS   As you move the triangle close to the head, notice whether or not the triangle slips underneath the square head or slides on top of the head, blotting out the face. What you're noticing are *layers*, and all image programs use them in order to add each element to the picture. The square is clearly the bottom layer. The eye is the next layer.

And the triangle body is the third layer. New elements to your sprite will always go on top of the last layer, so plan accordingly when building a sprite. It helps to draw out a sprite on paper and figure out the order you want to draw it on the screen. For instance, it makes sense to draw the face first and then the eyes, and not the other way around. If you draw the eyes first, they'll be covered up when you go to draw the larger head.

Skip the next tool (you'll return to the Remove Background tool at the end of this chapter) so you can give the cat a second eye with the final tool on the Side Toolbar.

DRAWING WITH THE DUPLICATE TOOL

It's time to give your poor cat a second eye. You could have drawn a second circle, but those two circles may not have been the same size. The way you can ensure that the circles are the same size, as they are in figure 2.19, is to use the Duplicate tool.

Figure 2.19   The Duplicate tool makes it easy to have both eyes be identical.

To make a second eye using the first eye

1 Click the stamp icon to choose the Duplicate tool in the Side Toolbar (not the Grey Toolbar).

2 Use the mouse to draw a small box around the first eye and release the mouse button.

3 Click inside the blue outline and drag your mouse pointer. Although it may not seem as if anything happened when you first released the mouse button, you'll now see the copy of the circle appear.

4 Release your mouse button when you get the new eye to the spot you want, similar to the Select tool.

Now your cat has two eyes.

FINISHING THE CAT

You are almost done with your cat. Begin with the tail, which you'll make in the same way that you made the two ears. Do you remember which tool you used to make those triangles? Make a triangle again, this time coming off the cat's body, as shown in figure 2.20.

Switch to the Line tool to make the tail:

1 Make sure your color is still set to the orange used for the cat's body and head.
2 Draw a set of two diagonal lines.
3 Switch to the Paint Bucket tool.
4 Click inside the triangle to fill the shape with color.

Figure 2.20   A simple triangle becomes a tail for the cat sprite.

Your cat now has an orange tail.

Next, navigate up to the face so you can make the mouth and whiskers, or nose and whiskers. It's up to you how you want to view this cartoonish dot on the finished cat's face, shown in figure 2.21.

To finish the cat's face

1 Switch to the black paint sample square in the Color Toolbar.
2 Switch to the Circle tool on the Side Toolbar.

Figure 2.21   A mouth (or nose?) and six whiskers finish off the cat's face.

3 Draw a tiny black circle underneath and between the two eyes.
4 Switch to the Line tool.
5 Make six straight lines radiating out from the dot in the middle of the face.

Congratulations, you made your first sprite! Now that you know how to use each of the tools on the left sidebar, feel free to play around and make other sprites. When you're ready, keep reading, because there is a second way to build sprites, getting even closer to the look of those old Atari games.

Making your own cat, pixel-by-pixel

You can also enlarge the Art Editor and draw your sprites pixel by pixel. Let's make a cat like the one in figure 2.22.

Start by making the canvas a little bigger. You can either clear the canvas and start fresh or draw this sprite next to your other sprite. To enlarge the canvas

Figure 2.22   The pixelated cat is outlined with dots and then filled using the Paint Bucket tool.

1 Navigate to the Color Toolbar and choose a darker orange (in the second column of the paint sample squares) for the outline of the cat.

2 Notice the two magnifying glass icons underneath the canvas on the right side of the screen. The one on the right allows you to zoom into the image, and the one on the left allows you to zoom out.

3 Zoom in by clicking the magnifying glass with a plus sign (seen in figure 2.23) three times to make the canvas 800% its normal size.

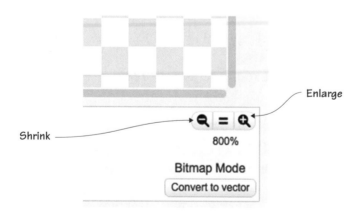

Figure 2.23   The two magnifying glasses at the bottom of the Art Editor are your friends when you get ready to make pixelated art.

ANSWER THIS   SHOULD YOU WORRY ABOUT SPRITE SIZE?

Question: does it matter how big you make your sprite?

Answer: not really. You can always use the Grow tool in the Grey Toolbar (or, if your sprite is too large for your game, the Shrink tool) after the sprite is made. You learned how to use these tools back in chapter 1. You'll see your sprite growing on the Stage as you add each pixel, so you'll be able to judge whether you're getting close to the size you want. But don't start over if you realize in the middle of making your cat that it's too big or too small.

You'll use the darker shade of orange to make the outline for the cat and then fill in the body and face of the cat in a lighter shade of orange.

Start again by making a square for the head, only this time you'll make it out of dots:

1 Select the Paintbrush tool on the Side Toolbar.

2 Navigate to the Line Width tool, shown in figure 2.24, on the left side of the Color Toolbar.

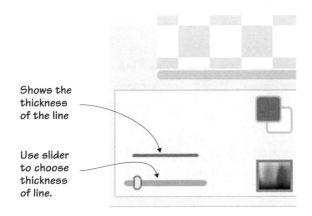

Shows the thickness of the line

Use slider to choose thickness of line.

Figure 2.24   The Line Width tool in the Color Toolbar controls the thickness of the line.

3 Increase the line size until one click of the Paintbrush tool leaves a dot instead of a square. To test the size of the brush, make a single dot on the canvas. Why a dot instead of a square? It gives the cat a rough edge, almost like fur. Plus it makes it easier for you to see where to place the next dot by following the edges of the dots on the canvas.

4 Move the mouse pointer to the canvas and start making a square out of dark orange dots. Make your square with six dots on each side.

5 Make two dots, side by side, directly over the top corners of the square.

6 Crown these two dots with another single dot in the center, as shown in figure 2.25. If you see any empty pixels at the top of the triangle, gently shift the mouse pointer and click again to fill them.

Next, move below the square to draw the cat's body and tail. Keep using the same shade of dark orange.

To draw the neck and top of the body

1 Navigate to the two center dots at the bottom of the square.

2 Draw two dots underneath those dots, side by side.

3 Build out the body by attaching a line four dots across to the neck. Build down from the edges of the line with two dots down on either side, as in figure 2.26.

Figure 2.25 This square head is made out of dots topped by two pixelated dot ears.

The body keeps getting wider as you move toward the bottom of the sitting cat. You'll extend the body by making dots to the side followed by dots going downward.

Figure 2.26 Strategically placed dots start forming the top half of the cat's body.

To draw the rest of the body

1 Draw a dot to either side of the descending lines and then make the new edge two dots down.

2 Do this a second time, drawing a single dot to the side and then one dot down.

3 Finish the bottom of the cat by drawing eight dots across to close off the tiered cat body.

4 Begin to the left or right side of the bottom tier and draw an unconnected line extending outward for the cat's tail.

In figure 2.27 you can see the outline of the cat.

You can now use the Paint Bucket tool to fill the body with lighter orange pixels.

To fill the cat's body

1 Choose a shade of orange slightly lighter than the shade you used for the outline.
2 Switch to the Paint Bucket tool.
3 Click inside the empty spaces to fill them with the lighter orange color. Make sure the paint bucket icon is always over the grey-and-white canvas inside the outline and not on the outline itself.

Your cat is now completely orange, with the darker outline giving your cat a little depth, as shown in figure 2.28.

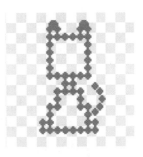

Figure 2.27   The cat outline is made up of dark orange dots.

Figure 2.28   The orange pixelated cat still needs a face.

FIX IT   IF YOU ACCIDENTALLY CHANGED THE OUTLINE COLOR   Every once in a while, you'll click the outline instead of the space inside the outline. When you do this, the outline will change to the same color as the inner pixels. Don't panic. Use the undo arrow in the Top Toolbar of the Art Editor, and it will rewind the project to before the last paint spill. Check where the paint bucket icon is positioned and try clicking again to fill the space.

Lastly, you need to make the face, and you'll do this using two line width sizes that you'll set with the Line Width tool.

To make the eyes, mouth, and whiskers

1 Switch to the black paint sample square in the Color Toolbar.
2 Make two dots in the center of the head for the two eyes.

3 Navigate down to the Line Width tool on the left side of the Color Toolbar.

4 Move the slider to the left to make the line thinner.

5 Switch to the Line tool.

6 Draw a line going down between the two eyes and make a small line across at the bottom, like an upside-down T.

7 Draw six lines radiating out of the cat's face for whiskers.

You now have a finished pixelated cat like the one in figure 2.29 on your Stage. Which cat do you like better?

Now that you know how to make sprites, you need to learn how to make the backdrops you'll use for your games. The two processes are similar, and the two Art Editors look a lot alike.

Figure 2.29   Your second sprite is now complete.

Making your first backdrop

The Backdrop Art Editor looks almost exactly like the Sprite Art Editor, so you don't need a second introduction to the Top Toolbar, Side Toolbar, and Color Toolbar. All tools will work exactly as they do in the Sprite Art Editor.

The only difference is the canvas. When you were working with the Sprite Art Editor, the canvas was pixelated with grey and white boxes. The Backdrop Art Editor's canvas is solidly white. If you're ever in doubt about whether you're making a sprite or a backdrop, check the canvas.

Navigating to the Backdrop Art Editor

To get into the Backdrop Art Editor

1 Start a new project and navigate down to the Sprite Zone.

2   Look at the left sidebar. You should see an option to create a new backdrop. Above the words "New backdrop" is an empty white box labeled Stage, as shown in figure 2.30.

The white box above the word Stage will take you to the Backdrop Art Editor.

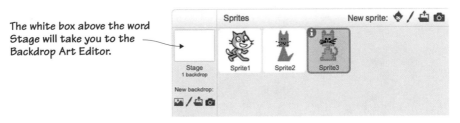

Figure 2.30   Click the white box in the Sprite Zone to get to the Backdrop Art Editor.

3   Click the white Stage box, go to the Block Menu in the middle of your screen, and select the Backdrops tab.

Designing the backdrop

The backdrops in retro-style games tend to be simple in order to keep the attention on the sprites. You don't want players to focus on tiny details you've put in the background; you want them to watch the sprite in the foreground. Let's make a field with a blue sky and green grass, as in figure 2.31.

Figure 2.31   The Scratch cat walks across a green field in this simple backdrop.

To begin, you'll need to set the horizon line and then fill the large areas above and below the line with the Paint Bucket tool. This horizon line gives the player a three-dimensional understanding of a two-dimensional space.

To make the horizon line

1   Return the Art Editor to normal size by clicking the magnifying glass with a minus sign in the bottom right corner. Make sure the Art Editor is set to 100%.

2 Click the Line tool and draw a black line across the screen, as in figure 2.32. As you draw on the canvas, you'll see the same line appear on the Stage. This is helpful because it lets you know whether the line you're drawing extends across the whole backdrop.

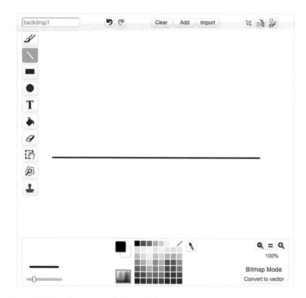

Figure 2.32   If your Art Editor is set to 100%, you'll be able to make the line go across the entire canvas.

FIX IT   MY LINE IS TOO SHORT!   If your line doesn't extend across the whole Stage, use the slider at the bottom of the canvas (not the slider for the Line Width tool) to extend the straight line. Scroll left and right (or up and down using the side slider) to continue drawing the line. You won't see the slider if your Art Editor is set to 100%. You'll only see it if you haven't zoomed out.

Now you need to fill the space above and below the horizon line with color to simulate a field and sky.

To fill the ground and sky

1 Switch to the Paint Bucket tool and choose any shade of blue from the paint sample squares in the Color Toolbar.

2 Move the mouse pointer to the section above the black line and click the screen once to fill the sky area with your chosen shade of blue.

3 Return to the Color Toolbar and choose any shade of green from the paint sample squares.

4 Move the mouse pointer to the section below the black line and click the screen once to fill the field area with your chosen shade of green.

You now have the simple backdrop shown in figure 2.33 to use in a game.

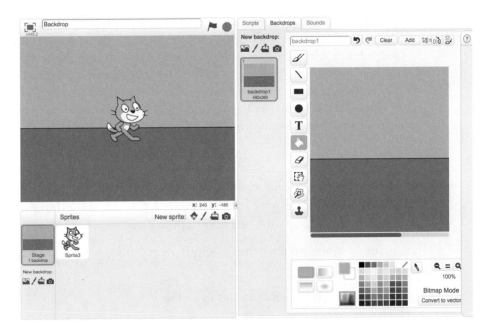

Figure 2.33   Backdrops are drawn in a similar manner to sprites.

Backdrops will always be the same size as the Stage, and the Stage is where your game will ultimately play. Therefore, each backdrop stretches over the whole background, much like a set on a theater stage.

Wrapping up the tour

You now know your way around the Scratch workspace *and* the Art Editor. Once again, if you ever get lost drawing your sprites, return to this chapter to remember where all the tools are located.

Play in the workspace

During the tour, I skipped a tool on the Side Toolbar. Between the Select tool and the Duplicate tool, there is a tool that you won't need for this book but that is still fun to try out. The Remove Background tool allows you to erase the background out of a photo and turn the subject of the image into a sprite.

CHALLENGE   Can you turn yourself or your pet into a sprite? Upload a photo to Scratch by using the open folder icon next to the words New Sprite in the Sprite Zone, click the Remove Background tool, and start outlining the part of the photo you want to keep. By clicking and holding the mouse button down, you can drag the green dot around the section of the photograph that will become the sprite. After you release the mouse button, you may see a dotted line appear. Outline the section again and then click anywhere else on the screen. The background will disappear, and you will be left with the picture inside the outline.

What did you learn?

We covered many topics on our tour of the Art Editor. Let's review before you move on to new information. If you see something unfamiliar on the list, back up and reread chapter 2.

Pause for a moment and think about everything you learned in this chapter:

- How digital space is measured in pixels
- How to navigate the Art Editor
- How to use the drawing tools on the Side Toolbar
- How to build a sprite pixel by pixel
- How to make a backdrop to go behind the sprites

Before you make your first game, Gabriel wants to introduce you to a few popular blocks and coding concepts that you'll be using a lot in each of the games you make in this book. I know you're excited to dive into making the games, and I promise that this is the final chapter in part 1. In chapter 3, you'll build tiny scripts to see how they work, and this will help you to dive into creating future games. Turn the page and get started.

3

Meeting Scratch's key blocks through important coding concepts

You want to make the games, right? I know. I want to jump straight to the game making too. But I also know that learning key computer science ideas first will make that whole game-making thing a lot easier. It will help you jump into the coding in this book, help you design your own games in the future, and even help you learn another coding language, such as Python or JavaScript. The ideas covered in this chapter apply to every programming language and every game you'll ever make.

Think of this chapter as the first day of school, and you're meeting your new classmates—except your classmates happen to be computer science concepts instead of humans. As you build the games and put these ideas into practice, you'll get to know them better. In fact, you'll re-meet these eight computer science ideas in every game you make in this book, so you'll know them quite well by the last chapter.

Here's what you'll encounter in this chapter:

- How to use the eight most common blocks you'll need to build games, and how these eight common blocks are tied to key computer science concepts
- How to make eight mini scripts to see computer science in action

You'll find all the blocks you need to meet in the center Block Menu. What are the eight most commonly used blocks, and what do they do inside a game? See table 3.1.

Table 3.1   **The eight most commonly used game-making blocks**

Name of block	Where you'll find It	What it looks like	What it can do
When Flag Clicked	Events menu	when ⚑ clicked	Tells the program when it should run
Change X by 10	Motion menu	change x by 10	Moves sprite on the screen
If/Then	Control menu	if ⬡ then	Triggers action if condition is met
Forever	Control menu	forever	Makes action continue in a loop
Variable	Data menu	Variable	Tracks points in a game
Touching Color	Sensing menu	touching color ▇ ?	Triggers action when two sprites touch
Create Clone of Myself	Control menu	create clone of myself ▾	Duplicate sprites mid-game
Broadcast Message	Events menu	broadcast message1 ▾	Allows separate scripts to communicate

IMPORTANT!   Make sure to clear your workspace of practice scripts at the end of each section either by using File > New in the Grey Toolbar or by clicking the top block in the script (usually When Flag Clicked), dragging all the blocks together to the Block Menu, and releasing the mouse button.

Let's start with a nice, clean default workspace. Go to File > New in the Grey Toolbar so the Scratch cat returns to your Stage, ready to do everything you instruct him to do with your code.

Ready to get started?

Starting a program with the When Flag Clicked block

The first block to meet is the When Flag Clicked block, in the Events block menu. Yes, you saw this block back in chapter 1, but now it's time to talk about how important it is for all the scripts you'll make in your games. This block, like the similar When Space Key Pressed block, tells the program the action that is required to get the program to run. It sets an "on" switch that the player can trigger (in this case, by clicking the green flag above the Stage) when they are ready to play the game. You'll use it to create a small script that makes the sprite move 100 steps to the right, as shown in figure 3.1.

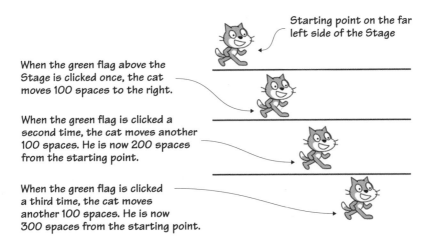

Starting point on the far left side of the Stage

When the green flag above the Stage is clicked once, the cat moves 100 spaces to the right.

When the green flag is clicked a second time, the cat moves another 100 spaces. He is now 200 spaces from the starting point.

When the green flag is clicked a third time, the cat moves another 100 spaces. He is now 300 spaces from the starting point.

Figure 3.1   The cat moves 100 steps to the right each time the green flag above the Stage is clicked. At 100 spaces per click, he can cross the Stage in four clicks of the green flag.

Finding your program's on switch

When Flag Clicked may seem like a self-explanatory block, but it's worth talking about because every script in the game needs its own on switch.

Try putting a Move 10 Steps block in the Script Area and then clicking the green flag above the Stage. What happens? Nothing, right? The cat can't move because the script doesn't have an on switch. All scripts — yes, every individual script in your game — need a way to start.

Scripting with the When Flag Clicked block

Let's build that small script that tells the sprite to walk 100 steps to the right, as the cat is doing in figure 3.2. You saw this script in chapter 1, but you need to understand what this block accomplishes.

Make the sprite move 100 spaces to the right.

Figure 3.2   Every program, including one that moves the cat 100 spaces, begins with an on switch.

To use the When Flag Clicked block

1 Navigate to the Block Menu and click the Events block option.

2 Click and drag a When Flag Clicked block and release it anywhere in the Script Area.

3 Switch to the Motion block menu and click the Move 10 Steps block.

4 Drag the Move 10 Steps block underneath the When Flag Clicked block and snap the two blocks together. Remember, if the two blocks aren't touching, the program will try to run but nothing will happen.

5 Change the 10 in the center of the block to 100 by typing inside the white bubble on the block.

The two blocks in figure 3.3 form a complete script. Click the green flag above the Stage. What happens to the cat sprite? You should see it move to the right.

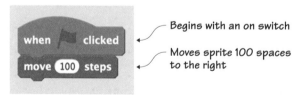

Begins with an on switch

Moves sprite 100 spaces to the right

Figure 3.3   A script using the When Flag Clicked block

This script in figure 3.3 is simple, but illustrates the idea that all scripts need a starting point. It begins with a When Flag Clicked block. That tells Scratch that you want the program to start when the green flag above the Stage is clicked. The next block (Move 100 Steps) tells Scratch what you want to have happen after the green flag is clicked: you want the sprite you programmed to move 100 spaces to the right. It will move the cat every time the green flag is clicked.

FIX IT   YOUR PROGRAM WON'T START!   Oh no! Your program won't start. If your game won't run when you test it out, your troubleshooting starting point is to look at each of your scripts and make sure they each have a block that triggers the code to run, such as the When Flag Clicked block or the When Space Key Pressed block. If not, add one and see if that fixes your problem.

Setting location with X and Y coordinates

In the last script, you asked Scratch to move the cat 100 steps, but these "steps" are actually coordinate spaces. Coordinates tell a program where the sprite is on the screen.

Many scripts use coordinates to position or move sprites, but coordinates aren't only a common part of computer programming. You've encountered X coordinates in math if you've ever jumped around on a number line. In figure 3.4, you can see how 100 steps and 100 coordinate spaces are the same thing in Scratch. Each time you click the green flag above the Stage, the cat moves 100 steps, meaning 100 coordinate spaces.

Coordinates are used in every area of STEAM, from grids in art to map making. Coordinates are how you state the exact location of a place or object.

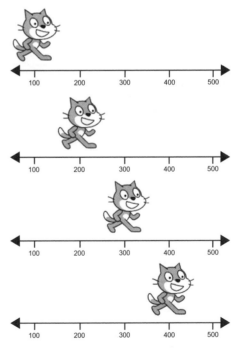

Figure 3.4   The cat jumps ahead 100 coordinate spaces each time the green flag is clicked.

Finding the sprite's location with X and Y coordinates

All programming languages use math (in this case, coordinate numbers) to tell the program what you want it to do. This makes sense because math is a constant; 2 + 2 always equals 4.

Scratch can understand a command such as "move the cat sprite 10 coordinates to the right" (which is clearly math-related), but it can't understand a command such as "move the cat sprite near the house." What house? Unless you assign the house a mathematical location, Scratch has no clue *where* that house is on the screen.

Your directions—where you want sprites to move or where you want objects to be positioned—all need to be described numerically in your program.

In the top right corner of the Script Area is a tiny picture of the sprite you're currently programming (the cat) and two letters (X and Y) next to a number, as in figure 3.5.

Figure 3.5   The top right corner of the Script Area shows the sprite and its X and Y coordinate position. X: 0 and Y: 0 is the center of the Stage.

Click the cat on the Stage and drag it around the Stage. The numbers next to the X and Y are changing, constantly logging the cat's new location.

The Stage is a grid constructed out of horizontal (X) and vertical (Y) lines, called the X-axis and Y-axis. Every location on the Stage can be plotted on those lines, which are its X and Y coordinates. In fact, you can see where those lines are on the Stage by using Scratch's grid backdrop, which shows the axis lines.

To use the grid backdrop

1   Go to the Sprite Zone. Navigate to the left sidebar of the Sprite Zone underneath the words New Backdrop.

2   Click the first icon of the painting to bring up a pop-up window with the Scratch backdrop library.

3   Scroll to the bottom and choose the option XY-Grid. Click OK.

You should now see horizontal and vertical lines behind the cat, as in figure 3.6, along with numbers where they intersect, such as 100 or –100. This is an open grid, only showing every hundredth coordinate. Ten coordinates or 10 steps is 1/10th of one of those squares on the grid. In order to have the cat move the length of one square on that grid, you need to program the cat to move 100 steps.

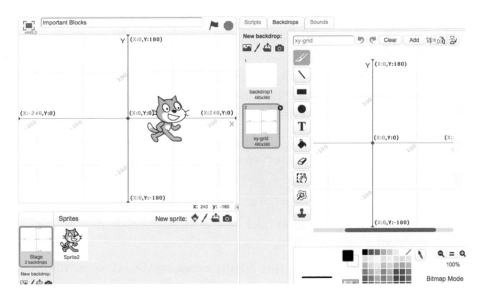

Figure 3.6   The XY-Grid backdrop

X coordinates run from left to right. Y coordinates run up and down. The dot in the center of the screen where the lines meet is zero for both the X and Y coordinates, which is why the numbers in figure 3.5 show

X and Y both set to zero (0). The cat sprite begins each new project in the center of the Stage:

- Positive numbers on the X coordinate (such as 10) move your sprite to the right.
- Positive numbers on the Y coordinate (such as 10) move your sprite up.
- Negative numbers on the X coordinate (such as –10) move your sprite to the left.
- Negative numbers on the Y coordinate (such as –10) move your sprite down.

Scripting with the Change X by 10 block

Let's build a small script that tells the sprite to go to a certain place on the screen. The cat in figure 3.7 is currently in the center of the Stage, but the script you'll write will send the cat to a new position when the green flag is clicked— namely, 100 coordinate spaces toward the top of the Stage.

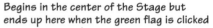

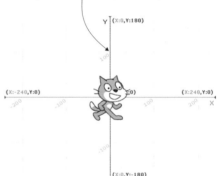

Begins in the center of the Stage but ends up here when the green flag is clicked

Figure 3.7   Send the cat 100 coordinate spaces above the center of the Stage.

To get your workspace ready to program the cat

1 Click the Scripts tab in the Block Menu in order to get back to the blocks.

2 Navigate down to the Sprite Zone and make sure the blue box is around the cat sprite.

You won't need to do this every time, but you do right now because Scratch is still in the backdrop menu.

Now you're ready to get started. To use the Set Y to 0 block

1 In the Block Menu, click Events.

2 Click and drag a When Flag Clicked block into the Script Area.

3 In the Block Menu, click Motion.

4 Click and drag a Set Y to 0 block into the Script Area and snap it onto the When Flag Clicked block.

5 Change the 0 inside the block to 100.

Once again, the two blocks in figure 3.8 form a complete script. Now click the green flag above the Stage.

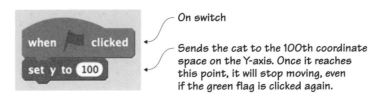

On switch

Sends the cat to the 100th coordinate space on the Y-axis. Once it reaches this point, it will stop moving, even if the green flag is clicked again.

Figure 3.8   A script using the Set Y to 100 block

FIX IT   YOUR SPRITE ISN'T MOVING   Wait a second! Your cat isn't moving even though you wrote a program. When things don't go according to plan with your program, chances are you didn't program the correct sprite. Did you check that the blue box was around the cat in the Sprite Zone? Because you added a backdrop before you started this script, Scratch switched the programming focus to that new backdrop. But you don't want the Stage to do the action; you want the cat to be the one moving to the new coordinate position! Troubleshoot programs that don't run according to plan by making sure the scripts are assigned to the correct sprite. You can check all the scripts assigned to a sprite by clicking the sprite in the Sprite Zone and then looking at the scripts in the Script Area.

The cat will go directly to the 100th coordinate slot on the Y-axis (or Y line). This is the type of program you'll use to position a sprite on the Stage at the beginning of a game.

ANSWER THIS   HOW DO YOU POSITION THE CAT 100 SPACES BELOW CENTER?

Question: you know how to move a sprite up, but can you figure out how to make the cat move down?

Answer: place a minus sign in front of the number (–100) to indicate that it is a negative number. Remember, negative numbers move the sprite to the left and down. Positive numbers move the sprite to the right and up.

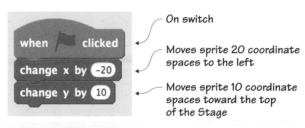

On switch

Moves sprite 20 coordinate spaces to the left

Moves sprite 10 coordinate spaces toward the top of the Stage

Figure 3.9   A script that changes both the X and Y position at the same time

You can also change the X and Y position of the sprite at the same time. To move the cat diagonally, swap out the Set Y to 100 block for two blocks: a Change X by 10 block and a Change Y by 10 block. Snap them underneath the When Flag Clicked block, one on top of the other, as shown in figure 3.9. Change the 10 in the X block to –20 to move the cat 20 coordinate spaces to the left, but keep the 10 in the Y block to move the cat 10 coordinate spaces up. The cat will move diagonally when you click the green flag because it is moving to the left and up at the same time.

Clear the script from the Script Area but keep the grid backdrop for the rest of the games in this chapter because it will help you to see the position of your sprite on the screen.

FIX IT   STEPS AND COORDINATES   In this case, the Move 10 Steps block and the Change X by 10 block accomplish the same thing. One block has a plain-English way of stating the instruction but is dependent on the direction the sprite is facing (move 10 steps), and the other has a mathematical way of stating the instruction (change the current X coordinate number by 10). Both do the same task of moving the sprite 10 spaces to the right and illustrate an important point: sometimes there is more than one way to accomplish the same task in programming, and the code choices are up to the programmer.

Using a conditional statement

You encounter conditional statements every day. Conditional statements state what first needs to be true for something to happen. For instance, your parents might say, "*If* you eat your vegetables, *then* you can have dessert." A condition is set. In order to get dessert, the vegetables need to be eaten. You know what you need to do if you want a piece of chocolate cake: eat your carrots.

How will your parents know if you've eaten your vegetables? They'll look on your plate. If the carrots are still there, the condition hasn't been met, and you won't proceed to dessert. If the carrots are not there (and I hope you're not hiding them under the table!), then you'll move to the next step: getting dessert.

Computers work in the same way.

Finding conditions to set in your game

You can set a condition in a game, such as "*If* the cat sprite is touching something red, *then* make it stop moving." The program checks the cat sprite, as it's doing in figure 3.10.

Figure 3.10   Is the cat touching a red pixel? Look at his foot.

Red pixels make up the outer edge of the rainbow. If the cat is touching the red band of the rainbow, the game will stop the cat from moving. But if the cat sprite is not touching that part of the rainbow, the game will have the cat keep moving until the condition is met.

How do you know if you are setting up a condition? It almost always begins with an If statement when you talk about the game aloud.

Scripting with the If/Then block

Conditional statements are set using the If/Then block. Let's build a script that notes where the sprite is on the screen and makes something happen when it moves past a certain point. In this case, you're going to have the cat stop moving when it moves past the X coordinate position of 50, marked on the backdrop in figure 3.11.

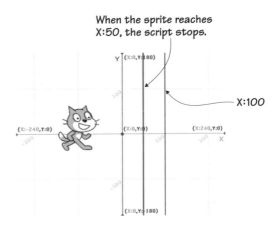

Figure 3.11   The cat will stop moving when it crosses over the X coordinate position of 50, marked by the red line.

To use the If/Then block

1 Click the Events block menu and grab a When Flag Clicked block. Drag it into the Script Area to begin your script.

2 Switch to the Control block menu.

3 Drag an If/Then block to the Script Area and snap it to the When Flag Clicked block. There is a similar-looking If/Then/Else block option, but you want the If/Then block.

4 Click the Operators block menu and choose the Square < Square block.

5 Place the Square < Square block inside the empty hexagonal space on the If/Then block, as in figure 3.12.

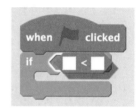

Figure 3.12   Placing the Square < Square block inside the hexagonal space in the If/Then block

6 Click the Motion block menu and scroll to the bottom of the menu.

7 Choose the X Position block and drag it inside the left square in the Operators block. This means that you've nested a Motion block in an Operators block in a Control block, as in figure 3.13.

8 Type the number 50 in the right square of the Operators block.

9 Scroll up in the Motion block menu and click and drag a Move 10 Steps block into the Script Area, placing it inside the open mouth of the If/Then block.

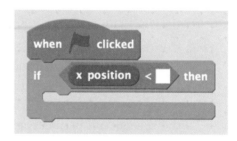

Figure 3.13   The X Position block inside the left square of the Operators block

Figure 3.14 shows a slightly more complicated script than you've made up until this point. Click the green flag above the Stage a few times and see what happens when the cat sprite moves too far to the right side of the Stage.

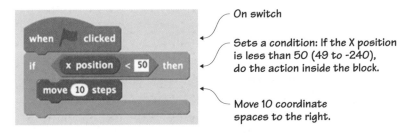

On switch

Sets a condition: If the X position is less than 50 (49 to -240), do the action inside the block.

Move 10 coordinate spaces to the right.

Figure 3.14   The If/Then block sets up a condition that only allows the sprite to move 10 coordinate spaces to the right if the X position is less than 50.

Once the cat's X position is 50 or higher, it no longer meets the condition, so the cat stops moving. If you want to try running this program again, drag the cat back toward the left side of the Stage.

Putting conditional statements into your game means that Scratch needs to constantly be evaluating whether or not the statement is true or the condition has been met. That means that by using a single block, you've set a lot of computational energy to work. This is a common way of making things happen in games, and you'll find that each computer language has its own unique way of writing conditional statements.

LEARN IT   LESS THAN (<), GREATER THAN (>), AND EQUAL (=)   A common practice in computer programming is to set up conditions that use operators, asking the computer to solve what amounts to a quick math problem as it runs. Three common Operators blocks are the Square < Square (less than), Square = Square (equal), and Square > Square (greater than), all seen in figure 3.15.

Figure 3.15   Three types of Operators blocks used in Scratch

These three Operators blocks allow for three different situations. In the first block, the statement is true if the sprite is in an X position less than 10. In the middle block, the statement is true if the sprite has an X position equal to 10. In the last block, the statement is true if the sprite has an X position greater than 10.

Making loops

Sometimes you want an action to happen once. Other times you want the action to happen over and over again. A *loop* is used when you want a piece of code to run until either a condition is met or the red stop sign above the Stage is clicked. For instance, you could make your cat spin round and round, as in figure 3.16, just by putting the blue Motion block inside the yellow Forever block.

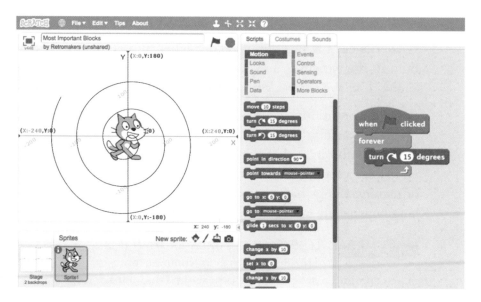

Figure 3.16   The Forever block in the script makes the cat continue turning without needing to click the green flag over and over again.

Finding places to use loops

There are a few loop blocks used in Scratch, all found in the Control block menu. The most common and flexible one is the Forever block. If you place other blocks inside a yellow Forever block, Scratch will repeat those actions over and over again.

Think about times when you would want an action to occur without needing player input, such as having the cat continue to move without needing to continuously click the green flag. Loops allow you to set up a situation once and have it run over and over again, bringing fluidity to the sprite's movement on the screen.

Scripting with the Forever block

Any blocks you put inside the Forever block will continue their action without you needing to click the green flag above the Stage more than once to get the loop started. Let's make that small script that will cause your cat sprite to spin indefinitely. See figure 3.17.

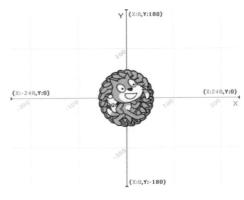

Figure 3.17   The cat is spinning so quickly due to the Forever block repeating the action over and over again that it looks like there are dozens of cats.

To use a Forever block

1 Navigate to the Events block menu and click and drag a When Flag Clicked block to the Script Area. Release the block near the top of the workspace.

2 Switch to the Control block menu. Drag a Forever block to the Script Area and snap it to the When Flag Clicked block.

3 Click the Motion block menu and choose a Turn 15 Degrees block. Put this blue block inside the Forever block, as seen in figure 3.18.

When you click the green flag above the Stage, your sprite will start spinning like a pinwheel. A circle is 360 degrees, so 15 degrees would be turning 1/24 of a circle. The action looks smooth because Scratch doesn't pause between each 15 degree turn.

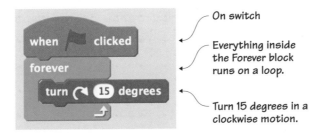

On switch

Everything inside the Forever block runs on a loop.

Turn 15 degrees in a clockwise motion.

Figure 3.18   This loop using the Forever block causes the cat to spin in a circle.

The example script consists of only three blocks, but with a single click of a button, it can run forever.

Using variables

A *variable* is a way of tracking information. That information, called a *value*, can be a number, word, or true/false condition. For instance, let's say you make a game and you want to give the player three chances to have the cat catch a balloon. Each time the cat misses the balloon, the game deducts a turn. To keep track of how many times the player has tried to catch the balloon, you could make a variable called Turns and give it a value of 3, meaning the player has 3 chances to catch the falling balloon. Each time the player misses the balloon, the value of the variable Turns decreases by 1. When the value hits 0, the game ends.

Check out the orange bubble at the top of the Stage in figure 3.19 showing that the player has three turns. That balloon is pretty far away from the cat. Do you think it will make it across the Stage in time?

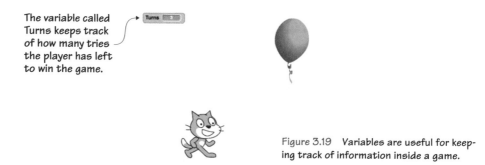

The variable called Turns keeps track of how many tries the player has left to win the game.

Figure 3.19   Variables are useful for keeping track of information inside a game.

You could also create a variable called Score and have the value of that variable *increase* by 1 every time the player gains another point. I like to imagine variables as empty boxes, ready to hold any number, word, or true/false value I place inside.

Finding types of variables

A game may have multiple variables at the same time. For instance, it may be tracking how many lives the player has with a variable called

Lives while simultaneously tracking how many points the player has earned with a second variable called Score. It may even have variables assigned to objects in the game so Scratch can know whether or not the sprite "picked up" a tool or a jewel. Anything you want to track in the game uses a variable.

Variables can have three types of values, as shown in table 3.2.

The variable in figure 3.19 has a *numerical value*. The variable starts the game with a value of 3, which means that the player has 3 tries. A variable can also have a *word* value, called a

Table 3.2   **The three types of values**

Type of value	Example of value
Numerical	3
Word (or string)	Diamond
True/False (or Boolean)	True

string in programming. A string is any word you could assign an object, such as having a variable called Jewel and having the value either be *diamond, ruby, sapphire*, or *emerald. Diamond, ruby, sapphire*, and *emerald* are all strings. A variable can also have a *true/false* value, called a *Boolean* in programming. You'll read more about these in the next section when you learn about Touching blocks.

Scripting with the Variable block

Programming the falling balloon part would make this script a little complicated, so let's simplify the idea and build a script that uses a variable called Lives and have it deduct a life every time the cat sprite reaches the right side of the Stage. See figure 3.20.

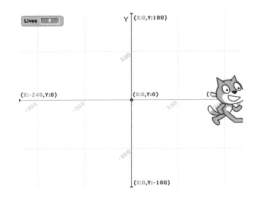

Figure 3.20   Oh no! The variable Lives goes from 3 to 2 when the cat hits the right wall.

Variables don't exist in Scratch until you create one. Once created, Scratch gives variables an initial numerical value of zero (0). You can change that value to be anything you want — numerical, string, or Boolean.

Before you begin, you need to create the variable. To create a variable block

1 Navigate to the Block Menu and click Data.
2 Click Make a Variable. This will cause a pop-up window to open.
3 Give your variable a name, such as Lives. Leave it For All Sprites. Click OK.

You should see your variable in two places: inside the Data block menu and as a little box in the top left corner of the Stage.

Now you need to use your variable and give it a value. To use a variable block

1 Click the Events block menu and drag a When Flag Clicked block into the Script Area.
2 Switch to the Data block menu and choose a Set Lives to 0 block. Click and drag it under the When Flag Clicked block in the Script Area until they snap together.
3 Change the value in the Set Lives to 0 block to 3 in order to give the player 3 lives.
4 Return to the Block Menu, choose Control, and grab a Forever block. Snap that underneath the Set Lives to 0 block.
5 Switch to the Motion block menu and click and drag a Move 10 Steps block inside the Forever block.
6 Go back to Control and move an If/Then block underneath the Move 10 Steps block inside the Forever block.
7 Click the Sensing block menu and drag a Touching block to the If/Then block. Drop it inside the empty, hexagonal space in the If/Then block. Open the drop-down menu in the new block by clicking inside its box, as seen in figure 3.21, and click Edge so that the block now says Touching Edge.

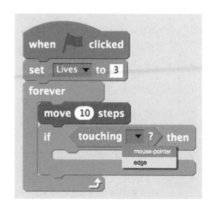

Figure 3.21   The drop-down menu that comes with the Touching block from the Sensing menu

Finally, you need the script to delete a life whenever the sprite hits the wall. To deduct a life, continue filling the If/Then block:

1 Open the Data block menu and choose the Change Lives by 1. Drag it inside the If/Then block in the Script Area.

2 Change the value from 1 to –1 in order to deduct (instead of add) a life.

3 Switch to the Motion block menu and grab a Set X to 0 block. Snap it underneath the Change Lives by –1 block inside the If/Then block. Change the value from 0 to –200 to send your sprite back to the left side of the Stage, because the –200 X coordinate is the far left side of the Stage.

You can see the completed script in figure 3.22. This is your first long script, and it completes a complex task. When you click the green flag above the Stage, the cat should move toward the right. When it touches the right wall, it should bounce back toward the left side of the Stage while simultaneously deducting a life. Because you didn't set an end point, you should see your life count move from 3 into the negative numbers.

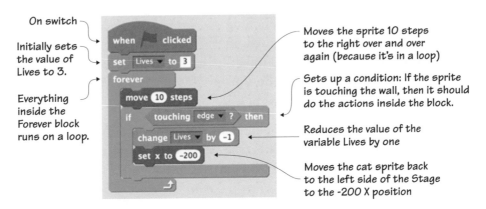

Figure 3.22   The script deducts a life every time the sprite touches the wall.

You'll notice every time you restart your game by clicking the green flag again, the value of Lives resets to 3. This is an important step. If you don't set that value at the start of the game, it will continue wherever the last player left off. It wouldn't be a fun game if the first player used up the three lives and every other player that came after that started with less than zero lives!

But the Set Lives to 3 block comes *before* the Forever block because it's something you only want to have happen once per game, right when the game begins. Everything inside the Forever block is something you want to have happen throughout the game.

Talking about variables leads directly into another place where you can use true/false or Boolean statements: touching blocks.

Using Booleans

As I mentioned earlier, a Boolean is a fancy programming term for a true/false statement. For instance, what if you add a unicorn sprite, and you want to check whether or not your cat sprite is touching the unicorn sprite, as shown in figure 3.23? It either is touching (true) or it isn't touching (false)—it can't both be touching and not touching the unicorn at the same time, right?

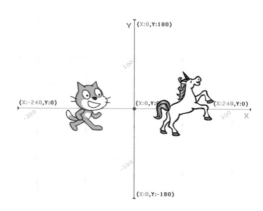

Figure 3.23   You can use Booleans in a script to figure out whether two sprites are touching.

You can set up conditionals with Booleans so Scratch will keep checking whether a statement is true or false. If it's true, it will do one thing, and if it's false, it will not do that action.

Finding uses for Booleans

It's easy to see why programmers like to use true/false statements. There is no grey area: either the cat is (true) or is not (false) doing the action established in the script, such as touching another sprite or touching the edge of the Stage.

Nowhere is this easier to see than when using the Touching Color blocks. The Touching Color blocks provide an easy way to see Booleans in action. If the sprite is touching even one pixel of a set color, the statement is true. If the sprite isn't touching the color, the statement is false. You can set certain actions to run if the statement is true.

Scripting with Touching blocks and Booleans

Let's make a script that looks at whether or not the cat is touching an apple sprite. If it is touching the apple, it will say, "Yum!" for two seconds, as in figure 3.24.

To add a new apple sprite from Scratch's premade sprite library

1 Navigate to the Sprite Zone. Click the little head icon next to New Sprite on the Top Toolbar, as you did in chapter 1 when adding the bananas.

2 Choose the apple sprite by double-clicking the picture.

3 Set up the Stage by dragging the cat sprite toward the left side of the screen and the apple toward the right side of the screen, as in figure 3.25.

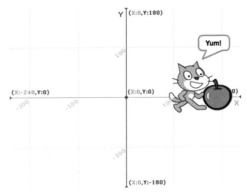

Figure 3.24 The cat says "Yum!" when it touches the black outline of the apple. If any part of the cat sprite is touching any part of the apple outline, the script will work.

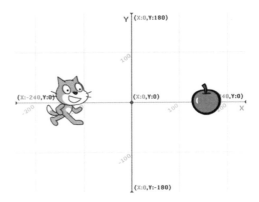

Figure 3.25 Setting up the Stage with the cat on the left and the apple on the right

The apple is surrounded by a black outline, which means in this script (because the cat is moving tiny amounts each time), the cat sprite will touch black pixels before it ever gets to the red pixels inside the black outline.

FIX IT   THE SPRITE TOUCHES THE WRONG COLOR   Uh-oh—have you made this mistake? The biggest mistake Scratchers make when setting the Touching Color block is to skip over the outline and use the overall color of the object, such as red for the apple. The sprite may touch the outline before it touches any internal color depending on the script, so note the color of the outline, too. Make the outline of any sprites that you make one uniform color instead of many colors if you're going to use a Touching Color block in your game.

Before you begin writing your program, check that the blue box is around the cat in the Sprite Zone. If not, you're programming the apple!

To use the Touching Color block

1 Navigate to the Events block menu and click and drag the When Flag Clicked block into the Script Area. Release it near the top of the workspace.

2 Go into the Control block menu and choose the Repeat Until block. It has an empty, hexagonal space in the block. Snap this block underneath the When Flag Clicked block.

3 Click the Sensing block menu and choose the Touching Color block. It will not have the name of a color listed, but instead has a square that contains a paint sample.

4 Set the color by clicking the tiny square inside the block so the cursor arrow changes into a hand. Move the hand to the Stage and click anywhere on the apple's outline so that the square turns black. Once the color is set, the hand will disappear and turn back to an arrow.

5 Return to the Block Menu and click Motion. Choose the Move 10 Steps block and place it inside the Repeat Until block.

6 Go to the Control block menu and choose an If/Then block. Place it inside the Repeat Until block, underneath the Move 10 Steps block.

7 Duplicate the Touching Color block by either right-clicking the block (on a PC) or control-clicking the block (on a Mac). A pop-up window will give you the option to duplicate your block, as seen in figure 3.26. Choose Duplicate and slide the copy of the Touching Color block inside the empty hexagonal space in the If/Then block.

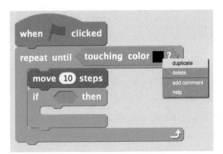

Figure 3.26   Duplicating a piece of code within a script

8 Switch to the Looks block menu and grab a Say Hello for 2 Secs block. Put it inside the If/Then block.

9 Change the word *Hello!* to *Yum!* by erasing and typing inside the small text window on the block.

Test the script shown in figure 3.27 by clicking the green flag above the Stage. When the cat touches the apple, it says "Yum!" for two seconds.

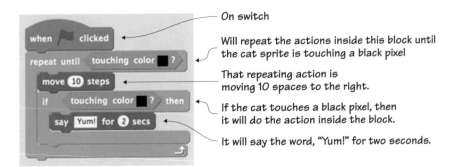

— On switch

Will repeat the actions inside this block until the cat sprite is touching a black pixel

That repeating action is moving 10 spaces to the right.

If the cat touches a black pixel, then it will *do* the action inside the block.

It will say the word, "Yum!" for two seconds.

Figure 3.27   If the cat is touching any black pixel on the screen, it will say, "Yum!"

It looks like the cat on the Stage can see the apple and exclaims, "Yum!" when it gets beside it. All this is done behind the scenes with Booleans and Touching Color blocks.

If there had been numerous other sprites on the Stage, all of which had black pixel outlines, the cat wouldn't have known whether it was touching the apple or a different sprite. Keep that in mind as you make tweaks to sprites in this book or build future games.

LEARN IT THINK LIKE A CODER   Sometimes you need to get up from the computer and do other things with your day, but that doesn't mean you can't keep thinking like a coder. Look around you and you'll see your world is full of Booleans, or true/false situations, where something either is or isn't. Make your life into a video game by looking for all the true/false moments. For instance, set a conditional while you eat breakfast: if my plate is empty, then breakfast is over. Now keep checking your plate. If it's empty, the condition is true. If you still have some toast in front of you, the condition is false. Practice thinking in Booleans to come up with creative video game ideas to use in the future.

You can get rid of the apple sprite (as well as your last script) by clicking the scissor icon in the Grey Toolbar and clicking either the apple on the Stage or in the Sprite Zone. Why do you need to clear the Stage? Because you're about to get a lot of cats popping up on the screen.

Cloning sprites

I'll let you in on a little secret: programmers love to find shortcuts to lessen their workload. If you've ever played a fixed shooter that has you blowing apart space rocks or played a reflex-testing game like Tetris, which has you guiding falling shapes, you've seen cloning in action. *Cloning* allows the programmer to make a few varieties of enemy—in those examples, space rocks or colorful shapes—

Figure 3.28   The falling balloons are generating mid-game using cloning. You only need to make one sprite. Scratch will keep reproducing new copies with a cloning script.

and then have the computer generate more copies as the game goes on, like all the falling balloons in figure 3.28.

Although you can make a duplicate of a sprite before a game begins using the stamp icon in the Grey Toolbar, cloning is about generating a new version of the sprite while the game is in action by writing it into the code.

Finding sprites to clone mid-game

This will be your first time making multiple scripts work together in order to perform an action. Cloning always requires at least two scripts that work together. The first script creates the clone. The second script uses the clone.

For instance, you may create one balloon for your game and then create a first script that tells Scratch to generate clones of the balloon mid-game. Next you have to create a second script that tells Scratch how to use those clones. Maybe you'll have them drop from the sky, one every second. In games, you may have many scripts assigned to the same sprite, each running one small part of what the sprite can do, so this is excellent practice for the games ahead.

You can clone any sprite, which means you can even create multiple copies of the cat mid-game. In fact, let's make a script that does that.

Scripting with Cloning blocks

This two-part script is going to fill your screen with identical cats. The first script will duplicate a new cat sprite every second. The second script will make those cats march to the left or right. Watch out! The Stage is about to get very crowded, as it is in figure 3.29.

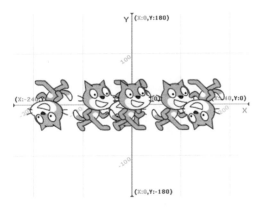

Figure 3.29 **The cats keep duplicating and marching across the Stage in a two-part cloning script.**

To clone a sprite during a game

1 Click the Events menu, choose the When Flag Clicked block, and drag it to the Script Area. Release it near the top of the workspace.

2 Go into Control and grab a Forever block. Snap the Forever block directly under the When Flag Clicked block.

3 Scroll down the Block Menu and click the Create Clone of Myself block. Drag it inside the Forever block.

4 Scroll up and choose the Wait 1 Secs block, and place that under the Create Clone of Myself block inside the Forever block.

The first script is complete. It's now time to start the second script, which will be placed right underneath the first script in the Script Area:

1 Begin a second script by leaving a small space between the first script and the second script. In the Control block menu, choose a When I Start as a Clone block and drag it to the Script Area.

2 Click a Forever block and snap it underneath the When I Start as a Clone block in the workspace.

3 Switch to the Motion block menu.

4 Slide a Move 10 Steps block inside the Forever block.

5 Slide an If on Edge, Bounce block underneath the Move 10 Steps block inside the Forever block.

Now click the green flag above the Stage and you should see dozens of cats march across the screen as a new one is added every second. Compare your scripts to the ones in figure 3.30.

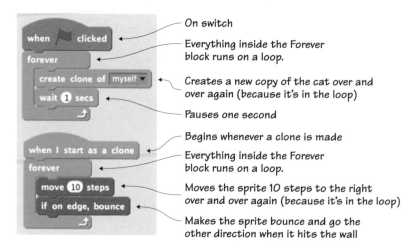

Figure 3.30   The completed clone scripts work together to create an infinite number of cats.

Why insert a one-second delay into the program? That small pause will make a space between the clones so you'll be able to see each individual version of the cat rather than having them all mash together on top of one another.

These two scripts will work together indefinitely because no end condition has been set. That means if you start this program and walk away, you'll return to a thick line of cat sprites on your Stage.

Congratulations! You now have a screen full of cats, but you can also use this script to make games more exciting while making your workload a bit smaller.

ANSWER THIS HOW CAN YOU KEEP THE CATS FROM FLIPPING UPSIDE DOWN?

Question: those upside-down cats are probably feeling a bit sick hanging in midair. Why are some cats upside-down and others are right-side-up?

Answer: when the cat reaches the right or left side of the screen, it bounces off the edge and switches direction. Rather than twist around, your cat hits the edge and flips over before it continues back in the other direction and generates again. If you want your cats to remain right-side-up, navigate to the Sprite Zone and click the lowercase *i* in the top left corner of the blue box around the sprite. That will open the pop-up menu seen in figure 3.31. Next to Rotation Style, click the straight left-and-right arrow instead of the curved arrow. To exit the pop-up menu, click the blue arrow in the top left corner of the box. Now click the green flag. Do your cats remain right-side-up?

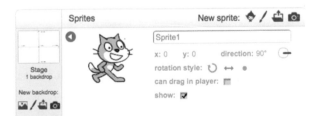

Figure 3.31 Click the *i* to change how your sprite moves.

You just made two scripts work together to make and use cloned sprites. The final script in this chapter will allow you to make *unrelated* scripts communicate with one another.

Broadcasting messages

Figure 3.32   You can use broadcasting to send a Game Over message when the player uses up all of the lives.

Have you ever been in a relay race where you are passed a baton and begin to run? Scratch has a way of sending messages between two unrelated scripts so one script can pass a virtual baton to the other script and tell it to run. For instance, a broadcasting script could be used to track the number of tries left in the variable Lives. When it reaches zero, it sends the second script a message to flash the Game Over sprite on the screen, as shown in figure 3.32.

Finding a message to broadcast

Broadcasting allows two scripts to speak to one another by letting the first script tell the second script (or more) that it's time to spring into action.

This is different from the way the two cloning scripts worked together. With cloning, an action happens that sets off another action, almost like dominos. In broadcasting, you set up one script to send the other script a message that it is time to begin without the first script making or doing anything.

You'll once again make two scripts. The second script won't do anything until it gets the signal from the first script. Then the second script will spring into action.

Scripting with the Broadcasting block

A cat walks up to a bear. When the cat reaches a certain point on the Stage, the first script will broadcast a message to the second script to spring into action, and the bear will call out, "Hello!" It's a friendly bear, as you can see in figure 3.33.

Figure 3.33   The bear sprite calls out "Hello!" to the cat when it passes over a certain point on the Stage.

So what is happening behind the scenes in Scratch? Script One tells the cat to (1) start walking. In fact, it sticks that walking command inside a loop so it keeps happening until a condition is met. And what is that condition? To do something when (2) the cat reaches the middle of the screen. That *something* is to send a message, which is the virtual baton being passed to the next script. Script Two receives that broadcasted message and begins going through a series of actions. Well, really, one action: that friendly bear says "Hello!" once it receives the message sent from the first script saying that the second script is ready to run. If you didn't set it up this way, the bear may be calling out, "Hello!" before the cat is nearby. And then how would the cat know that this is a friendly bear?

This example needs two sprites, and you'll need to be careful that you're programming the correct sprite. The sender is the cat, and the receiver is the bear.

Before you begin, you'll need to add a second sprite to the Stage. Navigate to the Sprite Zone and click the head icon next to New Sprite. Double-click the bear sprite. Now set up your Stage by dragging your cat to the left side of the Stage and your bear to the right side of the Stage. Now you're ready to program the cat. Make sure the blue box is around the cat in the Sprite Zone.

To make your first script

1 Navigate to the Events block menu and choose a When Flag Clicked block. Drag it over to the Script Area.

2 Click Control, choose the Forever block, and place it under the When Flag Clicked block.

3 Switch to the Motion block menu and click and drag the Change X by 10 block to the Script Area. Place it inside the Forever block.

4 Change back to the Control block menu and choose an If/Then block that goes under the Change X by 10 block inside the Forever block.

5 Go to the Operators block menu and choose a Square > Square block. Place it inside the empty hexagonal space in the If/Then block.

6 Return to Motion and scroll down until you find the X Position block. Slide it into the left square on the Square > Square block. Type a zero (0) in the right square.

7 Navigate back to Events and choose a Broadcast Message1 block. Open the drop-down menu and click New Message. Type *Hello* in the pop-up window.

8 Go back to Control and slide a Wait 1 Secs block underneath the Broadcast Hello block. Change the 1 to a 3. This will put a pause into the script so it will be easier to see the bear say hello.

The completed first script in figure 3.34 sets when the cat sprite will send out the message.

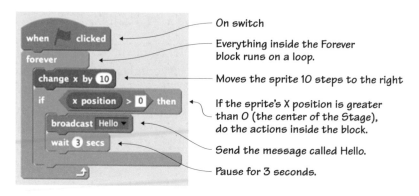

Figure 3.34 The first script broadcasts a message once the cat passes the center point on the Stage.

Now the bear needs to receive the message. Switch to programming the bear by clicking the bear in the Sprite Zone.

FIX IT YOUR SCRIPT DISAPPEARED! Watch out! Looking in your Script Area and seeing it empty may cause you a moment of panic, but don't worry. Your scripts are safe and sound; they're attached to a different sprite. The Script Area only shows the scripts applied to the sprite chosen in the Sprite Zone. When you click the bear, the script for the cat disappears. Click the cat, and the script reappears. If you ever have a script disappear, click each of the sprites in the Sprite Zone and check the Script Area. Chances are your script isn't gone; it's attached to a different sprite.

To start the receiving script

1 Navigate to the Events menu and choose a When I Receive Hello block. Drag it into the Script Area and release it near the top of the workspace.

2 Click Looks and drag the Say Hello! for 2 Secs block. Snap it underneath the When I Receive Hello block.

In figure 3.35, you can see the completed receiving broadcasting script. Click the green flag above the Stage. What happens when the cat starts moving?

Begins whenever the Hello message is sent

Says "Hello!" for two seconds

Figure 3.35   The brief receiving script has the bear say "Hello!"

These two scripts interact with one another to make the bear say "Hello!"when the cat crosses over the middle of the Stage. The first script sends the message, but it does more than that. It monitors where the cat is on the Stage, checking its X position to see if it is more than 0. It has instructions to send the message to the other script once the cat passes the center of the Stage, because 0 is the midway point on the X-axis. You should also see the cat slow down and move in small jumps after it gets to the midway point due to the Wait 3 Secs block, which you inserted so you could see the bear's script. It's not just pausing sending the message—it's pausing the cat's movement. It still moves 10 steps, but only every 3 seconds after it passes the midway point on the Stage.

And what is the bear's script? It's pretty simple. The first block, When I Receive Hello, is the receiver block. It's like the baton being put in the bear's hand and telling him it's his turn. It starts the action attached to this second on switch: to say "Hello!" for two seconds.

The ability to send messages between scripts means you can create some pretty complicated games in Scratch.

Learning in action

Welcome to the world of computer science. You learned eight computer science concepts in a single chapter. You'll explore these ideas in depth through the rest of the book as you make games. Getting comfortable with these ideas is important because they're the foundation for every coding language, from Scratch to Ruby to Java and beyond. Understanding them in Scratch will help you springboard later on into the larger programming world.

CHALLENGE Make sure you understand these coding concepts by making your own example scripts in the style of the exercises in this chapter. Can you make a simple conditional statement? Figure out a use for a variable? Set up directions to run in a loop?

Pause for a moment to think about how much you've already learned:

- How to set a starting point for your program so it can run
- How to find a sprite's X and Y coordinates to know its location on the Stage
- How to write conditional statements so you can have actions happen at a certain moment
- How to create loops to keep pieces of code running indefinitely
- How to build variables so you can track information
- How to understand Booleans and how important true/false statements are for programming
- How to make clones of sprites in the middle of a game
- How to broadcast messages between two scripts

You'll use all these programming elements in the games that appear in this book. In fact, let's get started with the first game, a two-player ball-and-paddle game called Breakfast Wars. Yes, it's time to conclude all the preparatory work that you accomplished in the chapters of part one, "Setting up the arcade," and move onto part two, "Turning on the machines." For the next two chapters, you'll learn how to make a game with step-by-step instructions and a lot of reminders. Ready to put this computer science knowledge to work?

Part 2

Turning on the machines

Now that you know your way around Scratch and grasp some basic ideas in computer programming, you're going to make a retro-style arcade game. We're going to hold your hand through this process, telling you where everything is located and which colors to choose.

The game is broken down into a two-chapter set. The first chapter is the art chapter where you'll make all the sprites for your game. The second chapter is the coding chapter where you'll learn how to piece together the game with small scripts.

Before you jump into making the game, you should know that your game won't be playable until you write your final script for the program. But that doesn't mean you have to cross your fingers and hope for the best. The way you check your work is to compare the scripts you create on your screen to the scripts in the book. If they match, you're good to go, and we'll help you make any tweaks in the trouble-shooting section.

4

Designing a two-player ball-and-paddle game

A fight breaks out over breakfast, and there is only one way to settle it: bounce a fried egg between two cast-iron skillets without letting it hit the wall. This two-player game ends when one person reaches seven points by making their opponent miss the egg. Breakfast Wars is a remake of the first ball-and-paddle game, *Pong*, though it replaces *Pong*'s white line paddle with a pan and its LED light with an egg, as seen in figure 4.1.

Breakfast Wars is all the fun of table tennis without leaving your living room.

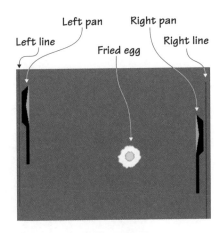

Figure 4.1   A game of Breakfast Wars means making a purple backdrop, a fried egg, two skillets, and two lines to serve as walls.

A unique game calls for unique sprites, and making them means learning some core art concepts. In this chapter, you will learn

* How the color wheel breaks down into primary, secondary, and tertiary colors

- How to balance color between backgrounds and sprites
- How to make color choices work together in your game

Let's start by making a simple, purple background.

Prepping the background while meeting the color wheel

Backgrounds usually set the scene, giving the player information about the type of game they're about to play. A game set in space may have a black background with little white dots for stars, whereas a game set on a farm is going to have pixelated green meadows. Breakfast Wars has a solid purple background to keep the player's focus solely on the fried egg.

Making the breakfast nook background

Imagine a breakfast nook with purple walls. You're going to make the simple, solid background in figure 4.2 using a single color that will help the fried egg visually pop on the screen.

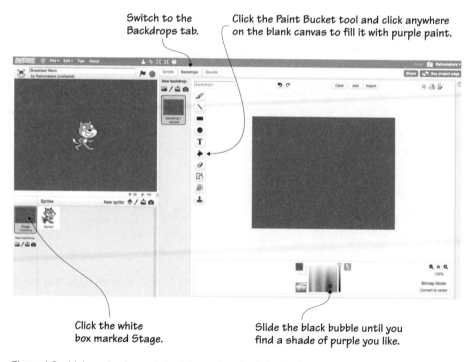

Switch to the Backdrops tab.

Click the Paint Bucket tool and click anywhere on the blank canvas to fill it with purple paint.

Click the white box marked Stage.

Slide the black bubble until you find a shade of purple you like.

Figure 4.2   Make a simple purple backdrop using the Paint Bucket tool.

To make a new backdrop

1 Navigate to the Sprite Zone and click the white box marked Stage on the left side of the screen. Move to the Block Menu and click the second tab labeled Backdrops.

2 Click the rainbow box in the Color Toolbar of the Art Editor and slide the black bubble around the box to choose a shade of dark purple.

3 Choose the Paint Bucket tool. Click anywhere on the canvas to fill the space with your chosen shade of purple.

This background provides contrast so the player can easily see where the egg is at all times, similar to how the original *Pong* paired a solid black background with the white dot.

Meeting the color wheel

If you could only afford three cans of paint, you'd be smart to buy red, yellow, and blue. These three colors can be used to make every other color, which is why they are called the *primary colors*. Locate them on the color wheel in figure 4.3 and you'll see that in between, there are secondary and tertiary colors. To make the secondary colors, you add two primary colors together. For instance, to make orange, you combine red and yellow. To make the tertiary colors, you add a primary and secondary color together.

A color recipe list:

- *Primary colors*—Red, yellow, blue

- *Secondary colors*—Orange (red + yellow), green (yellow + blue), purple (blue + red)

- *Tertiary colors*—Vermilion (red + orange), marigold (orange + yellow), chartreuse (yellow + green), teal (green + blue), violet (blue + purple), magenta (purple + red)

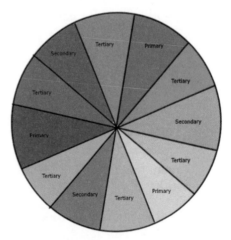

Figure 4.3   The color wheel showing primary, secondary, and tertiary colors

Sometimes you'll hear colors referred to as *hues*. The 12 hues are the pure versions of the primary, secondary, and tertiary colors seen on the wheel. You can change these colors into even more colors by adding white, black, or grey.

Understanding the layout of the wheel will be important in the next section when I talk about complementary colors (colors that contrast) and analogous colors (colors that work together).

Prepping the main sprites

The point to having a simple background is to keep the focus on your sprites: the fried egg and the two frying pans.

This game has no room for feline sprites, which means the cat on the Stage has to go. Navigate to the Grey Toolbar at the top of the screen, click the scissor icon, and click the cat on the Stage. You're now ready to start making the first sprite of this game.

Making the egg sprite

The egg sprite uses two color ideas you'll see a lot in this book: complementary and analogous color choices.

Complementary refers to the fact that they are directly across from one another on the color wheel. Return to figure 4.3 and take a look: red is across from green, and orange is across from blue. Each of these sets contains two colors that complement one another. *Complement*, in this case, means to complete each other and work together. Look at figure 4.4 to see the complementary colors of the purple backdrop and yellow egg yolk at work.

Figure 4.4 The purple contrasts with the yellow, making it stand out, which is important because you need the player to be able to visually track where the egg is on the screen at all times.

At the same time, unless you live with Dr. Seuss, egg yolks are yellow, and the darker the better. This yolk is a blend of orange and yellow, which are analogous colors.

Analogous colors are three or more colors that are all next to each other on the color wheel. For instance, the orange, marigold, and yellow that you'll use for the yolk are analogous colors, as seen in figure 4.5. Other example analogous color combinations are green, teal, and blue or purple, magenta, and red. Analogous color combinations make your eyes happy because the colors are all neighbors on the color wheel. Analogous color combinations are used in pixel art to create depth, and that is accomplished by

Figure 4.5 The three analogous colors used to make the yolk of the retro egg

using one color a little bit (the marigold in the yolk), another color a little bit more than that (the orange in the outline), and the final color even more than that (the yellow that fills the rest of the yolk). You're not only layering the colors; you're layering the amount of each color. Whenever you want to add a little variety to a monochromatic sprite (*monochromatic* means only using one color), layer in some depth by filling a few pixels with analogous colors.

Before you start making your yolk, let's talk about *staircasing*, a common method for creating curved, pixelated lines that you'll use a lot in this book.

 STAIRCASE METHOD Many times in pixelated art, you'll see what I call the staircase method being used to create curved lines. Nothing has more curved lines than a circular yolk! To use the staircase method, you place down two (or more) pixels side-by-side. Then you stack two pixels below the last pixel on the right. Next, you place another two pixels horizontally to the right of the new bottom pixel. This pattern will also repeat in reverse, making upward or upside-down staircases, as seen in figure 4.6. With staircasing, you'll always have two pixels running alongside each other, either side-by-side or one on top of the other.

Alternating between pixels downward and pixels to the side makes a staircase pattern used for curved lines.

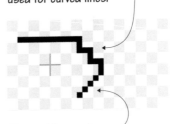

Diagonal line made up of single pixels

Figure 4.6 Staircasing is used for curved corners, though you'll sometimes use a diagonal line of pixels.

This is different from having two pixels touch on their corners to create a diagonal line, like the one in figure 4.6.

To make a new sprite, go to the Sprite Zone and click the paintbrush icon next to New Sprite. This will open up the grey and white pixelated canvas of the Sprite Art Editor:

1 Zoom in three times using the magnifying glass in the Color Toolbar. The canvas should be at 800%.

2 Choose the Paintbrush tool from the Side Toolbar. Keep the brush at its default size, which will create a small square (rather than the larger dot you used to make the cat in chapter 2).

3 Navigate to the Color Toolbar and choose the orange paint sample square.

4 Draw a line of eight orange pixels the length of four white or grey boxes on the canvas. If you are picturing a staircase, this line serves as the landing at the top of the stairs (or 12 o'clock on a circle when it comes to the yolk).

5 Starting at the far right of the line, draw two pixels down.

6 Extend the line two pixels out to the right. Alternate between two pixels going to the right and down to create the staircased corner shown in figure 4.7.

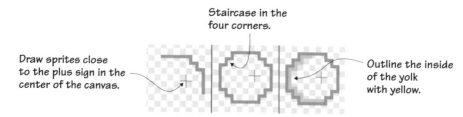

Staircase in the
four corners.

Draw sprites close
to the plus sign in the
center of the canvas.

Outline the inside
of the yolk
with yellow.

Figure 4.7   Using staircasing to create the curves of the circular yolk

7 Draw eight orange pixels straight down and then repeat the staircase method, working inward, making a line to the left, then a line down, to the left, and down.

8 Make an eight-pixel line across the bottom of the yolk, parallel to the one at the top.

9 Continue making two steps at each corner and longer lines in between, to connect the orange line in the shape of a pixelated circle.

10 Click the Paintbrush tool and switch to the yellow paint sample square. Begin outlining the inside of the yolk, starting midway across the top of the yolk and finishing across the full bottom of the yolk. Check the third step in figure 4.7 to see this idea in action.

11 Complete the yolk by switching to the rainbow box and sliding the bubble upward to choose a lighter shade of yellow. Use the Paint Bucket tool to fill the remaining space on the yolk.

Now you need to make the egg white that surrounds the yolk. If you've ever fried an egg, you've seen that the edge gets a bit crispy and darker than the rest of the whites, which means your egg needs a grey or brown outline:

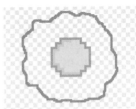

Figure 4.8 The brown outline of the egg before the egg white is filled

1 Switch to grey or brown to draw a wavy circle around the yolk to serve as the edge of the egg white, as seen in figure 4.8.

2 Select the white paint and fill the egg using the Paint Bucket tool.

> **FIX IT**   THE PAINT FILLED THE SCREEN! Are you looking at a completely white canvas instead of an egg? Remember, if you have even one pixel open, the paint will spill outside the edge of the egg when you use the Paint Bucket tool. Use the Undo arrow to erase the spilled paint and then check your edge. You may need to zoom in by clicking the magnifying glass in the bottom right corner of the Art Editor to find the open pixel and use the Paintbrush tool to close the outline.

You now have a pixelated egg, like the one in figure 4.9. Navigate to the Sprite Zone, click the blue *i*, and name this sprite Pixel Egg.

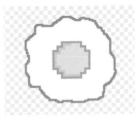

Figure 4.9 The completed Pixel Egg sprite

> **LEARN IT**   COOL COLORS AND WARM COLORS Sometimes you'll hear people talk about cool colors and warm colors. Knowing which colors are considered "cool" and which are "warm" can help you choose a good color scheme for your game. If you want to keep your players calm, go

for *cool colors* such as green, blue, and purple. If you want to make your players riled up, go for *warm colors* such as red, orange, and yellow. Colors make us feel calm or excited, so think about which feeling you're going for with your game. You'll notice that with complementary colors, one color is always warm (yellow), and the other is always cool (purple). This is one more contrast that makes these colors work well with one another, each making the other more vibrant in comparison.

Making the greyscale pan sprites

You also need to make the pans. You will save yourself a little bit of time by making one pan, duplicating it, and making it switch direction, a math move known as *reflection*. The pan will be black and grey, as seen in figure 4.10, and you'll use those specific colors when you write your program in the next chapter.

Figure 4.10   The grey opening of the pan isn't just for looks; you'll use the grey pan opening and the black handle when writing your program in the next chapter.

LEARN IT   GREYSCALE   *Greyscale* is a range of greys from white to black. Start at the white end of the spectrum and add in a drop of black. You now have a pale, pearly grey. Add two drops of black to the next block and the grey grows slightly darker. This continues until the midway point, where there are equal amounts of white and black, and ends completely in black, without a bit of white in sight. Are white and black colors? No, though I call them colors in this book. White is all the colors pulled together into a single color. Black is what you get when there is no light or color. Grey is what happens in between.

To make the pan

1 Navigate to the Sprite Zone and click the paintbrush icon to create a new sprite.

2 Start in the Color Toolbar and choose the black paint sample square.

3 Click the Line tool. To make a perfectly straight line that goes up and down or left to right, hold down the Shift key on the keyboard while you draw the lines in the next step. Unfortunately, this trick

won't work with diagonal lines, and you'll need to make your line with a steady hand.

4 Draw a trapezoid on its side: a short diagonal line, a slightly longer line, another short diagonal line, and a longer line connecting the shape, as in figure 4.11.

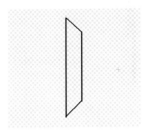

Erase extra pixels using the Eraser tool. It is easier to erase small portions of a sprite if you zoom in using the Magnifying Glass tool.

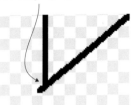

Figure 4.11   A sideways trapezoid

Figure 4.12   Erase extra pixels if two intersecting lines don't perfectly align.

FIX IT WHAT DO YOU DO WITH EXTRA PIXELS?   Sometimes when you're drawing a shape with the Line tool, you'll end up with extra pixels where two lines don't perfectly match up, as in figure 4.12. Switch to the Eraser tool, zoom into the image, and gently remove those extra pixels to give your picture crisp lines.

1 Starting at the bottom left corner, draw a thin rectangle under the trapezoid to make the handle, as in figure 4.13.

2 Switch to a medium grey and draw a diagonal line from the top left corner toward the center of the pan.

3 Continue the grey line from the middle of the pan to the bottom left corner of the pan. Draw a grey line over the black line that marks the front of the pan.

4 Click the Paint Bucket tool and click inside the grey triangle to fill in the front of the pan with color.

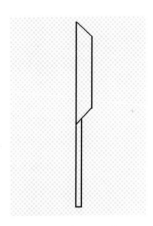

Figure 4.13   A rectangle underneath the trapezoid becomes the pan's handle.

5 Switch back to the black paint sample square. Continue to use the Paint Bucket tool to fill in the rest of the trapezoid and rectangular handle in black, as in figure 4.14.

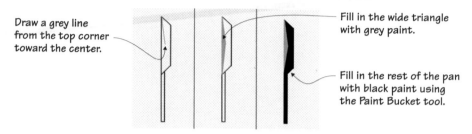

Draw a grey line from the top corner toward the center.

Fill in the wide triangle with grey paint.

Fill in the rest of the pan with black paint using the Paint Bucket tool.

Figure 4.14   The pan is complete after the spaces are filled in with grey or black paint.

Navigate to the Sprite Zone, click the blue *i*, and name this sprite Right Pan.

LEARN IT   TINT, SHADE, AND TONE   Three other color terms you'll hear a lot when it comes to art are tint, shade, and tone. *Tint* is adding white to a pure hue. For instance, take orange and add white to make peach. *Shade* is the opposite: it's adding black to a pure hue. For instance, take orange and add black to make brown. Finally, *tone* is adding grey. For example, take orange and add grey (a blend of black and white) to make beige. You can digitally create tints, shades, and tones by using the greyscale slider directly to the right of the rainbow box. Move the slider up and down *without* moving the bubble over the rainbow. You should see the selected color get darker and lighter.

Even though you need two pans in the game, you don't need to draw a second pan. You can duplicate the first pan and then flip it so it's facing the other direction.

To duplicate and flip the pan

1 Make sure the pan is not touching the egg on the Stage. If it is, slide over the sprite to an unoccupied space on the Stage.

2 Navigate to the Grey Toolbar and click the stamp icon.

3 Click the pan on the Stage to make a copy.

4 Go to the Sprite Zone and make sure the blue outline is around Right Pan2, the new copy of the pan.

5 Navigate to the top of the Art Editor. Click the Flip Left-Right button in the top right corner, as shown in figure 4.15.

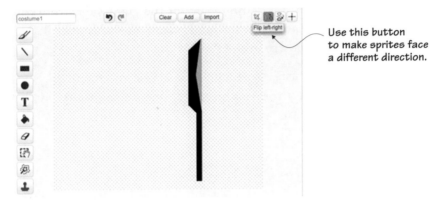

Use this button to make sprites face a different direction.

Figure 4.15   You can draw one pan and then duplicate it and flip it in order to create the other.

Return to the Sprite Zone, click the blue *i*, and rename this sprite Left Pan. You now have two pan sprites, one facing toward the left and the other facing toward the right. You're almost ready to start programming your game, but you still need to create some odds and ends that will help you with the coding.

Prepping the odds and ends

Sometimes you'll need to make sprites that are solely created to work with the code rather than serve as game pieces. In this case, you'll need two lines to use as boundaries in the game.

Making the wall sprites

Making the wall sprites involves drawing two lines: one on the far right side of the Art Editor, and the other on the far left. In both cases, you will need to start in the Sprite Zone, clicking the paintbrush to create a new sprite.

To make a wall

1 Choose the Line tool. Make sure the Art Editor is at 100% and not zoomed in.

2 Select a dark violet paint sample square, slightly darker than the purple you used for the background.

3 Draw a straight line running down the right side, from top to bottom. You may not see the line appear on the Stage, depending on how far over you are in the Art Editor.

Navigate to the Sprite Zone, click the blue *i*, and name this sprite Right Line. You can see the straight, violet line on the right side of the Art Editor in figure 4.16.

Figure 4.16   The line sprite drawn in the Art Editor

You now need to do the same thing on the left side. Once again, start a new sprite and draw a violet line on the far left side of the canvas. Name this second line Left Line.

There will be times when you draw a sprite and it doesn't appear on the Stage even though you can see it in the Sprite Zone. Don't worry! If you see the sprite in the Sprite Zone, it exists. This is especially true when you're drawing on the far edges of the canvas, such as the far left, far right, or bottom.

Preparing to code

You're almost ready to code, but before you skip ahead to making the game, take a second to build on what you learned in this chapter.

Play in the workspace

You currently have a solid purple background, but what if you want to use a different color? How would you have to change the egg?

CHALLENGE   Yellow and purple isn't the only complementary color combination you could use for your game. If Dr. Seuss showed up for breakfast and demanded green eggs and ham in the game, what color should you make the background in order to make the egg visually pop on the screen? If you guessed red, you're correct. What other complementary color combinations can you make?

What did you learn?

How does knowing about color help you with coding or any of the other sections of STEAM? Making new colors is a simple addition problem: red + blue = purple. Understanding color means also understanding fractions as you consider how much white, black, or grey to add to create tints, shades, and tones. Scripts, like colors, interact with one another to contrast instructions (like complementary colors) or work in harmony (like analogous colors) with other parts of the program. Okay, some of this is a bit of a stretch, but you get what I mean: thinking deeply about your color choices will help you think deeply about every decision you make in your code. There always needs to be a reason for why you're putting two blocks together, and the same goes for colors.

Pause for a moment to think about everything you learned:

* How to divide up the 12 base hues into primary, secondary, and tertiary colors

- How to make sprites pop on the screen by pairing complementary colors
- How to use analogous colors to make games visually pleasing
- How to use tints, shades, and tones to create all other possible colors

You have five sprites ready to be programmed. I'm going to pass you over to my brother who will teach how to make our version of *Pong*, called Breakfast Wars.

5

Using conditionals to build a two-player ball-and-paddle game

Pong was the first *popular* arcade game. For many people, this ball-and-paddle game was the first video game they ever got to play.

In the early 1970s, a new company named Atari hired a guy named Al Alcorn to make a game called *Pong*. They placed the arcade cabinet inside a restaurant in California, and by the next day, people were lining up to play it. When other game makers saw how much people loved *Pong*, they raced to make their own games. And the rest is history.

Which brings us to an important point: how did people know how to play if they had never seen a video game before? The answer to that question is the secret of *Pong*'s success. First and foremost, the point of *Pong* was easy to understand because it was a digital version of something the average person already knew: Ping-Pong. You hit the LED light back and forth between two "paddles." In fact, the directions that came with the game gave a single objective: "Avoid missing ball for high score." To rack up points, don't miss the ball, as in Ping-Pong.

Additionally, in the beginning, computer chips and graphic cards could only hold so much information. Keeping things simple made *Pong* easy to pick up because there were only three things on the black screen: two white paddles and a single white ball. No colorful, distracting background. No disorienting, first-person perspective. *Pong* made it simple for people to drop their quarter into the machine and know what to do, even if it took some time to figure out how to work the controls well in order to not miss the ball.

And that is the recipe for a good video game: make it easy to understand, possible to improve with practice, and challenging enough to hold the player's attention. Too complicated, and you risk having the player give up before they've even inserted their quarter in the machine. Too easy, and you risk players growing bored. *Pong* is in that Goldilocks zone—just right.

You're about to make an exciting version of *Pong* using two cast-iron frying pans for the paddles and a fried egg for the ball, as shown in figure 5.1.

You're going to borrow what works from *Pong*—simple concept, basic background, uncomplicated graphics—and customize the code so you can make your game challenging and fun.

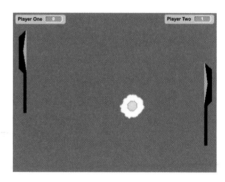

Figure 5.1   In Breakfast Wars, the player will move the paddle up and down while the egg bounces across the screen. The code you'll write will also keep score for the player.

In this chapter, you will learn

- How to use conditional (or if/then) statements to power the game
- How to determine the location of game pieces on the screen
- How to make the sprites move
- How to work with angles to mimic the way a ball moves off a paddle

Open up your Breakfast Wars project where you made your sprites in chapter 4 and get ready to snap some blocks together.

Preparing to program

You're almost ready to begin writing code, but first there are a few steps you need to take to prepare the Stage.

Missing sprites

If you skipped chapter 4 and don't have sprites made, you can download our sprites from the official Manning site. Although you should make your own, we also know that sometimes you want to jump straight into programming. Make sure you download the egg, both pans, and both lines.

Once you've downloaded the sprites, go to a new project in Scratch and navigate to the Sprite Zone. Click the folder icon in the Top Toolbar for that section, as seen in figure 5.2. This will open a window that shows where you keep your documents on your hard drive. Open the folder where you've stored the downloaded sprites and select all the sprites by clicking each sprite while holding down Control (Windows) or Command (Mac).

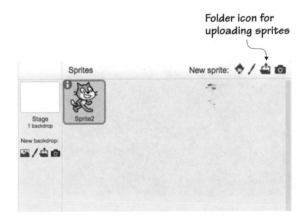

Figure 5.2   Use the folder icon to upload sprites from your hard drive to Scratch.

Preparing the Stage

Get the Stage ready by dragging the left pan to the left side of the Stage (so the grey opening faces the middle of the Stage) about a half-centimeter from the edge, and the right pan to the right side of the Stage, also a half-centimeter from the edge. You can click and drag the egg to any space in the center of the Stage.

This is a good time to take a look at the size of the pans and the size of the egg and adjust accordingly. Shrink the egg six clicks using the Shrink tool in the Grey Toolbar. Shrink the pan three clicks and leave the lines as they are.

Programming the cast-iron pans

The two pans are like the two paddles in *Pong*. You'll use them to hit the egg back and forth across the screen. Because the paddles only do one thing—move up and down—you'll only write one movement script for the pans. Click to place the blue box around the left pan sprite in the Sprite Zone. Remember, the names or values on *your* blocks may differ slightly from time to time, so use the completed script images to make sure you chose the correct block.

Making a paddle movement script

Right now, the paddle in figure 5.3 is about to miss the egg! You need to make it possible for the player to move their paddle so they can block the egg when it comes sailing toward their side of the Stage.

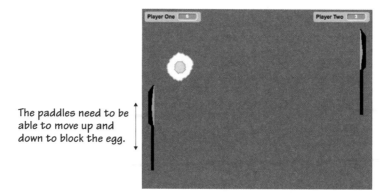

The paddles need to be able to move up and down to block the egg.

Figure 5.3   Write a program that allows the player to move the paddle up and down.

This script will allow the left paddle to move up and down when certain keys are pressed on the keyboard. To program the left pan

1   Navigate to the Block Menu and click the Scripts tab to access all of your blocks.

2   Click Events and drag a When Flag Clicked block to the Script Area. Release it near the top of the workspace.

3   Switch to Control and drag a Forever block under the When Flag Clicked block. Snap them together so the two blocks are touching. A Forever block, if you'll recall, means that you are setting up a loop.

4 Add an If/Then block inside the Forever block. This sets the condition for the loop.

5 Click Sensing and drag a Key Space Pressed block into the empty hexagonal space of the If/Then block.

6 Open the drop-down menu on the Key Space Pressed block by clicking the little arrow. Scroll down and choose W, as seen in figure 5.4. The W key will be the key the player presses on the keyboard to move the pan up.

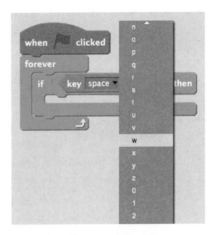

Figure 5.4 *The opened drop-down menu for the Key Space Pressed block*

7 Click Motion and drag a Change Y by 10 block inside the If/Then block. Change the value to 5, because 10 will be too fast. Remember, positive numbers on the Y-axis go up, and negative numbers on the Y-axis go down.

8 Return to the Control block menu and place another If/Then block under the first If/Then block, inside the Forever block, as seen in figure 5.5.

9 Click Sensing once again and drag a Key Space Pressed block into the new If/Then block's empty hexagonal space.

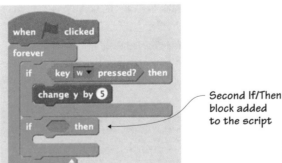

Second If/Then block added to the script

Figure 5.5 *The second If/Then block is also placed inside the Forever block, adding to the loop.*

10 Open the drop-down menu in the Key Space Pressed block and change the value to the letter S. The S key will be the key the player presses on the keyboard to move the pan down.

11 Go to the Motion menu and grab a Change Y by 10 block. Change the value to –5.

ANSWER THIS   WHY USE THE W AND S KEYS?

Question: up and down arrows make sense, but using W and S for up and down is a little weird. Do you have any clue why you've used these random letters to serve as your control keys?

Answer: WASD are four keys that are often used in gaming when you have two players and need two spaces on the keyboard used for moving sprites, or when you're using both keyboard keys and a mouse at the same time. W and S are used for up and down, and A and D are used for left and right.

Congratulations! This first script is finished. You set your first condition for this game. Figure 5.6 shows the completed script along with what each block accomplishes in the program. Does your script match the one in figure 5.6?

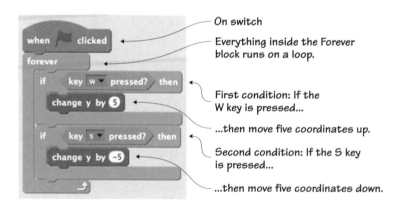

Figure 5.6   A movement script to move the left pan sprite up or down when a key is pressed

Remember in chapter 3 when you learned about conditional statements? This is a straightforward conditional statement that lets the player move the paddle. If the W or S key is pressed, the sprite moves five coordinates up or down. If the W or S key isn't pressed, nothing happens.

Duplicating the paddle movement script

Often when you have a two-player game, you can write a script for Player One and then duplicate it for Player Two, because you want both pans to be able to do the same thing. By dragging the script to another sprite, the same script can exist in two places.

To duplicate the movement script from the left pan to the right pan

1 Navigate to the Script Area and click the When Flag Clicked block.

2 Click and drag the entire script to the Sprite Zone. If you drag it by its top block (When Flag Clicked), the blocks will move together.

3 Hover over the other pan sprite in the Sprite Zone. A blue box *will not* appear around the new sprite (Right Pan), as you can see in figure 5.7, but the script *will* transfer when you release the mouse button.

4 Check that the script has transferred by clicking the right pan and making sure the script appears in the Script Area.

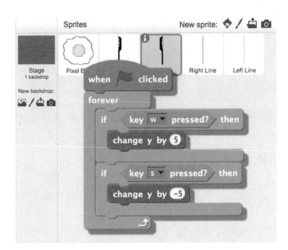

Figure 5.7   Hovering over the Right Pan in the Sprite Zone

But watch out! You don't want the script for the right pan to use the same keys as the left pan.

Use the drop-down menu to change the Key Space Pressed block from W to Up Arrow in the first If/Then block, and the S to Down Arrow in the second If/Then Block, as in figure 5.8.

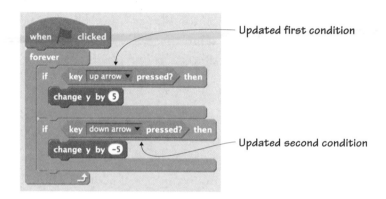

Figure 5.8   *The duplicated and updated movement script moves the other pan.*

Those two scripts are all the scripts you'll need for the cast-iron pans. The egg, on the other hand, like *Pong*'s LED ball, is a little more complicated because it needs to be able to bounce in multiple directions and move on its own across the screen. There will be more scripts attributed to the egg sprite.

Programming the egg

The egg is like the LED light that bounces across the screen in *Pong*. You will need many scripts to control the egg sprite:

- A starter script to tell the egg where to go at the beginning of the game
- A receiver movement script to tell the egg how to move
- A bounce script to keep it moving
- A boundary script to award points
- A game-ending script to set an end point
- A reflection script to make the egg ricochet off the pans

All these scripts will use conditional statements to determine the location and movement of the egg on the screen. Make sure you place the blue box around the egg sprite and do not move it until you are finished writing all the scripts in this section.

Making a starter script

Pong's original game instructions came with a second note: "Ball will serve automatically." Although it wasn't as instructive as the game objective—"Avoid missing ball for high score"—this one line summed up something important: if you want to make a game that people connect with immediately, make it easy to begin.

Right now, your egg may be on one side of the Stage, as in figure 5.9, and therefore puts one side at an unfair advantage. Poor Player Two has a fraction of a second to move their pan when the game begins to keep the egg from hitting the wall.

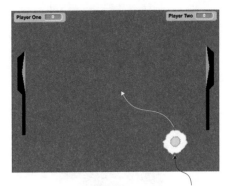

Send the egg to the center of the Stage to start the game.

Figure 5.9   *The egg is off to the side at the start of the game. You can fix this with a starter script that sends the egg to the center of the screen.*

You can fix this problem with a starter script to tell the egg how to kick off the game. It sends the sprite to the center of the screen, sets an angle, and sends a message to another script through broadcasting that will tell the egg to start moving in that angle's direction.

To make the starter script

1   Navigate to Events, grab a When Flag Clicked block, and slide it to the Script Area. Release it near the top of your workspace.

2   Click Motion and drag a Go to X/Y block under the When Flag Clicked block until they snap together. Change the values in the bubbles to zero (0) for both X and Y. X:0 and Y:0 is the center of the Stage, so you're sending the egg to the center of the screen.

3   Grab à Point in Direction 90 block. Snap it under the Go to X/Y block.

4 Change the value from 90 to 45. If you open the drop-down menu, you won't see the number 45 as a choice. Instead, delete the 90 from the bubble and type in 45. This part of the script tilts the egg so when it begins moving, it will move on the diagonal.

5 Switch to Control and get a Wait 1 Secs block. Snap it under the Point in Direction block. This block gives the player time to get their fingers on the keyboard.

6 Go to Events and grab a Broadcast Message block. Snap it to the Wait 1 Secs block.

7 Use the drop-down menu on the Broadcast Message block to choose New Message. Name that message Start Moving.

Figure 5.10 shows the completed script.

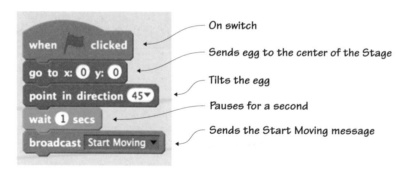

Figure 5.10   The completed starter script tells the egg what to do at the beginning of the game.

It's important to understand that all scripts with the same on switch start at the same time, so all scripts you write for this game that use the When Flag Clicked block will begin running simultaneously when the green flag above the Stage is clicked.

Remember learning about broadcasting in chapter 3? This is a script that sends a message, passing the baton to another script and telling it to start running. You haven't set up a script to receive it yet, so right now this script is shouting to the other scripts, but none of them is listening... yet. This script tells the egg to move to the center of the Stage, tilt, and send out that broadcast message. The script that receives that message will do all the other egg movements in the game.

This script also uses angles. If you kept the Point in Direction block at 90 degrees, it would be a pretty boring game. If the angle was 90 degrees (instead of the current 45), once the game began, the egg would go back and forth along the same horizontal line. You wouldn't even need to move your paddle.

To understand angles, draw a central point and then make two lines off that dot. The space between those lines is an angle. Angles are measured in degrees.

The easiest way to understand angles is to think about a pizza. The connecting "dot" is the center of the pizza, and a full pizza (or circle) consists of 360 degrees. Take a pizza cutter and make two lines, cutting the pizza into quarters. Each slice is 1/4th of 360 degrees, or 90 degrees. Cut those slices in half again, making 8 slices as in figure 5.11, and each slice is 1/8th of 360 degrees, or 45 degrees.

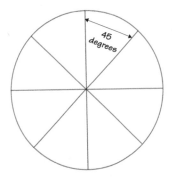

Figure 5.11   Each slice of pizza equals 45 degrees.

Understanding angles in Scratch is important if you want to make movement interesting. Now look at the game. The starter script sends the egg to the center of the screen and sets it at a 45 degree angle. When the egg starts moving, it's going to move along that 45 degree line, just as the second cat moves along the 45 degree line in figure 5.12. Pay attention

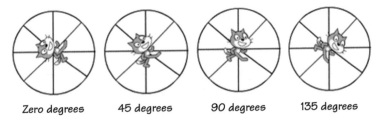

Zero degrees   45 degrees   90 degrees   135 degrees

Figure 5.12   The cat turns 45 degrees in each picture.

to the cat's face to see which direction it will move. You could change the number in the block in the script to be a different angle—for instance, 135 if you want the egg to start moving down and to the right, as you can see in the fourth cat in figure 5.12. Play with this number, making it any number between 1 and 360, because there are 360 degrees in a circle.

Making an egg movement script

A message was sent out with the last script telling the egg to get ready to move, but you still need another script to receive that message so the egg can spring into action, like the egg in figure 5.13.

This script is a receiver script that works with that broadcast message block. It will tell the egg to start moving so the players can begin playing the game.

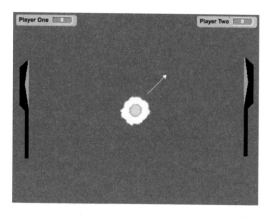

Figure 5.13   The egg will start moving at that 45-degree angle when it receives the broadcasted message.

ANSWER THIS   DOES THE ORDER OF THE SCRIPTS MATTER?

Question: does it matter where you place each script in the Script Area?

Answer: although you want to keep your workspace neat, it doesn't matter where the various scripts for the sprite are in the Script Area. Although order is important when it comes to lining up the blocks in each individual script, it's less so when it comes to how you line up all the scripts applied to a single sprite. The main concern is to not have two scripts touching, but other than that, feel free to work from top to bottom or left to right. Your Script Area will expand to hold all of your scripts.

Heads up: a lot of layering happens in this script. You've put a block inside a block before, and that creates two layers. You can nest blocks inside those new blocks, which creates a third layer. This script contains a conditional with four block layers! Go slowly as you make this and follow the pictures. I'll discuss it on the other end when the script is complete.

To make a receiver script

1   Go to Events and choose a When I Receive Start Moving block. Drag it to the Script Area and release it a centimeter underneath your last script. You don't want the two scripts to touch, but they can be close to one another. This is the receiver block that picks up the message sent in the previous script. You only want this script to be active after the message has been sent. If you used the When Flag Clicked block, it would be active from the moment the game begins. Using this receiver Events block means that it's only active after the message has been sent.

2   Use the drop-down menu to switch the value to Start Moving if it's not already set to this message.

3   Switch to the Control block menu and drag a Forever block under the When I Receive block.

4   Go to Motion and grab a Move 10 Steps block. Slide it inside the Forever block and change the value to 7. Moving 10 coordinate spaces at a time would make the egg move quickly. Moving only seven coordinate spaces at a time slows it down.

5   Return to the Control block menu and grab an If/Then block. Slide it under the Move 7 Steps block inside the Forever block.

6   Open the Operators block menu and get a Hexagon or Hexagon block. You are going to nest Hexagon or Hexagon blocks inside one another. It begins with a single block placed inside the empty hexagonal space in the If/Then block. Then take two more Hexagon or Hexagon blocks and place them inside the two hexagons of the first Hexagon or Hexagon block. You should now have four empty green hexagons, as shown in figure 5.14.

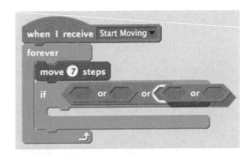

Figure 5.14   Two Hexagon or Hexagon blocks nested inside a Hexagon or Hexagon block.

7 Slide two Square = Square blocks into the right hexagon in each pair, as shown in figure 5.15.

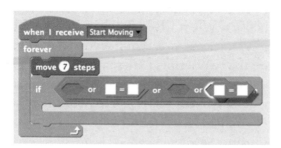

Figure 5.15   Another Operators block is nested in the right hexagon of each pair.

8 Click Sensing, grab two Touching blocks, and put one in the left hexagon of each pair, like figure 5.16.

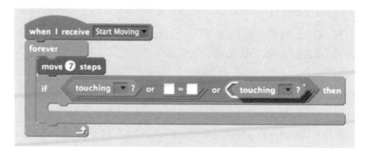

Figure 5.16   Touching blocks fill the left hexagons in each pair.

9 Change the value in the drop-down menu of the left Touching block to Left Line. Change the value in the drop-down menu of the right Touching block to Right Line.

10 Click Motion and scroll down. Choose two X Position blocks and slide them into each of the left squares in the Square = Square block.

11 Type a value in the final empty squares of the Square = Square block. In the square connected to Left Line, type –240 because that coordinate position is the far left side of the Stage. In the square connected to Right Line, type 240 because that coordinate position is the far right side of the Stage.

12 Go to Control and grab a Stop All block. Use the drop-down menu to change the value to This Script so that if this condition comes true, it only stops this particular script and not all scripts in the game.

That was a complicated script with many layers! Check that your script matches figure 5.17 and then give yourself a pat on the back for making such a complicated script.

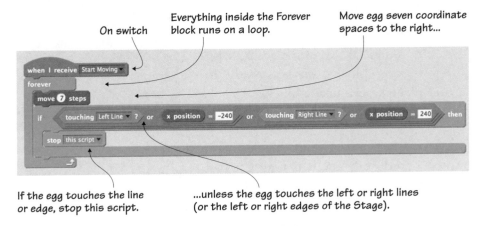

Figure 5.17   The completed egg movement script tells the egg to keep moving seven steps unless it hits one of four possible conditions.

With one script, you set up four possible situations that will stop this script if any of them is true: if the egg is touching the Left Line sprite, the far left edge of the Stage, the Right Line sprite, or the far right edge of the Stage. Those lines are flush with the left and right walls of the Stage, so why give two versions of the same condition—left line or left wall (or right line or right wall)? It's a more accurate way of defining the edge. Because the wall plays a very important role in the game, it's better to define it with a sprite.

What if the egg isn't in any of these four situations? For instance, what if the egg is touching one of the pans or not touching anything at all? Then the script continues because it is on a loop. That's how your game will continue and the egg will be able to bounce back and forth. In fact, let's make an additional bouncing script to make sure your egg pops off the top and bottom walls, too.

Making a bounce script

What happens if your egg hits the top or bottom edge of the Stage, as in figure 5.18? You don't want the egg to stop or sail off the screen; you want it to bounce.

This script will make the egg rebound. It's another script with nesting blocks, so get ready to place blocks inside blocks.

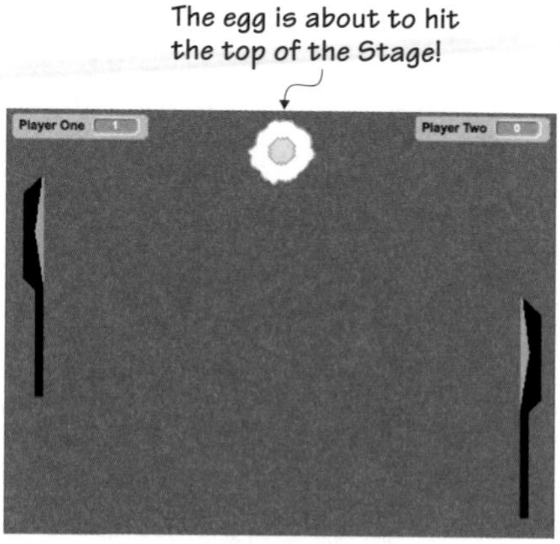

To make your egg bounce

1 Open the Events block menu and grab a When Flag Clicked block. Drag it to your workspace to start a new script. Again, don't have it touch any existing scripts, but place it near the other two scripts already in the Script Area.

The egg is about to hit the top of the Stage!

Figure 5.18   Making the egg bounce off the top and bottom edge so the game can continue

2 Switch to the Control menu and grab a Forever block. Snap it under the When Flag Clicked block. Anything inside this block will run on a loop.

3 Grab an If/Then block and place it inside the Forever block.

4 Go to the Operators menu, grab a Not Hexagon block, and place it inside the empty, hexagonal space in the If/Then block.

5 Drag a Hexagon or Hexagon block into the empty Not Hexagon block, nesting a block inside a block.

6 Switch to Sensing and choose two Touching blocks. Slide each into the empty hexagons on the Hexagon or Hexagon block.

7 Use the drop-down menu to change the left Touching block to Left Line and the right Touching block to Right Line. You're setting up a negative condition. This is what you want to have happen in the game if the egg is *not* touching the left or right lines.

8 Click Motion and slide the If on Edge, Bounce block inside the If/ Then block. This will make the egg bounce off the top or bottom of the Stage and keep the egg in motion.

You can see the completed script in figure 5.19.

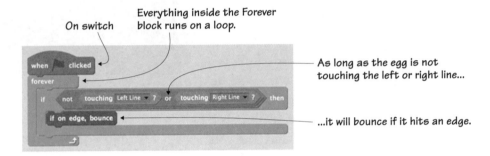

Figure 5.19   As long as the egg isn't touching the left or right lines, this script will allow the egg to bounce.

The condition in this script is that as long as the egg sprite is not touching Left Line or Right Line, it will bounce if it hits an edge. You don't need to include the additional X position = –240 or X position = 240 because that set of coordinates is contained in the action inside the block: the "edge" is that –240 or 240 position (or the Y position of 180 or –180).

If the egg sprite is touching Left Line or Right Line, that *not* in the Operators block is no longer true; therefore, the rest of the script won't run. This means that you need to set up another script with a condition for what will happen if the egg sprite *is* touching Left Line or Right Line.

FIX IT   WHAT IF THE BLOCKS WON'T NEST?   Sometimes when you try to put a block inside a block, you forget to check for the white halo that appears to show where the block will land when released. Quickly dragging and dropping sometimes means that a block ends up in the wrong place. To fix this, remove the messed up blocks and place them next to the script in your workspace. Then carefully transfer them back in, one at a time.

Making a right-side boundary detection script

Oh no—the condition you set up in the earlier egg movement script (to stop running if the egg sprite is touching Left Line, Right Line, or either the left or right edge of the Stage) is about to happen in figure 5.20.

This script will award a player one point if they get the egg to touch the opposite wall—meaning the right-side player will get a point if the egg touches the left wall, and the left-side player will get a point if the egg touches the

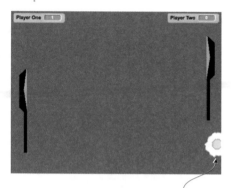

The egg got past the pan and is now touching the right wall.

Figure 5.20   The right paddle misses the egg, and the egg touches the right wall.

right wall. This script will also start the next round of the game by sending the egg back to the center of the stage and sending it into motion again. This script adds to that start script's *Pong*-like instruction—"Ball will serve automatically"—and makes it true even in the middle of a game.

To make a boundary detection script

1 Open the Events block menu and drag a When Flag Clicked block to the Script Area.

2 Switch to Control and snap a Forever block under the When Flag Clicked block. Everything inside the Forever block will run on a loop.

3 Grab an If/Then block and place it inside the Forever block to set another condition.

4 Click Operators and drag a Hexagon or Hexagon block and place it inside the empty, hexagonal space in the If/Then block.

5 Switch to Sensing and grab a Touching block. Place it inside the left hexagon in the Hexagon or Hexagon block.

6 Use the drop-down menu to change the value to Right Line. This will set a condition that checks if the egg is touching the right line.

7 Return to Operators and drag a Square = Square block into the right hexagon in the Hexagon or Hexagon block.

8 Go to Motion. Scroll down and slide an X Position block into the left square of the Square = Square block. Type the number *240* in the right square because this is the coordinate position of the far right side of the Stage.

9 Click Data. It's time to make two variables that will be used to track the points of Player One and Player Two. Click Make a Variable and name your first variable Player One. Keep the default For All Sprites setting. Click Make a Variable again and name your second variable Player Two. You will see boxes appear for both variables on your Stage in the top left corner. You can position these boxes by dragging them across the Stage, one in either corner, as in figure 5.21.

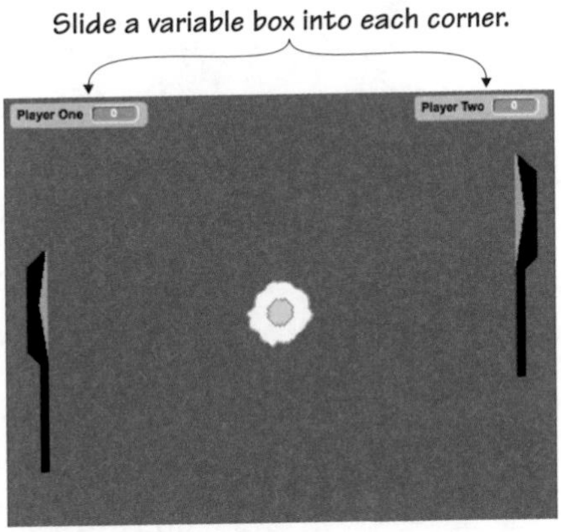

Slide a variable box into each corner.

Figure 5.21 *Two variable boxes in either top corner of the Stage*

10 Drag a Change Player Two by 1 block and place it inside the If/ Then block. Switch the variable name to Player One using the drop-down menu in the block. This will now give Player One a point if the egg touches the right line or the right edge of the Stage.

11 Go back to Motion and grab a Go to X/Y block. Place it under the Change Player One by 1 block. Type a zero (0) value into each of the bubbles, so X:0 and Y:0. This will send the egg back to the center of the Stage so the next round can begin.

12 Switch to Events and drag a Broadcast Message block. Make sure the message is set to Start Moving in the drop-down menu on the

block. This will repeat the step that begins the game, sending out a message to the Egg Movement script to kick into action.

That's the whole script, which you can see in figure 5.22. This script makes sure that each new round of Breakfast Wars begins the same way, similarly to how real Ping-Pong always begins the round by serving the ball over the net.

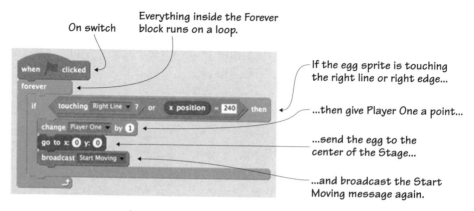

Figure 5.22   This script states what happens if the egg gets past Player Two's pan.

Duplicating the boundary detection script for the left side

Once again, you're duplicating a script, just as you did earlier when you duplicated the Paddle Movement script, and then tweaking a few values or variable names.

This will work a little differently because you're copying the script for the same sprite. To duplicate the Right Side Boundary Detection script (and turn it into the Left Side Boundary Detection script), control-click (Mac) or right-click (Windows) the When Flag Clicked block and choose Duplicate. You will see a second copy overlap with the first. Click the top copy and drag it to a new space in the Script Area.

All you have to do now is tweak the blocks so they are the opposite of the original script: Right Line becomes Left Line. Instead of 240, it's –240, and Player One becomes Player Two. You can see in figure 5.23 that it is the exact same script with a few changes.

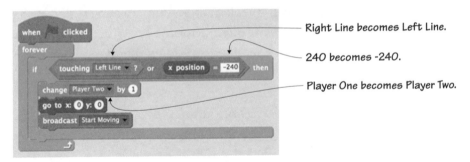

Right Line becomes Left Line.

240 becomes -240.

Player One becomes Player Two.

Figure 5.23   *The duplicated script sets a boundary on the left side, too.*

ANSWER THIS   WHY NOT JUST WRITE ONE SCRIPT?

Question: there are two similar but separate conditions set in the last two scripts, and it would be possible to combine them into one single script with two If/Then blocks on top of each other. So why not do that?

Answer: it can be easier to see how your program is unfolding if you break your larger program down into bite-sized scripts. By keeping these two scripts separate, I remind myself as a coder that I've taken care of scoring for the left and right side. Think about places where you can break down a script into smaller parts to make it easier for you to scan your program and make sure you've accounted for all tasks.

Making a game ending script

A game of *Pong* didn't go on forever, and a game of Breakfast Wars has to end at some point, too. This script will set an end point for the game by checking the score and noting when one player reaches 7 points, as in figure 5.24. (Congratulations, Player One!)

To make a game ending script

1 Click Events and choose the When Flag Clicked block. Slide it over to the Script Area to start a new script.

The game ends when one person reaches seven points.

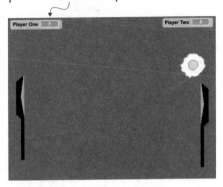

Figure 5.24   *The game ends when one player reaches seven points.*

2 Switch to the Data block menu, take two Set Player Two to 0 blocks, and snap them, one on top of the other, beneath the When Flag Clicked block. Use the drop-down menu to ensure one block is set to the Player One variable and the other is set to the Player Two variable.

3 Make sure the value in both orange blocks is zero (0). This means both players begin the game with zero points because the value for the variable Player One and Player Two is 0.

4 Go to Control and slide a Forever block under the bottom Set Player Two to 0 block. Inside the Forever block loop, start setting a condition by adding an If/Then block.

5 Click Operators and place a Hexagon or Hexagon inside the empty hexagonal space in the If/Then block.

6 Choose two Square = Square blocks and slide one each into the hexagons in the Hexagon or Hexagon block. You should see four squares that you need to fill.

7 Switch back to Data and place a Player One block in the far left square. Type the number 7 in the next square. Slide a Player Two block into the next square and type the number 7 again in the last square. This makes the condition if either Player One or Player Two reaches seven points. The game is tracking those points with the Player One and Player Two variables and checking those variables for a value of 7.

8 Return to Control and choose a Stop All block. Slide it inside the If/Then block. This will stop all the scripts in the game when one player reaches seven points.

Figure 5.25 shows the completed game ending script.

The points in this game are tracked by a variable. (If you need a refresher on variables, turn back to chapter 3.) The number you see in the score boxes in the top corners of the Stage is the current value of the variable. You can think of the variable Player One (or Player Two) as being like a box that collects the score. At the beginning of the game, the number in the virtual box will be zero (0). You've also created a script (the boundary detection script) that adds a point every time the

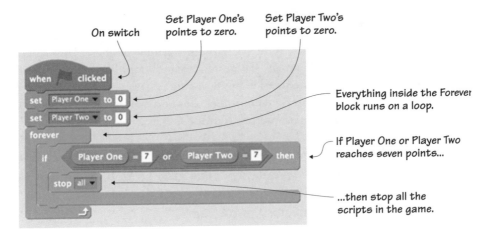

On switch

Set Player One's points to zero.

Set Player Two's points to zero.

Everything inside the Forever block runs on a loop.

If Player One or Player Two reaches seven points...

...then stop all the scripts in the game.

Figure 5.25   This script tells Scratch what to do if either player reaches seven points.

egg hits the left or right side of the screen and not the pan, so that score number will change over the course of the game.

As the value for the variable increases, this script continuously (due to the Forever block loop) checks the score, waiting for the value to reach 7.

You're almost ready to play Breakfast Wars. But first, you need to make a sound script that will run when the egg hits the pan.

Making a reflection script

What sound do you think an egg would make when it bounces off the pan? I went with a little popping noise whenever the egg ricochets off the cast-iron surface or handle. It won't show you the word *POP!* that was added to figure 5.26, but it will make a sound that will remind you of a tennis ball hitting a racket.

Okay, it's not *only* a sound effect script. This important part of the program will also make the egg bounce off the pan and change direction.

Figure 5.26   Every time the egg hits the pan, it will make a popping noise.

LEARN IT   CHIPTUNES   *Chiptune*, named for the sound chip, is another name for arcade music. Thirty years ago, computers couldn't make complex sounds, only beeps with various pitches. Those beeps were used to create simple music. Chiptunes are still popular today, and those retro beeping sounds are included in modern games such as *Disney Crossy Road*. If you want to make your own chiptunes that you can put in your Scratch games, try using beepbox.co, an online chiptune maker.

With this long script, you'll understand that sometimes your sprites are designed to enhance game play. The grey section of the pan isn't only to give the visual effect of the top of a pan. It plays an important role in determining the trajectory of the egg.

To make a reflection script

1   Begin in Events and choose a When Flag Clicked block. Slide it to the Script Area.

2   Switch to Control, grab a Forever block, and snap it underneath the When Flag Clicked block.

3   Place an If/Then block inside the Forever block so you can set a condition.

4   Go to the Operators block menu and choose a Hexagon or Hexagon block. Place it in the empty hexagonal space on the If/Then block.

5   Click Sensing and grab two Touching blocks, placing one inside each of the empty hexagons of the Hexagon or Hexagon block.

6   Use the drop-down menu to change the left Touching block to Left Pan and the right Touching block to Right Pan.

7   Return to the Control block menu and choose two If/Then blocks. Slide them inside the existing If/Then block, stacking them on top of one another. In the end, you should have two If/Then blocks inside the original If/Then block, as shown in figure 5.27.

8   Drag a Wait 1 Secs block underneath the bottom If/Then block inside the original If/Then block. The stack of three blocks inside the original If/Then block is a top If/Then, a bottom If/Then, and a Wait 1 Secs block. Change the number in the bubble from 1 to 0.01 to make it a fraction of a second. This sets two more conditions inside the larger condition of whether or not the egg is touching one of the pans.

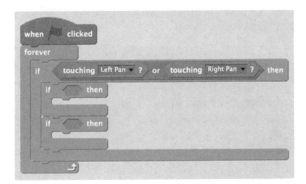

Figure 5.27 *Two more conditions are inside the larger condition of if the egg is touching the left or right pan.*

9 Switch to Sensing and grab two Touching Color blocks. Remember, it won't have the name of the color on the block. It will have a square filled with a random color. Place each block inside the two empty hexagonal spaces in the two new If/Then blocks. This will enable you to have different things happen if the egg is touching the black part of the pan or the grey part of the pan.

10 Change the color in the top Touching Color block by clicking the colorful square, going over to the Stage, and clicking the black part of the pan. Make sure the square in the block changes to black, too.

11 Change the color in the bottom Touching Color block by clicking the colorful square, going over to the Stage, and clicking the grey part of the pan. Make sure the square in the block changes to grey, too.

12 Click Motion and slide a Turn Clockwise 90 Degrees block into the top If/Then block. Make sure the arrow is going in the same direction as a clock. Change the number from 90 to 180. This will look at the angle of the egg and change it by 180 degrees.

13 Grab a Turn Counterclockwise 90 Degrees block and put it into the bottom If/Then block. Make sure the arrow is going in the opposite direction as a clock. Keep the number 90 in the bubble or change it to 90 if it's currently another number. This will look at the angle of the egg and change it by 90 degrees.

14 Go to Sound and add a Play Sound Pop block above the Wait 0.01 Secs block. This will cause the egg to make a popping sound every time it hits a pan.

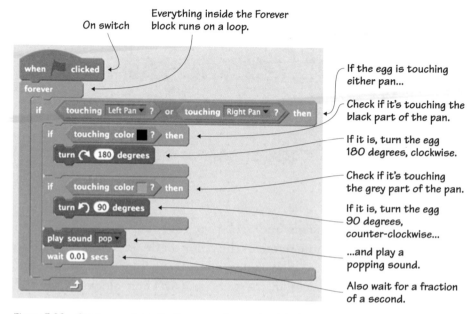

Figure 5.28   This long script tells the game what to do with the egg if it hits either pan.

Figure 5.28 shows the completed reflection script. It's a longer script that accomplishes many tasks at the same time.

What is up with that fraction of a second pause at the end of the script? That pause is inserted to give your computer a chance to catch up. Without that tiny pause, the game may glitch, and you'll see the egg trapped in a spinning loop against the pan. With that fraction-of-a-second delay, the egg has time to bounce off and escape the clutches of the loop.

There's only one last script to make before you can play your game.

Programming odds and ends

Right now, your lines are probably in the center of your Stage, as in figure 5.29. Because they serve as barriers, this will make for a very short game unless you send them to their correct positions.

By setting their X coordinate and Y coordinate positions instead of dragging them into place, the two boundary lines will always be properly aligned with the left and right side of the Stage. Make sure the blue box is around the Left Line sprite in the Sprite Zone.

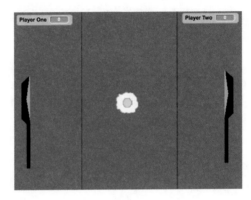

Figure 5.29 **The two lines need to be positioned on the far left and far right sides of the Stage.**

To make this tiny positioning script

1 Click Events and grab a When Flag Clicked block. Drag it into the Script Area and release it.

2 Switch to the Control menu and choose a Forever block. Snap it under the When Flag Clicked block in your workspace.

3 Go to Motion and grab a Go to X/Y block. Place it inside the Forever block. Switch the number for X to –240. Make sure the number for Y is zero (0). The X coordinate position is the far left side of the Stage. The Y coordinate position is centering the line so it covers the whole left side.

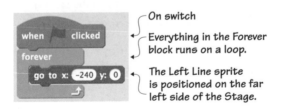

On switch
Everything in the Forever block runs on a loop.
The Left Line sprite is positioned on the far left side of the Stage.

Figure 5.30 **This script positions the left line in the correct place on the far left side of the Stage.**

And that's it, the whole script, as you can see in figure 5.30.

This script needs to be duplicated for the other line, and the number for the X coordinate position needs to be tweaked. Do you remember how you send a script to a different sprite?

Click the When Flag Clicked block at the top of the proper script in the Script Area and drag the entire script to Right Line in the Sprite Zone. Hold it over the sprite and release the mouse button. Remember, the blue box won't appear around the sprite, but trust that the script is being dropped into the sprite that you are hovering over.

Click Right Line to make sure that the script shows up in the Script Area. Tweak the script by changing –240 to 240 in order to position the right line over to the far right side of the Stage.

Congratulations! You've completed your first game, and you're ready to play. Go grab a second player and see who wins the Breakfast Wars.

Troubleshooting your game

Glitches happen. Even when you copy code block-by-block, there's still a chance for bugs. This section will help you fix any issues you're having with your game, though your first step is to go sprite by sprite, comparing the completed script examples in the book with the scripts on your screen. Once you've done that, here are some other tweaks you can try to get your game running smoothly.

Fixing layering issues

Each sprite comes with a transparent layer. Think of it like this: take a sheet of plastic wrap and place a real fried egg in the middle. Now set another piece of plastic wrap on top of it so the egg is sandwiched between two sheets of plastic. What would happen to that fried egg if you tried to nudge it with a real cast-iron pan? I'm willing to bet that it wouldn't move around a lot because it's trapped between layers of plastic. The same thing can happen to your fried egg sprite. The transparent layer attached to one sprite may negatively affect another sprite.

This is an easy fix. Click the egg on the Stage and move it slightly to the left or right. Doing so means that the egg is now the top layer on the Stage. If you move anything else on the Stage, make sure you always end by going back to the egg and jiggling it slightly to make it the last thing clicked on the Stage.

Fixing a glitching egg

Sometimes when the egg hits the pan, you will see it buzz for a moment before launching back into action, almost like a real egg sizzling against a frying pan! This is not an intended effect of the code; it's the sprite getting confused for a moment and glitching before it remembers where to go.

The reflection script is where you're going to want to go to fix this possible bug. Look at the two angles you've set for turning the egg before launching it again: 180 degrees clockwise or 90 degrees counterclockwise. The glitch is the code having a hard time using those angles due to the size of your sprite.

There are two solutions: click the Shrink tool in the Grey Toolbar and make your egg a little smaller, or play with those numbers until the glitch stops. It is easier to begin by shrinking the egg one or two clicks, but if you want your egg to be that size, try swapping a 90 for the 180 and see if that fixes the problem.

Learning in action

Now that you've completed your first game and officially become a programmer, it's time to play with the code. Try some of these challenges to change the game play of Breakfast Wars.

Play with the code

Speed plays a big role in a player's enjoyment of a game. There are two main places you can play with speed in the game: the movement of the paddles and the movement of the egg.

CHALLENGE   Can you figure out how to make the paddles move faster or slower? In the Paddle Movement script, change the value of 5 in the Change Y by 5 blocks. The lower the number, the slower the paddle will move. The higher the number, the faster the paddle will jump across the screen. Experiment when you're ready to make the game harder or easier to play.

CHALLENGE   Can you figure out how to make the egg move faster or slower? In the Egg Movement script, the Move 7 Steps block is controlling how fast the egg moves in the game. The higher the number, the faster the egg. If you find the egg is moving too quickly, lower that number to 3 or 5. If you find the game too easy, increase that number to 10 or 12. How high can you get that number and still win at this game? Additionally, you can make two difficulty levels with two versions of your game: a slow version for younger players and a faster version for older players.

CHALLENGE Right now the egg makes a popping sound when it hits the pan, but that's not the only sound Scratch can make. Can you poke around and find Scratch's sound library? Navigate to the Block Menu and switch to the Sounds tab to get to the sound screen. The speaker will allow you to choose from Scratch's sound library, and the microphone icon will allow you to record your own sound.

What did you learn?

Before you race back to playing your game, take a moment to reflect on which common computer science ideas from chapter 3 were used in this game:

- Using an on switch for every script in the game
- Sending the egg to the center of the Stage by stating X and Y coordinates
- Writing conditional statements to control where the egg goes on the screen
- Setting up loops so an action will run indefinitely without additional player input
- Creating variables and using them to track the players' scores
- Working with Touching Color blocks and Booleans to change the direction of the egg when it hits the pan
- Broadcasting a start message to make the egg start moving

You put into action seven out of eight common programming ideas. The rest of the games in this book will give you more examples of computer science in action. Additionally, you learned

- How to use angles in programming to change the direction of the egg and make the game more challenging
- How to make virtual paddles that can move up and down
- How to add a sound to your game
- How to create a points system in a game

After you enjoy a few more rounds of Breakfast Wars, take a deep breath and turn the page. You're going to make a fun, reflex-testing game called Wizards vs. Ghosts that will turn you into a wizard, blasting ghosts with your magic wand.

Part 3

Coding and playing games

You'll make four more games in the final nine chapters following the same format used for part two, with one important distinction: the training wheels are off, because at this point, you're familiar enough with Scratch that you can make design decisions and easily find the blocks for your code.

What if you're not quite ready to move on? That's okay. We created a set of extra practice chapters for a game called Salad Catch. If you're reading the print version, this extra practice can be downloaded at the Manning site, or you can register your book and download a free e-book version that contains the extra practice. If you're reading the e-book version, this extra practice is at the back of the book.

But if you are ready to move on, there are four more games to make. You'll finish off the book learning a bit about how to share your games with others as well as how to be a good member of the Scratch community.

Designing a fixed shooter

You are a powerful wizard with one annoying enemy: ghosts. The only way to destroy the ghosts is to blast them with magic using your wand. One night, you decide to rid the world of these pesky apparitions. You go out in an open field and wait for the ghosts to descend. Moments later, they're swooping down on you. As the ghosts fall from the sky to attack, you cast a spell with your wand and fire the red sparks seen in figure 6.1, hitting the ghosts with magic before they reach the ground.

Sparks   Wizard   Ghost

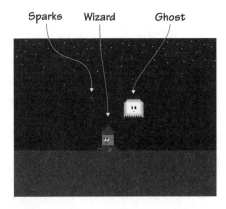

Figure 6.1   A game of Wizards vs. Ghosts means making an open field and night sky backdrop, the wizard, a ghost, red sparks, and a barrier line (not shown in image).

Wizards vs. Ghosts is a fixed shooter like Intellivision's *Astrosmash*. In *Astrosmash*, you're a space cannon with blasters, and you need to shoot down falling asteroids before they hit the ground. In Wizards vs. Ghosts, you're a wizard, shooting down ghosts with sparks from your wand. The wizard moves left and right across the grass. The ghosts fall from the sky. The goal is to avoid the ghosts. Scoring moves in two directions, removing points if you miss a ghost and giving you points if you hit a ghost.

Once again, as you make the sprites for the game, you'll learn some key art concepts, such as proportion and scale.

In this chapter, you will learn

- How to realistically size sprites
- How to keep sprites scaled to their surroundings
- How to proportion elements of a sprite to keep it visually in balance
- How to make a background that uses the rule of thirds
- How to predict where the eye will go when looking at the screen

Once again, you'll start off by making a simple nighttime background.

Prepping the background and learning about proportion, scale, and the rule of thirds

Ghosts come out at night, and the dark blue or black backdrop will make the white ghosts pop on the screen. A scattering of stars across the top of the screen and a field of green grass at the bottom break up the background into three distinct sections.

Making the nighttime backdrop

The backdrop in figure 6.2 sets the tone for the game. It's not the visual focus of the game, like the ghosts and wizard, but instead plays a supporting role.

In Wizards vs. Ghosts, it's nighttime and the goal is to *avoid and shoot* the ghosts. That twist in the goal steps up the intensity of the game, and the backdrop matches that feeling. Night is when everything creepy and crawly comes out to play...or haunt.

Figure 6.2   The empty field and the night sky set the scene for Wizards vs. Ghosts.

Open the Backdrop Art Editor and get ready to make the nighttime backdrop:

1 Select the darkest green paint sample square and the Line tool.

2 Draw a horizontal green line about a third of the way from the bottom of the Stage.

3 Switch to the Paint Bucket tool and click anywhere in the bottom third of the screen to fill the area with green paint.

4 Choose either the darkest blue or black paint. Click anywhere in the empty, top section of the canvas to fill it with either dark blue or black for the sky.

5 Switch to a pale yellow or white paint. You are about to draw the stars, so choose a color that contrasts nicely with the night sky. If the sky is dark blue, choose pale yellow. If the sky is black, choose white.

6 Click the Paintbrush tool and make random dots in the top third of the Stage, as in figure 6.3. Don't try to create any order—unless you happen to know a few star constellations. (Then feel free to draw them in the night sky, making tiny dots for stars.) Group the stars close

Figure 6.3   Close up of the tiny yellow dots indicating stars at the top of the Stage

together at the top of the Stage, and diffuse the stars as they move toward the bottom of the upper third of the Stage.

You now you have a big empty field for your wizard.

ANSWER THIS   WHICH IS BETTER? THE BLACK SKY OR THE BLUE SKY?
Question: is it better to make the sky black or blue?

Answer: there is no right answer to this question, though thinking about these types of decisions will make you a better artist. So much of art is going with your gut and making decisions based on what looks good *to you*. Art is about trying out a few options and seeing which one feels best when you look at it. If you made the sky black, duplicate the backdrop and use the Paint Bucket tool to turn the sky blue (or vice versa). Ask yourself which one you like best, and go with that option. Congratulations; you're now thinking like an artist.

Before you draw the wizard and ghosts, you need to understand the difference between scale and proportion in order to make your sprites fit the Stage.

Figuring out scale and proportion

I made a drawing of my family when I was younger that is in our living room. My mother is a short woman, but in the picture, I made her the biggest person in the family. My father is super tall, but I made him the smallest person in the family. I made myself as tall as my mum, and I drew Gabriel half off the frame. We were clearly not scaled properly.

You may have heard people talk about scale and proportion. *Scale* compares two items, like making sure if you draw a person next to a giant oak tree that the tree is much larger than the person, as in figure 6.4. Scale requires the artist to judge all the objects or people in the picture and make them work with one another. For instance, you may look at a person holding a balloon and notice that the balloon is slightly smaller than the person's head. When you draw the picture, you use a slightly smaller oval for the balloon than the face. Scale makes your picture look realistic.

This cat is not scaled properly. It is too big next to the tree to be realistic.

This cat is scaled properly to the tree. It is much smaller than the tree.

Figure 6.4   The cat on the left is scaled properly in comparison to the tree from the sprite library. The cat on the right is way too big to look realistic.

Proportion looks at the parts of the whole, such as how the eyes are sized to the whole face. Proportion creates balance within the object so that each element of the object is properly placed. For instance, did you know that the space between your two eyes is the length of one eye? Place your index finger and thumb on the two corners of your left eye. Now, keeping your fingers the same distance apart, move them so the thumb is on the corner of your left eye, and the index finger is on the corner of your right eye. That space over the bridge of your nose is one eye-length long. Hold your hand over your face with your fingers out. Your hand is probably slightly smaller than your face. What about your feet? They should be longer than your hands. When you draw a person, you need to look at the size of the two eyes and space them properly on the face. You need to look at the size of the head and proportion the hands and feet accordingly, as in figure 6.5. And yes, even pixel drawings follow some proportional rules.

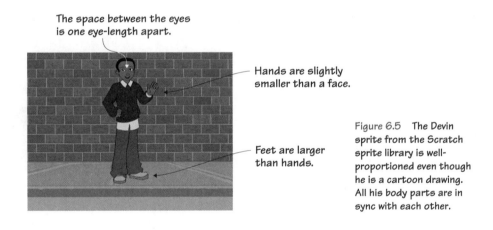

The space between the eyes is one eye-length apart.

Hands are slightly smaller than a face.

Feet are larger than hands.

Figure 6.5   The Devin sprite from the Scratch sprite library is well-proportioned even though he is a cartoon drawing. All his body parts are in sync with each other.

Scale is outwardly focused, looking at two objects and how they work together. Proportion is inwardly focused, looking at how the parts relate to one another. When you create your sprites, you need to think about creating proportional sprites and scaling all objects in the image and background to work together in harmony.

Your background is scaled well, with the ground placed in the bottom third of the screen and the stars' tiny pinpricks of light at the top of the screen. But the way you divided the screen is more important than only supporting good scale. It also helps you to use the Rule of Thirds.

Learning the Rule of Thirds

Take a piece of paper and hold it horizontally. Fold it into thirds, bringing the sides toward the middle of the paper. Open it up and turn the paper, now holding it vertically. Fold it into thirds the other way, bringing the two longer sides toward the center of the paper. If you did this correctly, you should have your paper divided into nine squares, as in figure 6.6.

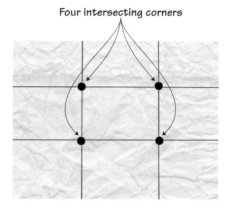

Four intersecting corners

Figure 6.6   The two sets of parallel lines divide the paper both ways into thirds, while dots mark the four important intersections.

This illustrates the *Rule of Thirds*. What it means is that centering important visual items on those four intersections creates a visually interesting picture. Everyone's eyes are super picky. We don't like to see objects out of balance on the screen. We don't mind objects in the center column, though we think that's a little boring. We definitely don't like an item in the left or right column. But we love it when an item is right on one of those lines, using

Figure 6.7   Instead of putting the cat and tree in the center of the Stage, position the cat and tree on one of the invisible third lines.

those intersections, as in figure 6.7. Layouts that use the Rule of Thirds make our eyes happy.

You're going to have to estimate those creases on the Stage because you can't fold the screen. You've made your life a little easier, though, with this particular background. The ground covers one third of the bottom, and the stars cover one third of the top. It will be easy to have the sprites extend over those intersection points on the virtual creases. In fact, let's make a wizard so you can position him on one of those sweet spots on the screen.

Prepping the main sprites

The Rule of Thirds is about how to lay out all the elements in a game, but you can also work that magic number three into your wizard, breaking up the sprite into three equal parts. You'll repeat that number by creating three smoky grey layers on the ghost. Think about various ways you can incorporate *three* into your game. You can remove the default cat on the Stage by clicking the scissors in the Grey Toolbar and clicking the cat.

Making the wizard

The wizard in figure 6.8 is wearing purple robes and a matching purple hat and he's carrying a wand that will fire sparks at the ghosts.

Figure 6.8   The finished wizard with purple robes and a matching purple hat

Keep proportion in mind as you make your sprites. Okay, ghosts and magical wizards aren't the most realistic beings in the world, but you can still keep general rules about proportion in mind. For instance, after you make the wizard's eyes, use them to determine how big to make the mouth, or look at the size of the wizard's head to decide how big to make the hat.

Open the Art Editor to make the wizard:

1 Zoom in to 800%. Select the Paintbrush tool and a skin tone using the rainbow box shown in figure 6.9.

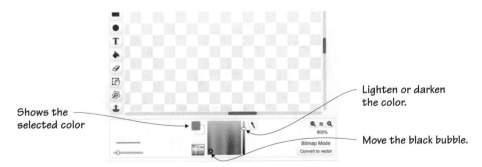

Figure 6.9   Choose the wizard's skin tone using the rainbow box.

Ten square dots

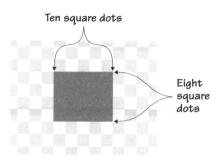

Eight square dots

Figure 6.10   The wizard's head begins with a simple square made out of pixels from the Paintbrush tool.

2 Draw a 10-by-8-pixel head close to the plus sign in the center of the canvas. Fill in the center of the square, like the one in figure 6.10, using the Paint Bucket tool.

3 Switch to the paint sample squares and choose the second darkest shade of purple and the Paintbrush tool. Draw a purple, 10-pixel line directly underneath the line of skin tone pixels that form the bottom of the wizard's head.

4 Start a pixel staircase from the right end of the purple line. Make one pixel underneath the line, then one pixel to the right. Again, make one pixel underneath that new, dangling pixel, and again, make one pixel to the right. Do this six times, as shown in figure 6.11. Make sure you end with one pixel going down, but don't make the final pixel to the right.

5 Make a horizontal line beginning underneath the single purple pixel at the bottom of the staircase on the right side of the wizard's robe, and make it parallel to that top row of purple pixels under the head. You're drawing the bottom of the wizard's robe, which can also be seen in figure 6.11.

6 Make a final vertical line of pixels closing off the left side of the wizard's robe, and fill in the middle of the robe either pixel-by-pixel or save yourself some time with the Paint Bucket tool. You should see the finished purple robe.

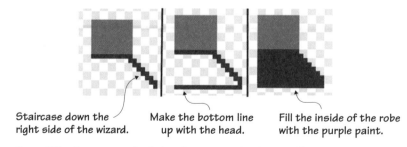

Staircase down the right side of the wizard.

Make the bottom line up with the head.

Fill the inside of the robe with the purple paint.

Figure 6.11   Create a purple pixel staircase to make the wizard's robe.

7 Move to the top of the wizard's head and draw a similar line of purple pixels going across the top of the skin tone pixels, as you did in step three, to make the neck of the wizard's robe. The line should be 10 pixels long.

8 Starting at either end of the new purple line, draw three square dots going up. Repeat this line of three pixels on the opposite side.

9 Make four diagonal square dots from the top of both lines, moving toward the center. You should end with two pixels touching each other, as in figure 6.12. Place a single pixel on top of that double pixel line to form a point.

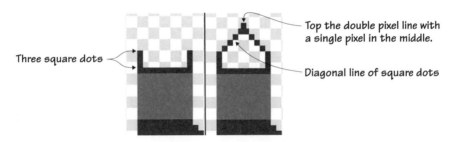

Three square dots

Top the double pixel line with a single pixel in the middle.

Diagonal line of square dots

Figure 6.12 The wizard's hat is formed by drawing a pentagon out of pixels.

10 Fill the hat using the Paint Bucket tool. The hat should be a solid purple pentagon. It's now time to make the wizard's arms.

11 Navigate back to the Color Toolbar and look for the Eyedropper tool seen in figure 6.13. This eyedropper will allow you to set your color by clicking anywhere that color already appears on the screen.

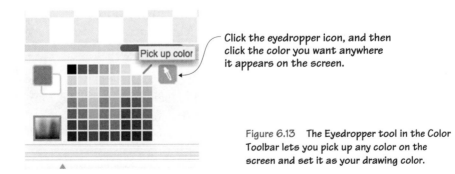

Pick up color

Click the eyedropper icon, and then click the color you want anywhere it appears on the screen.

Figure 6.13 The Eyedropper tool in the Color Toolbar lets you pick up any color on the screen and set it as your drawing color.

12 Click the eyedropper and then click anywhere on the wizard's face in the Art Editor. This sets your current color as that skin tone color.

13 Return to the Paintbrush tool and draw three diagonal square dots in the middle of the robe. Next, visually judge the height of the top of the arm and draw four pixels coming out of the front of the wizard's robe. Finally, switch to a dark brown paint sample square and make a four-pixel vertical line so the wand intersects with the left arm, as shown in figure 6.14.

14 Choose the white paint sample square for the wizard's eyes. Make two small squares, four pixels each, in the middle of the wizard's face, like step one of figure 6.15.

15 Switch to the black paint sample square and make a single black

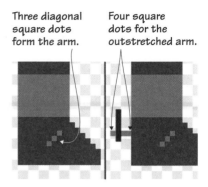

Three diagonal square dots form the arm.

Four square dots for the outstretched arm.

Figure 6.14   A few pixels make the wizard's arms, either diagonally or horizontally.

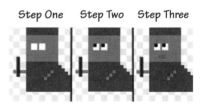

Step One   Step Two   Step Three

Figure 6.15   The wizard's eyes are two white-and-black squares, and his mouth is a worried-looking, two-pixel red line.

square dot in each white eye. You can decide where to place it. I placed mine in the top left corner, as in step two of figure 6.15.

16 Switch to the red paint sample square and make a two-pixel red line toward the bottom of the face, as in step three of figure 6.15.

That's it! You should have a worried-looking wizard like the one in figure 6.16. Make sure you go to the Sprite Zone and rename your sprite Wizard.

Right now, the wizard is probably somewhere near the middle of the Stage. But if you want to draw the player's attention to the wizard, you want to position him in a visually interesting place.

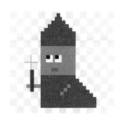

Figure 6.16   The wizard sprite is ready to fight some ghosts.

Use the Rule of Thirds and put him on one of the imaginary creases dividing the Stage into nine invisible, equal parts. To better understand this concept, I drew real lines on the background and placed the wizard right on the crease, as shown in figure 6.17. Look at the general area where that wizard is standing and drag your wizard to match that on your Stage.

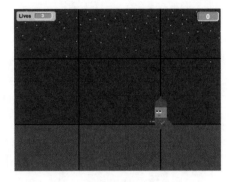

Figure 6.17 Place the wizard at a visually interesting place at an invisible intersection on the Stage.

ANSWER THIS IS THE WIZARD IN PROPORTION?

Question: is this pixelated wizard in proportion?

Answer: yes...and no. On the one hand, you've kept in mind that both arms should be the same size, and certain features—such as the body—should be larger than other features—such as the mouth. But the wizard is a great example of how you can exploit proportion to convey an idea once you understand how proportion works. For instance, I made the wizard's eyes oversized to make him look vulnerable. It's scary to fight ghosts, and I wanted to make sure that the wizard looked the part. You can enlarge or shrink certain features to immediately clue the viewer in to a part of their personality, such as making a neutral-looking creature have enormous teeth to make it seem scary, or giving a person a longer-than-usual neck to make them look more elegant. Think about ways you can tweak proportion to tell a story.

Making the ghost

You now need to make the ghosts that fight the wizard. You only need to make the one ghost as shown in figure 6.18 for Wizards vs. Ghosts. You'll once again code many copies to generate during the game.

Figure 6.18 The completed ghost doesn't look that scary when it's not in motion, but look out when the ghosts start swooping down from the sky.

Make a new sprite and return to the Art Editor:

1 Zoom in to 800%. Select the Paintbrush tool and the fourth lightest shade of grey (four over from the left). You are going to use three shades of grey to make your ghost, so make sure you have room to move lighter and lighter for the next three layers.

2 Make a 12-pixel horizontal line near the center of the canvas. The ghost is *symmetrical*, which means that if you divided him down the middle, both sides would be exactly the same. Keep this in mind as you work, because any pixel you make on the right side of the ghost should match with a pixel you make on the left side.

3 Make a diagonal line three pixels down on either side of the horizontal line.

4 Draw a vertical line, 13 pixels long, on either side of the ghost using the end of the diagonal line as a starting point.

5 Finish the ghost by connecting pixels on the diagonal across the bottom in an in-and-out pattern, as shown in figure 6.19.

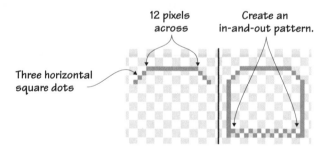

Figure 6.19   The darkest grey is used to form the outline of the ghost.

6 Switch to a slightly lighter shade of grey and outline the inside of the ghost, touching the new lighter grey pixels to the existing darker grey pixels, as shown in figure 6.20.

7 Switch again to the lightest shade of grey and outline the inside of the ghost, touching the lightest grey pixels to the medium light grey pixels.

8 Choose the white paint sample square and the Paint Bucket tool. Click anywhere in the center of the ghost to fill the empty space, as in figure 6.20.

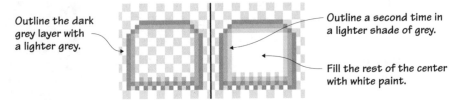

Outline the dark grey layer with a lighter grey.

Outline a second time in a lighter shade of grey.

Fill the rest of the center with white paint.

Figure 6.20   Two shades of grey outline the inside of the ghost, and a white center finishes off the sprite.

FIX IT   HELP! I CAN'T SEE WHERE THE PIXELS SHOULD GO!   It can be hard to see the three versions of grey pixels against that grey and white canvas of the Art Editor. If you're having trouble making the ghost, use three shades of blue. Then, when you are finished with the sprite, use the Paint Bucket tool to change each blue section to a corresponding grey. For instance, use the darkest blue in place of the darkest grey in the sprite. Once the sprite is complete, switch to the correct shade of grey and the Paint Bucket tool and click one of the dark blue pixels. This should spill that new color through all the connecting dark blue pixels without spilling over into any of the other lighter blue sections of the ghost. Repeat this with each layer to make the ghost a little easier to draw against the grey and white canvas.

9 Choose the black paint sample square and Paintbrush tool. Draw eyes that are two vertical pixels in the center of the ghost.

10 Switch to the red paint sample square and make a single red pixel underneath the eyes to serve as the mouth.

You should now have a finished, spooky, transparent-looking ghost, as shown in figure 6.21.

Rename the sprite Ghost by going into the Sprite Zone and clicking the blue *i* on the sprite. Now that the wizard and the

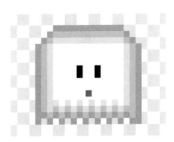

Figure 6.21   The ghost sprite is ready to swoop down from the sky.

ghost are ready to square off, it's time to give the wizard some red sparks to blast out of his wand.

Making the wand sparks

Your wizard is holding a wand, but right now it can't cast a spell. Give the wand the ability to shoot red sparks, like the ones in figure 6.22, from the end when the wizard is squaring off against the ghosts.

Make a new sprite and get ready to make the sparks in the Art Editor:

1 Choose the red paint sample square and Paintbrush tool.

Figure 6.22   **The wizard looks with surprise at the sparks coming out of his wand.**

2 Make a shower of sparks, placing spaces between each pixel. You'll want the sparks to come to a point at the bottom and spread out toward the top because they're coming out of the wand.

3 You should now have a little cluster of red pixels, as shown in figure 6.23.

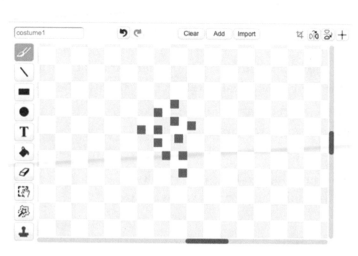

Figure 6.23   Tiny square dots with spaces in between become the sparks shooting out of the wizard's wand.

Finish off the main sprites by navigating once again to the Sprite Zone and clicking the *i* to rename this sprite Sparks. Look at the sparks on the Stage and click and drag them so they hover over the wizard's wand.

Prepping the odds and ends

You still have to make the single line that will serve as a barrier when you start coding your game. It's a boring sprite, but it will make coding your game a little more precise.

Making the barrier line

You'll want this single horizontal line at the bottom of the Stage, so once again draw it at the bottom of the Art Editor's canvas:

1 Select the darkest green paint sample square and Line tool. Zoom out to 100%.

2 Draw a line that starts at the bottom left corner of the canvas and ends at the bottom right corner. Hold down the Shift key on the keyboard as you drag your mouse to make the line completely straight, as in figure 6.24.

Figure 6.24 Draw your green line at the bottom of the Art Editor; it will be a barrier when you code your game.

Go to the Sprite Zone and rename this sprite Barrier Line.

Preparing to code

You've learned a lot of design concepts in this chapter, so let's review them and play with them before you jump into coding your game.

Play with the game

Right now, everything should be in balance on your Stage. But what if you take all your sprites out of scale with one another or play with proportion?

CHALLENGE   The mood of the game, believe it or not, is influenced by the scale of the sprites. Make the ghost enormous and think about how the game feels with the ghost looming over the little wizard. Turn it around and make the ghost small and the wizard enormous. Do you still feel sympathy toward the wizard when he is clearly so much larger than his enemy?

CHALLENGE   Your wizard has big eyes to show his vulnerability and a little, worried mouth. Can you reopen the wizard sprite and play with his features to make them more in proportion for an actual face? While you're in there, can you add a nose? What do you think of this version of the wizard versus the original one?

CHALLENGE   Right now, the stars fill the top third of the screen. What happens if you extend the stars to the midway point on the Stage or all the way to the green grass? Does it change the feel of the game? Does the game feel off-balance?

CHALLENGE   The sparks are all one version of red, but you can make them more visually interesting by blending a few shades of red, or even incorporating a few orange or yellow pixels to make them feel more like fire.

What did you learn?

Proportion and scale are important in other areas of STEAM. What if an engineer designing a new mobile phone didn't take into account the size of a person's hand and scaled their device for a giant? What if elements of a house were built out of proportion and no one could get inside because the door was too small? Well-made inventions are not only proportional, but they're also scaled toward the people who will use them.

Pause for a moment and think about everything you learned in this chapter:

- How scale is different from proportion
- How to tweak proportion to convey an idea about a sprite
- How scale affects the difficulty of a game
- How to use the Rule of Thirds to make the game visually interesting

You now have a crew of four sprites ready to be coded. Continue on to the next chapter to learn how to make this reflex-testing game.

7

Using conditionals to build your fixed shooter

You've probably figured out by now that the way people invent new video games is to look at old video games. If a video game is a big success, other game companies try to imitate it, making small changes to the visuals or goals of the game while keeping the same mechanics. That's what happened when Intellivision noticed the popularity of Atari's *Asteroids*.

Asteroids was released in 1979 and was a huge success. The player controlled a space cannon flying in outer space that could spin around and shoot at the rocks falling around them. Intellivision made its version — *Astrosmash* — in 1981, moving the space cannon to the ground, the colorful rocks to the sky, and adding a few extra enemies such as spinning bombs.

But don't think that Intellivision is just a copycat. *Asteroids* was based on the game *Spacewar!* And *Spacewar!* probably would have been based on something else if it wasn't one of the first video games. The game industry has a long history of creating similar games, which makes it easy for players to pick up a new game and immediately understand their goal and how to move their sprite.

Like *Astrosmash*, the goal of Wizards vs. Ghosts is to shoot the ghosts coming at you with sparks from your wand while trying not to get hit by any of the apparitions. The ghosts won't break apart like the rocks in

Asteroids or *Astrosmash* but instead disappear from the screen when blasted by the wizard's spell, as shown in figure 7.1.

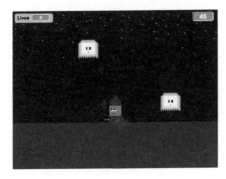

Figure 7.1   In Wizards vs. Ghosts, the player moves the wizard back and forth while blasting ghosts with his wand. The player loses a life whenever he touches a ghost, loses points whenever a ghost touches the ground, and gains points whenever he blasts one away.

Wizards vs. Ghosts is a fixed shooter, which means the sprite doing the blasting (in this case, the wizard) can only move back and forth on one fixed plane on the screen. You can't make the wizard fly above the ghosts, and you can't get him to hide in the grass. He can only move across the ground while fighting the ghosts. Additionally, the scenery is fixed and remains the same—a big, open field—throughout the whole game rather than changing as the player moves through a larger universe. The player is looking at the action from the side as if it is happening in front of them.

There are lots of types of shoot-em-ups, all of them named based on the way you're viewing the action or the abilities of the main sprite, such as side-scrolling shooters (games where the action makes the player keep flying in the same direction), rail shooters (where the game moves the sprite so you can concentrate on the single action of blasting away the enemy), and multidirectional shooters (where the main sprite can move in any direction).

You'll notice that all of these types of games include the word *shooter*. Violence plays a big role in video games, and it's common to have the player fighting against an enemy. Although games can be a safe way to explore something you would never do in real life (such as shoot at rocks!), you also don't have to make your game violent. The most creative fixed shooters move away from guns and cannons and use other methods for fighting the enemy. For instance, in this game you'll use a magic wand to blast your enemy, the ghosts.

In this chapter, you will learn

- How to use conditionals to check whether the player is pressing the spacebar
- How to use loops to keep sprites continuously moving
- How to use the same variable to reward and remove points

If you didn't get your letter from Hogwarts, here is your chance to not only get to be a wizard, but to rid the world of pesky ghosts like Peeves. Open up your Wizards vs. Ghosts project where you made your sprites in chapter 6 and get ready to code.

Preparing to program

You are steps away from being ready to write the code for this program, but there are a few small tasks you must complete before you're ready to go.

Missing sprites

If you skipped chapter 6, either flip back and complete it or go to the Manning site and download the background and sprites for Wizards vs. Ghosts. The directions for importing are the same as chapter 5. You should have a wizard, a ghost, a group of sparks, and a barrier line, as well as the nighttime background.

Preparing the Stage

You'll need to increase the size of your wizard and ghost. The wizard needs eight clicks with the Grow tool from the Grey Toolbar, and the ghost needs six clicks. The sparks and line are both the correct size.

If your wizard is not already standing on the grass, click and drag the wizard on the Stage to pull him onto the green third of the screen. You don't need to move any other sprite because they will all be coded into position.

Programming the wizard

The wizard is the equivalent to the space cannon in *Astrosmash*. You will move him back and forth along the grass using the arrow keys while you press the spacebar to fire spells from his wand. Three programs power the wizard: a movement script, a life deducting script, and a game ending script. All scripts in this section are applied to the wizard, so go put the blue box around the wizard sprite in the Sprite Zone and don't move the blue box until you program the ghost in the next section. Remember, the names or values on *your* blocks may be slightly different from time to time, so use the completed script images to make sure you choose the correct block.

Making a movement script

The wizard is standing in the grass, but he can't go anywhere. It's going to be hard to catch that falling ghost in figure 7.2 if he's unable to move.

You need to write a script that will give the player the ability to move the wizard left and right when the arrow keys are pressed.

To give the wizard the ability to move

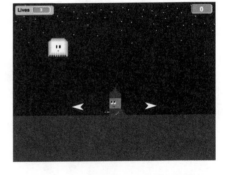

Figure 7.2   The wizard is currently unable to move beneath the ghosts in order to shoot sparks at them.

1 Start with a When Flag Clicked (Motion) block.

2 Snap a Forever (Control) block underneath to start a loop.

3 Move two If/Then (Control) blocks inside the Forever block. Stack them atop one another. You're going to set two conditions.

4 Slide a Key Space Pressed (Sensing) block into each of the empty, hexagonal spaces in the If/Then block. Change the top Key Space Pressed block to Left Arrow using the drop-down menu and the bottom Key Space Pressed block to Right Arrow. This sets what will happen if the left or right arrow keys are pressed on the keyboard.

5 Place a Change X by 10 (Motion) block inside each If/Then block. Change the number in the first Change X by 10 block to –10. This will move the wizard 10 coordinate spaces to the left. You don't need to make any changes to the second Change X by 10 block because positive numbers move toward the right.

The first script is now complete. Does your script match the one in figure 7.3?

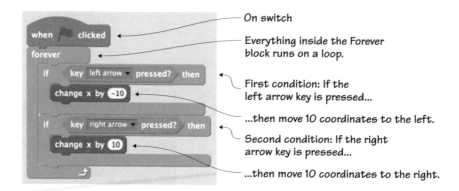

Figure 7.3   The movement script allows the player to move the wizard left and right along the grass.

ANSWER THIS   WHY 10 COORDINATES?

Question: why have the wizard move ten spaces at a time instead of one space?

Answer: you know that negative numbers move to the left and positive numbers move to the right, but you also need to think about the speed at which you're setting the wizard to move. The lower the number, the slower the wizard will move across the Stage. The higher the number, the faster the wizard will move. Jumping eight coordinate spaces at a time ensures that the wizard doesn't miss a falling ghost by overshooting the space, nor does he inch forward at a glacial speed. Ten is good for this game, though you can experiment with other numbers at the end of the chapter.

You've set the wizard to jump 10 coordinates at a time. Remember, the higher the coordinate number, the faster the sprite will move.

Making a life deducting script

Currently, the ghosts can swoop straight through our wizard without anything happening. But the ghost is the wizard's sworn enemy! Shouldn't something happen if the ghost touches the wizard, as in figure 7.4?

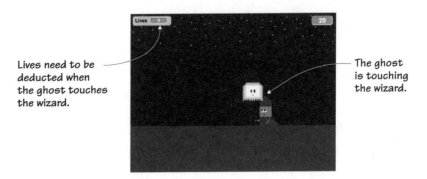

Lives need to be deducted when the ghost touches the wizard.

The ghost is touching the wizard.

Figure 7.4 The ghost is touching the wizard, but nothing is happening.

You need to write a script that will deduct a "life" every time a ghost touches the wizard. The player will start out the game with three lives, or turns.

To make this life deducting script

1 Start with a When Flag Clicked (Events) block.
2 Add a Forever (Control) block underneath to start a loop.
3 Slide an If/Then (Control) block inside the Forever block to set a condition.
4 Place a Touching (Sensing) block in the empty hexagonal space on the If/Then block. Use the drop-down menu to set the sprite to Ghost. You've now set a condition: if the wizard is touching the ghost sprite.
5 Go to Data and create a variable called Lives. Keep it on the default For All Sprites setting. Position the variable in the top left corner of the Stage.
6 Drag a Change Lives by 1 (Data) block inside the If/Then block. Change the 1 to a –1 because you want to deduct, not add, a life.

You've now set the action that will happen if the condition is met: change the value of the variable Lives by –1.

7 Slip a Wait 1 Secs (Control) block under the Change Lives by –1 block. Change the 1 to a 2, which will give the game two seconds to get rid of the ghost so the same ghost doesn't glitch and remove multiple lives at a time.

You now have the script, shown in figure 7.5, that will remove one of the player's three chances whenever a ghost sprite touches the wizard.

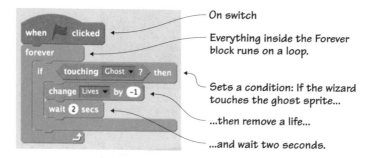

Figure 7.5 The completed life deducting script removes one of the player's three chances when a ghost touches the wizard.

Making a game ending script

This is the final script for the wizard, and it solves a big problem: the game currently doesn't have an end point. Sure, you're planning on giving the player three chances to get the ghosts, but currently, they can keep going long after they've used up their three chances, like the scoreboards in figure 7.6.

This script will check how many lives the player has left, and once it is less than 1, it will stop the game.

The player has taken 39 turns!

Figure 7.6 The game can go on forever unless you set an end point.

To make the game ending script

1 Start with a When Flag Clicked (Events) block.

2 Add a Forever (Control) block underneath to start a loop.

3 Slide an If/Then (Control) block inside the Forever block to set a condition.

4 Place a Square < Square (Operators) block inside the empty hexagonal space in the If/Then block. Fill the left square with a Lives (Data) block and type a 1 in the right square. You've set a condition: if the value of the variable Lives is less than 1, then do *something*. You'll define that "something" with the next step.

5 Slide a Stop All (Control) block inside the If/Then block. That is the action that will happen if the condition is met: all the scripts will stop, and the game will end.

The game ending script shown in figure 7.7 is now complete. Check your work against the image because this is the final script for the wizard sprite.

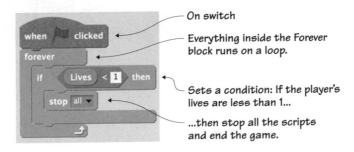

Figure 7.7   *The completed game ending script tells Scratch when to end the game of Wizards vs. Ghosts.*

There are three scripts for the wizard sprite and three loops. Wizards vs. Ghosts is a fast-paced game, and loops enable a set of actions to run indefinitely with the click of a single on switch—in this case, the When Flag Clicked block.

The ghost will have its own set of loops because you'll want the ghosts to continuously generate and fall during the game.

Programming the ghosts

Once again, you only have one ghost, but I keep using the plural: ghosts. This is your clue that you're about to make many copies of the ghost, by cloning them with code. The ghosts are the equivalent to the asteroids that fall during *Astrosmash*, and they require three scripts: a positioning script, a cloning script, and a movement script. Put the blue box around the ghost in the Sprite Zone and leave it there for all three scripts.

Making a positioning script

Where do ghosts hang out when they're not swooping down and haunting the wizard? In this game, they live in the sky, so they're in the perfect position to descend on our wizard, as you can see in figure 7.8.

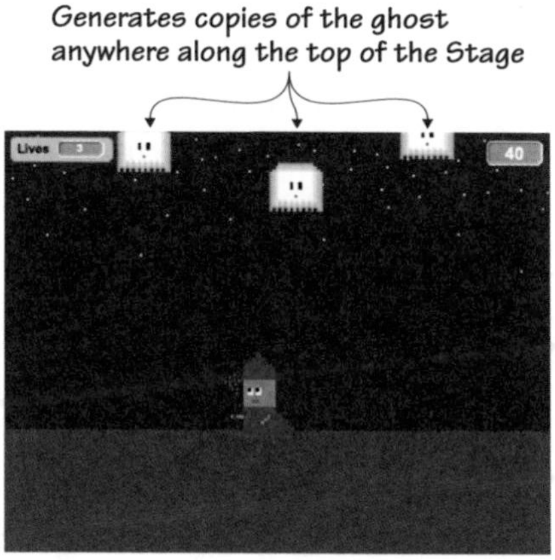

This script will make the ghost sprites generate at a random point at the top of the Stage.

To create the positioning script

Generates copies of the ghost anywhere along the top of the Stage

Figure 7.8   Watch out, wizard! The ghosts are coming down from the top of the Stage!

1 Start with a When Flag Clicked (Events) block.

2 Add a Forever (Control) block underneath to start a loop.

3 Place a Go to X/Y (Motion) block inside the Forever block. This will set the coordinate (or point on the screen) where the ghost will go. But you want the ghosts to pop out from different places at the top of the Stage, not the same place, so you're going to slip a block into the X slot.

4 Put a Pick Random 1 to 10 (Operators) block inside the first circle for the X coordinate, as in figure 7.9. This will allow you to set a range of coordinates and have Scratch choose a different one each time a ghost forms. Change the two numbers in the Pick Random block to –240 and 240 to indicate the range of coordinates along the

top of the Stage. Type 180 in the Y coordinate slot because you want all the ghosts to generate from the top of the Stage and not random spots along the Y-axis.

You now have your first script for your ghosts and yet another script using a loop. This time, the loop in figure 7.9 is causing Scratch to choose a new spot for each ghost sprite to use as a starting point at the top of the Stage.

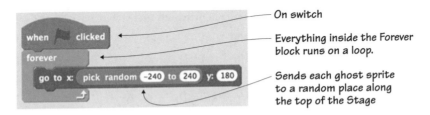

Figure 7.9   The completed positioning script sets a random starting point for each ghost sprite.

Making a cloning script

You currently only have one ghost. It's going to be a brief game unless you make some more. Right now, once the wizard blasts away that one ghost (as seen in figure 7.10), he's not going to have a lot to do.

Figure 7.10   The wizard scores 10 points for shooting down the ghost and then stands in the field indefinitely with nothing more to do.

You can make the game a lot more exciting by cloning the ghost and making the enemy constantly regenerate new copies during the game. This script will make copies of the ghost sprite, one every second.

To make this cloning script

1 Start with a When Flag Clicked (Events) block.
2 Slide a Hide (Looks) block underneath the When Flag Clicked block. This block hides the ghost while it generates so the player can't predict where the ghost will start falling.
3 Add a Forever (Control) block underneath to start a loop.
4 Place a Create Clone of Myself (Control) block and a Wait 1 Secs (Control) block inside the Forever block, one on top of the other. The task happens on a continuous loop while the game is in action, creating a clone and then pausing for a second.

The brief script in figure 7.11 gives the wizard plenty of ghosts to fight during the game.

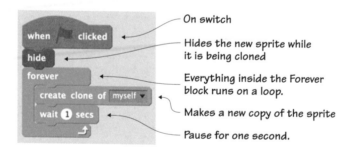

Figure 7.11   The completed cloning script creates new copies of the ghost sprite.

 WHAT DOES THE ONE SECOND DELAY DO?

Question: the script ends with a Wait 1 Secs block, but do you need it?

Answer: let's put it this way: would you rather fight an army of ghosts that are coming at you one per second, or would you rather deal with a million ghosts at once? Be kind to the little wizard and give him a fighting chance against the ghosts by staggering them one per second. Without that delay, the ghost copies will start generating one on top of the other and falling in clumps. You can change the length of the delay by typing a new number in the bubble. Changing the 1 to a 2 would make the game a little easier for young players. Changing the 1 to a .5 would make the game more intense.

Making a movement script

You've made a lot of ghosts, and they're positioned at the top of the Stage, but right now they're only hiding. Our little wizard is waiting nervously at the ready, as you can see in figure 7.12.

This movement script will do double duty, not only sending the ghosts down from the top of the Stage but setting up a scoring system, too.

This is the final script for the ghost, and it's a long one. Check your script against the one in the book every few steps. This script uses two variables and a complicated loop to keep track of where the ghost is on the screen and whether it is touching the wizard or the sparks:

The ghosts are hidden at the top of the Stage. You need to make them visible and start moving.

Figure 7.12   The wizard is ready, but the ghosts have no way to move.

1 Start with a When I Start as a Clone (Control) block. I bet you thought I was going to send you to the Events menu, but this script only kicks into action if the ghost clone has been made by the last script.

2 Snap a Show (Looks) block under the When I Start as a Clone block. This will make the clone visible.

3 Place a Repeat Until (Control) block under the Show block. This is a new kind of loop. You're going to have an action repeat until a condition is met.

4 Drag a Touching (Sensing) block into the empty space on the Repeat Until block. Use the drop-down menu to set it to Barrier Line. This means that everything you put inside the Repeat Until block will keep happening until the ghost sprite reaches the bottom of the screen and therefore touches the barrier line.

5 Slide a Change Y by 10 (Motion) block and place it inside the Repeat Until block. Change the 10 to –3. Any negative number will make it move down the Stage, and –3 is a good speed for the ghost. You can play with this number once your game is done. Low numbers, such as –1, will make the ghost fall slower, and higher numbers, such as –5, will make the ghost fall faster.

6 Stack three If/Then (Control) blocks underneath the Change Y by –3 block, as seen in figure 7.13. You're going to set up three conditions.

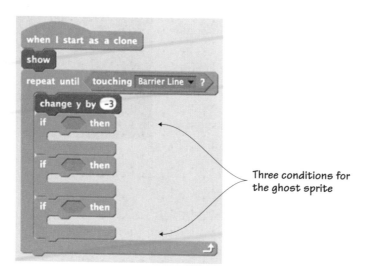

Figure 7.13 Stacking three If/Then blocks inside the Repeat Until block allows the game maker to set three different conditions.

7 Grab three Touching (Sensing) blocks and place one each inside the empty hexagonal space in the If/Then blocks. Use the drop-down

menu to change the first one to Touching Barrier Line, the second one to Touching Sparks, and the third one to Touching Wizard, as shown in figure 7.14.

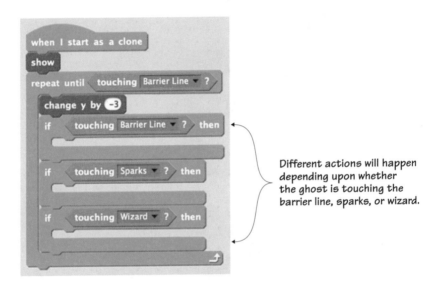

Different actions will happen depending upon whether the ghost is touching the barrier line, sparks, or wizard.

Figure 7.14 The loop contains three different conditions: if the ghost is touching the barrier line, sparks, or wizard.

8 Click Data and make a variable called Score. Position the variable in the top right corner of the Stage. Right-click (or control-click, if you're using a Mac) the score bubble to bring up the menu. Choose Large Readout so the score appears as a number on the screen.

9 Drag three Change Score by 1 (Data) blocks and place one in each of the If/Then blocks. Keep the variable set to Score in the first block, but change the value to –10. If the ghost reaches the barrier line without being shot down by the sparks, it will deduct 10 points from the player's score. Keep the variable set to Score in the second block, but change the value to 10. If the sparks make contact with the ghost, it will add 10 points to the player's score. Change the variable to Lives in the third block and change the value to –1. If the

ghost touches the wizard, it will remove a life. You can see all these variables and their values in figure 7.15.

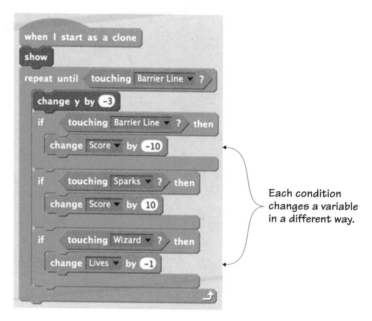

Figure 7.15   Each condition changes the variable and its value.

10 Slide a Delete This Clone (Control) block underneath each of the Change Score by –10 blocks (or whatever the variable and value is on the block). This will delete the copy of the ghost after it touches the barrier line, sparks, or wizard.

11 Place a fourth Delete This Clone (Control) sprite underneath the Repeat Until Touching Barrier Line block at the very bottom of the script. Just in case the If/Then inside the Repeat Until block misses deleting the sprite, this backup block will get rid of the ghost so you don't have copies lingering at the bottom of the screen.

You can see in figure 7.16 that it's a long script, but it gives the ghosts the ability to move and it sets up a scoring system.

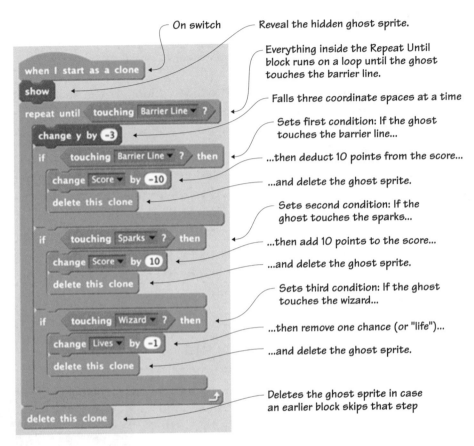

On switch

Reveal the hidden ghost sprite.

Everything inside the Repeat Until block runs on a loop until the ghost touches the barrier line.

Falls three coordinate spaces at a time

Sets first condition: If the ghost touches the barrier line...

...then deduct 10 points from the score...

...and delete the ghost sprite.

Sets second condition: If the ghost touches the sparks...

...then add 10 points to the score...

...and delete the ghost sprite.

Sets third condition: If the ghost touches the wizard...

...then remove one chance (or "life")...

...and delete the ghost sprite.

Deletes the ghost sprite in case an earlier block skips that step

Figure 7.16 The completed movement script not only allows the ghosts to fall but also sets up a scoring system.

The Repeat Until is another type of loop. It's one that comes with a condition rather than being open-ended.

ANSWER THIS   HOW DO YOU DECIDE THE NUMBERS IN A SCORING SYSTEM?

Question: each game sets a guideline for how points are gained or lost, but how do you decide how many points to reward or remove? Answer: this is a decision in the hands of the game maker, and there are no right or wrong answers. In fact, feel free to change the values in the Change Score blocks. Maybe you want to deduct only 10 points if the player misses the ghost but reward 20 points if the player gets the ghost. Or you can take the opposite path, deducting more points than you reward. Think about whether you want to make it easy, medium, or hard to rack up points.

The ghost is now complete. It's time to look at the sparks and set up scripts that will allow them to shoot from the wizard's wand.

Programming the sparks

The wizard is always holding his wand, but nothing comes out of it until he casts a spell. You need to code this sprite so the sparks will shoot up toward the ghosts when the player presses the spacebar on the keyboard. Once again, you'll use cloning to make unlimited sparks for your wizard to use. The sparks for the wand use four scripts: a positioning script, a cloning script, a movement script, and a clone deletion script. Place the blue box around the red sparks in the Sprite Zone.

Making a positioning script

The wizard can move back and forth, so he can dodge out of the way of the falling ghosts. But right now, he can't cast a spell and get *rid* of the ghosts. The wand in figure 7.17 is dormant—only a little stick of wood.

The wand is just a stick until sparks can fly out.

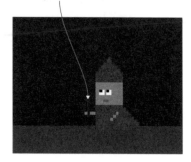

This script will send the sparks to the wand. The wand is drawn as part of the wizard sprite, whereas the sparks are a separate sprite. This script brings the two sprites together.

Figure 7.17   The wand is part of the wizard sprite, but the sparks operate with their own scripts.

To create the positioning script

1 Start with a When Flag Clicked (Events) block.

2 Slide a Hide (Looks) block under the When Flag Clicked block. This will keep the sparks invisible until the player is ready to use them.

3 Add a Forever (Control) block underneath to start a loop.

4 Drag a Go to Mouse Pointer (Motion) block inside the Forever block. You don't want the sparks to go to the mouse pointer. You want them to go to the wizard, so open the drop-down menu and choose the Wizard option.

Figure 7.18 shows the whole script. It's a small but important script that gives the wizard a lot of power in his fight against the ghosts.

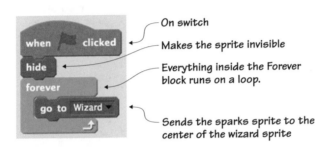

On switch

Makes the sprite invisible

Everything inside the Forever block runs on a loop.

Sends the sparks sprite to the center of the wizard sprite

Figure 7.18   The completed positioning script sends the sparks to the wizard's wand.

FIX IT   MY SPARKS ARE COMING FROM THE WIZARD'S HEAD!   When you sent the sparks to the wizard, you sent them to the center of the sprite, which could be anywhere on the wizard and not necessarily where you want them, such as coming from the wand. Remember how the sprite is the size of that canvas, with some parts in color and other parts transparent? The center of the canvas is the center of the sprite. Knowing that, you can draw your sprite so it's near that little grey plus sign always seen in the center of the Art Editor (figure 7.19).

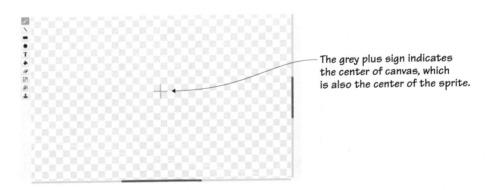

The grey plus sign indicates the center of canvas, which is also the center of the sprite.

Figure 7.19   The light grey plus sign marks the center of both the canvas and the sprite.

But don't worry if you drew your sprite somewhere else on the canvas. You can always center it. Go to the Sprite Zone and click the wizard. Navigate to the tab marked Costumes in the middle of the Block Menu. Look at the plus sign in the top right corner of the Art Editor, marked in figure 7.20. Click it, and a cross should appear on the canvas.

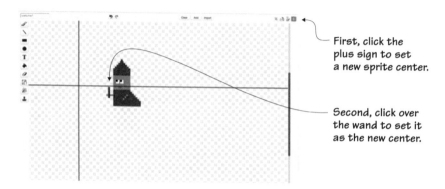

First, click the plus sign to set a new sprite center.

Second, click over the wand to set it as the new center.

Figure 7.20   First click the plus sign in the top right corner, and then click a point on the screen to set a new center.

Zoom in using the magnifying glass to enlarge the wizard if you have trouble seeing his wand. Now click the top of the wand (also marked in figure 7.20) to set that space as the new center. You should see the grey plus sign on the canvas over the wand, as in figure 7.21. Now the sparks will come out of the wand and not the wizard's head.

The plus sign is now over the top of the wand.

Figure 7.21   The center of the sprite is now the space over the wand, which is where the sparks will be sent from once you clone the sprite.

Making a cloning script

Right now, you have one spark. But the wizard is going to need an unlimited number of sparks in order to fight the ghosts so the sparks can continuously shoot from the wand, as in figure 7.22.

This script will clone the sparks that will come out of the wand. It will make a new copy of the sparks every time the spacebar is pressed. This is the only script so far that doesn't contain a loop.

Each time the spacebar is pressed, red sparks jump out of the wand.

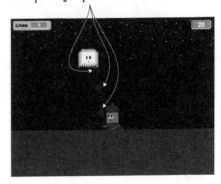

Figure 7.22   The wand emits sparks every time the spacebar is pressed.

If you checked the center of the wizard sprite with the last Fix It, make sure you go back to the Sprite Zone and put the blue box around the sparks. You're still programming the sparks sprite. Click the Scripts tab to continue programming.

To create the cloning script

1 Start with a When Space Key Pressed (Events) block. This is a different type of on switch, and it runs the next part of the script whenever the player presses the spacebar on the keyboard.

2 Slide a Create Clone of Myself (Control) block under the When Space Key Pressed block. This creates a clone of the sparks every time the player presses the spacebar.

And that's it! The whole script in figure 7.23 is only two blocks long. One block sets the starting point (pressing the spacebar) and the other block clones the sprite.

On switch

Makes a copy of the sprite

Figure 7.23   The completed cloning script is brief but is an important part of the game.

Making a movement script

Right now the sparks are ready to come out of the wand, but the sprite has no instructions to move. In figure 7.24, the sparks are piling up on the tip of the wand, unable to shoot toward the ghosts above.

This script will make the sparks that you clone shoot upward, out of the wand. To make the movement script

1 Start with a When I Start as a Clone (Control) block.

2 Snap a Show (Looks) block under the When I Start as a Clone block. This will make the clone visible.

3 Place a Forever (Control) block under the Show block. You're starting a loop that will put the sparks into continuous motion until a condition is met.

4 Drag a Repeat Until (Control) block inside the Forever block. It's a double loop! The outer loop (Forever block) controls how many times the inner loop (Repeat Until block) runs through its actions. The inner loop will run, and then the outer loop will check where things are with the script and run again. Putting a loop inside a loop is called a *nested loop*. In this case, the inner loop sets up a situation for the individual copy of the sparks, and then the outer loop applies those tasks to all the copies made of the sparks.

5 Place a Hexagon or Hexagon (Operators) block inside the empty hexagonal space on the Repeat Until block.

6 Put a Touching (Sensing) block in each of the empty hexagons in the green Operators block. Using the drop-down menu, choose Ghost for the first block and choose Edge (as seen in figure 7.25) for the second block. This sets a limit for the loop: repeat the actions inside until the sparks are touching either the ghost or an edge. In this case, the edge is always going to be the one at the top of the Stage because the sparks go straight up.

The cloned sparks are piling up on the end of the wand. You need to make them move.

Figure 7.24   **New copies of the sparks are being cloned, but they have nowhere to go.**

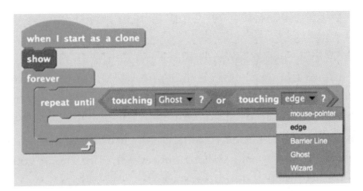

Figure 7.25   Use the drop-down menu to set the two limits for the Repeat Until block.

7 Place a Change Y by 10 (Motion) block inside the Repeat Until block. You can keep it as 10 because this will make the sparks slightly faster than the ghosts. Because it's a positive number, the sparks will go up.

8 Slide an If/Then (Control) block under the Change Y by 10 block, as in figure 7.26. You're about to start setting a new condition that will apply to the individual sparks.

9 Put a Touching (Sensing) block in the empty hexagonal space in the If/Then block. Use the drop-down menu to set the option to Ghost.

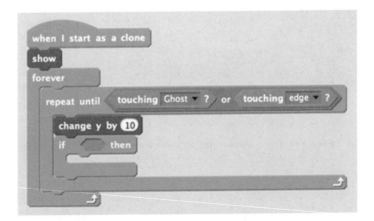

Figure 7.26   The If/Then block goes under the Change Y by 10 block.

This condition looks at what happens if the sparks make their target and hit a ghost.

10 Snap a Wait 1 Secs (Control) block inside the If/Then block. A second is a long time, so change that number to 0.01. You only need a fraction of a second pause to ensure that Scratch has enough time to recognize that the sparks have touched the ghost.

11 Slide a Delete This Clone (Control) block underneath the Wait 0.01 Secs block. If the sparks make contact with the ghost, you want the sparks to disappear from the screen.

The movement script shown in figure 7.27 sends the sparks shooting upward out of the wand and sets up what happens next if the sparks hit a ghost.

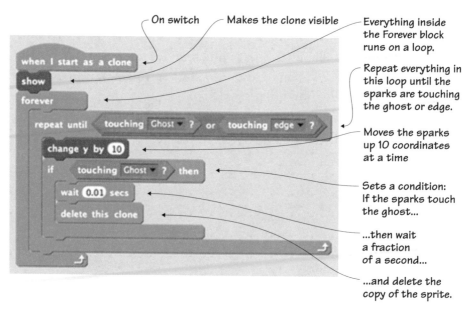

Figure 7.27   The completed movement script contains a nested loop—a loop inside a loop.

Making a clone deletion script

You set up a way for the sparks to disappear from the screen if they hit the ghost, but what about all the sparks that miss the ghost? After a few minutes of playing, the top of your Stage will be a sparks graveyard, as in figure 7.28.

This script will make the sparks disappear when they hit the top of the Stage. This task has been separated out from the last script to give you space to create two different situations when the sparks hit the ghost or the top of the screen.

To make the clone deletion script

1 Start with a When I Start as a Clone (Control) block.

The sparks need to delete when they reach the top of the Stage.

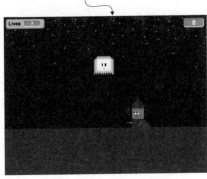

Figure 7.28   **The sparks are collecting at the top of the Stage.**

2 Add a Forever (Control) block underneath to start a loop.
3 Place an If/Then (Control) block inside the Forever block to set a condition.
4 Put a Touching (Sensing) block inside the empty hexagonal space in the If/Then block and use the drop-down menu to change the option to Edge. This will detect any edge, though the sparks will only come in contact with the top of the Stage because they move upward.
5 Drag a Delete This Clone (Control) block inside the If/Then block. This will remove the copy of the sparks from the screen.

Figure 7.29 shows the final script for the sparks. Does your script match the one in the figure?

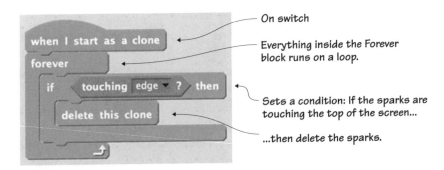

Figure 7.29   **The completed clone deletion script detects the edge of the Stage.**

Programming the odds and ends

You have two more scripts to write, both of them brief. One applies to the line, and the other script applies to the background. Yes, even the background is programmable in Scratch.

Making a positioning script for the line

Although there is a bottom edge on the Stage, marked by a Y coordinate number of –180, you're going to use a boundary line to ensure that Scratch always knows when the ghosts have reached the bottom of the screen. Right now your line is probably somewhere random on the screen, as in figure 7.30.

You need to position the barrier line at the bottom of the Stage.

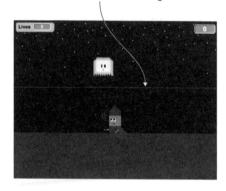

This script will position the line at the bottom of the Stage. Place the blue box around the line sprite in the Sprite Zone.

Figure 7.30   It's going to be hard for those sparks to reach the ghost with the barrier line in the way.

To make the line positioning script

1 Start with a When Flag Clicked (Events) block.

2 Add a Forever (Control) block underneath to start a loop.

3 Place a Go to X/Y (Motion) block inside the Forever block and change both numbers to zero (0). This will send the center of the sprite to the center of the Stage.

> **ANSWER THIS**   WHY SET THE X AND Y COORDINATES TO ZERO WITH THE BARRIER LINE?

Question: isn't X:0 and Y:0 the center of the Stage? Why use those numbers if you want the line to be at the bottom of the screen?

Answer: remember that every sprite comes with a transparent background. The barrier line sprite may look like a tiny two-dimensional line, but the sprite is the size of the whole Stage (or Art Editor). To imagine this with real objects, cut out a tiny strip of black paper and put it at the bottom of a square piece of plastic wrap. That's how Scratch processes your sprite. Because you drew the line at the bottom of the Art Editor, exactly where you wanted it to be for the game, you can use that as the transparent center of the sprite, which matches the center of the Stage.

The script in figure 7.31 sends the line to the bottom of the Stage because the line was drawn at the bottom of the Art Editor. It is matching the center of the sprite with the center of the Stage, and therefore the line is positioned exactly where it is drawn.

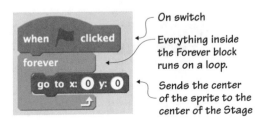

On switch

Everything inside the Forever block runs on a loop.

Sends the center of the sprite to the center of the Stage

Figure 7.31   The completed positioning script sends the line to the bottom of the Stage.

Making a scoring script for the background

You can also program the background, which may sound a little odd. It's not that you want your background to be able to run around the screen, but there are times when you'll want to tuck pieces of code into the backdrop. Sprites aren't the only programmable piece in your game.

Sometimes assigning too many starting tasks to a single sprite can slow down a game. Imagine your game as a swim race, and all the sprites are the swimmers. They all have a starting task, lining up on the side of the pool and getting into position. They can do their single task and be ready at the same time. But what if you asked one swimmer to pass out goggles to all the other swimmers before the race as well as get in position? Now that swimmer is going to be delayed and unable to start the race at the same time as the other swimmers.

That's what can happen if you load one sprite with too many "getting ready" tasks that start a game. Because you're already giving almost every sprite a starting task—from cloning to positioning—you can give this setting-the-initial-score task to the backdrop. While the sparks are cloning and the ghosts are hiding up at the top of the screen, your game can simultaneously set the score to 0 and the lives (or game chances) to 3. And now every part of your game is ready to run at the same time.

To program the backdrop, navigate to the Sprite Zone and click the picture of your backdrop on the left side so the blue box is around the thumbnail, as it is in figure 7.32.

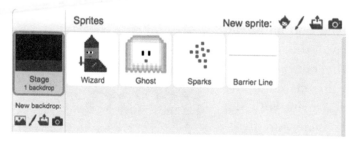

Figure 7.32   The blue box is around the Stage thumbnail in the Sprite Zone.

You will now build your scoring script in the Script Zone, the same as programming any sprite. You need to set the starting values of your Lives and Score variables. The value of Lives should be set to three to give the player three chances to get a high score fighting the ghosts. The value of Score should be set to zero (0), as in figure 7.33, so the player can start building their points as they shoot down ghosts.

The lives variable needs to begin with a value of 3.

The score variable needs to begin with a value of 0.

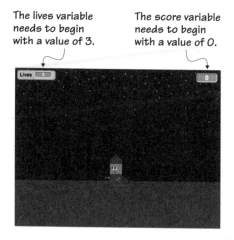

Figure 7.33   The two variables of Lives and Score need to be set before the game begins.

You may notice as you look at the Block Menu that certain blocks are missing. Don't worry—you still have them. Scratch doesn't display them with the backdrop to streamline the menu, including only the blocks you're able to use. Click around the menus for a moment and see what's missing. All those blocks will be back when you return to programming sprites; they're only missing when you program the backdrop because the backdrop can't move or touch anything.

To make the scoring script

1   Start with a When Flag Clicked (Events) block.

2   Move two Set Score to 0 (Data) blocks and stack them, one on top of the other, under the When Flag Clicked block. Open the drop-down menu on the top block and set it to Lives. Type a 3 in the value box. This will give the player three chances to fight the ghosts. Open the drop-down menu on the bottom block and set it to Score. Type a zero (0) in the value box. This will give your player a blank slate for points when the game opens.

This final script should match the one in figure 7.34.

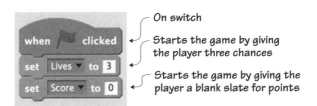

Figure 7.34   The completed scoring script sets the initial values for the two variables in the game.

Your game is finished and ready to be played! Click the flag and start blasting those ghosts, and then keep reading in case you run into problems with your game.

Troubleshooting your game

Our game went off without a hitch, but that doesn't mean that *your* game will work the same way. Use the ideas in this section to get your game working properly.

Checking your scripts

The first thing to do whenever a game doesn't work according to plan is to go back through the chapter and check your scripts against our scripts. Look carefully at each block because there are many similarly named blocks. Also look at values: do your numbers match the ones in the book?

Sprites not centered

You learned how to center your sprites when writing the scripts for the sparks. Turn back a few pages and reread those instructions if sprites are not behaving properly. If it's not a layering issue, it may be a centering issue, especially when it comes to the sparks lining up with the wizard's wand.

Eliminating blocks

Sometimes you may be inclined to delete a block that seems redundant, wondering if it's necessary for making the game. But wait! There is always a reason a block is included in a game, or code is broken up into two or more chunks, so please go back and follow the directions in the book if your game isn't working properly. An example is the seemingly redundant loop inside a loop that comes with the spark's movement script. When the Forever block is removed, it causes sparks to randomly generate in strange places on the screen and then shoot off on their own accord. Unless you're looking to produce phantom sparks in your game, stick to our instructions, because we've already troubleshot for you.

Learning in action

These challenges once again play with the existing code, making the game function in new ways. By playing with values, you can see how the script controls the various sprites.

Play with the code

This fixed shooter is also a reflex-testing game, and you can play with the values to make the game harder or easier to play.

CHALLENGE   What happens if you slow down the wizard but speed up the ghosts? Remember, the lower the number, the slower the sprite will move. The higher the number, the faster the sprite will move. How high can you score when the ghosts can fall 20 coordinates at a time but the wizard can only glide 2 coordinates at a time?

This is your second game, and you're ready to go beyond playing with values and tweaking the speed. Can you figure out how to change the way the ghosts move?

CHALLENGE   Each ghost currently moves in a straight line from the place
where it generates at the top of the screen toward the bottom
of the Stage. What if you want the ghost to move at a diagonal, so it's more difficult to position the wizard underneath the target?

You can do this by adding a Change X by 10 block to the ghost movement script, as in figure 7.35. By slipping in the extra block and changing the value to a much smaller number, such as –1, the ghost will
gently drift to the left as it falls. Additionally, you can change those values to have the ghost fall sharply to the side.

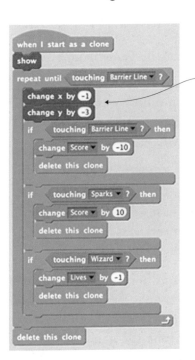

Adding the Change X by -1 block with the
Change Y by -3 block makes the ghost
move at an angle instead of straight down.

Figure 7.35 An extra block in the ghost's
movement script causes it to move in a
diagonal line instead of straight down.

What did you learn?

Before you go back to your game and get a high score blasting down
ghosts, take a moment to reflect which common computer science ideas
from chapter 3 were used in this game:

- Using an on switch for every script in the game, including the more
  unusual When I Start as a Clone block and the When Space Key
  Pressed block

- Moving the ghosts down and the sparks up with X and Y coordinates
- Writing conditional statements to detect if the value of the Lives variable is at zero (0) so the game will end
- Setting up a loop (in all but two scripts!) to accomplish many tasks, including cloning the ghosts and giving the wizard unlimited sparks for his wand
- Using a variable to keep track of the number of ghosts the wizard blasts down with his wand
- Working with touching blocks and Booleans to check if the sparks make contact with a ghost
- Cloning all the ghosts and sparks for the game from a single copy of each sprite

Once again, you put into action seven out of eight common programming ideas. You'll continue to put these computer science ideas into action in future games. Additionally, you learned

- How to make multiple clones occur in the same game
- How to apply loops to solve many varied coding tasks
- How to use a single variable to increase or decrease, depending upon the situation in the game, to make a two-way point system
- How to make a fixed shooter

Okay, go blast away some ghosts. But after you're done getting your high score, turn the page because it's time to make another game. This one's based on the Atari game *Breakout*. You're back to working with the ball and paddle format, only this time the game is one player, and you need to remove pieces of a soccer net while bouncing a ball against a shoe paddle. Goal!

8

Designing a one-player ball-and-paddle game

It's a boring Saturday afternoon, and all your friends are away. You decide to entertain yourself by shooting some goals into the soccer net in your backyard. How many times can you kick the ball into the net shown in figure 8.1?

Dribble is a ball-and-paddle game based on the famous Atari hit *Breakout*. In *Breakout*, you control a line that represents a tennis racket, and you need to hit a single, white pixel—the ball—at a wall made of rainbow blocks. The section vanishes when the ball hits the "bricks." Dribble

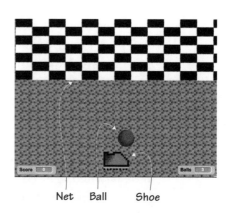

Net   Ball   Shoe

Figure 8.1   A game of Dribble means making a grassy field backdrop, red shoe, blue ball, net, scoreboard, and barrier line running across the bottom of the Stage.

plays with the theme by turning the rainbow blocks of *Breakout* into a black-and-white soccer net. Instead of a white dot, ball, and line paddle, you have a blue ball bouncing off a shoe. Players rack up points by removing sections of net whenever the ball hits one of the black or white blocks. The game ends either when the board is cleared or if the player misses the ball three times.

175

This chapter will teach you how to make all the sprites you'll need for the game—and make them come alive by giving them texture, such as building smooth surfaces or rough surfaces out of pixels. Images are bland without texture.

In this chapter, you will learn

- How to create an illusion of texture using pixelated shading
- How to blend shades of the same color together to create depth
- How to add realism to even cartoon-like drawings

You'll start by making a field of multicolor grass.

Prepping the background and learning about texture

In *Wizards vs. Ghosts*, you made a field by drawing a green line and dumping green paint into the lower section of the Stage. You're now going to step up your field creation by blending green pixels to make the grass on the ground. Your backdrop will provide contrast and texture at the same time.

Making the grass backdrop

Have you ever played *Minecraft* and spawned in a world covered in grass and trees? The grass isn't a solid green sheet across the screen. It's a patchwork of pixels in many different shades of green. Figure 8.2 shows the Dribble background, in case you're not familiar with this look.

This background only requires you to make a tiny section of pixels. You'll then duplicate this green block many times. You can make the green pixels in your square pattern as large or as small as you wish.

The background on the left is made up of hundreds of the 5 x 5 pixel boxes seen here. The textured grass is created by blending shades of green in a pattern.

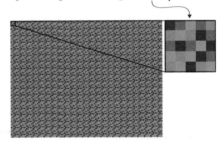

Figure 8.2   **The bright green grass background for Dribble**

Open the Backdrop Editor and zoom in to 800%. Move the sliders on the sides to the top right and bottom left corners of the editor, as seen in figure 8.3. You want to begin building your backdrop in the top left corner of the Art Editor:

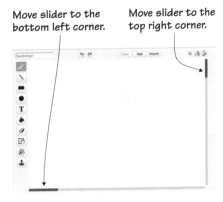

Move slider to the bottom left corner.   Move slider to the top right corner.

Figure 8.3   The sliders moved to their ends in order to start building the backdrop in the top left corner of the Art Editor.

1 Select the darkest green paint sample square and the Paintbrush tool.

2 Go to the top left corner of the Art Editor and make a small dark green pixel.

3 Switch to a different shade of green (you will be working with all four shades of green in the paint sample squares) and make a second green pixel to the right of the first green pixel.

4 Change shades of green again and make a third green pixel to the right of the second green pixel. Do this two more times, switching shades each time, to make a row of five green pixels, as in figure 8.4. You will need to use one shade of green twice because there are four shades of green in the paint sample squares. Make sure the two end pixels are different shades of green. You can use any shade of green in any order as long as you stick to different shades of green on the end of the row.

Figure 8.4   Five green pixels in a line. The far left and far right pixels are two different shades of green.

5 Create a second line of green pixels directly underneath the first line of green pixels following the same steps and rules. Make sure that

Correct

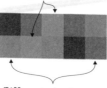

The same shade can
be diagonal, but not
side-by-side.

Different shades
of green on the ends

Incorrect

Do not use the same
shade on the ends.

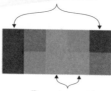

Do not use the
same shade
side-by-side.

Figure 8.5   Two shades of
green can touch in the corner,
but pixels above, below, or to
the side should be different.

any pixels that share an edge are not the same shade of green. Using the same shade diagonally is okay, as in figure 8.5.

6 Do this a third time with another new row. You can begin placing down pixels in two places before switching colors, as seen in figure 8.6.

7 Repeat this process two more times until you have a five-pixel-by-five-pixel square like in figure 8.7. In the same way that you always check that the left and right ends of a row don't repeat the same shade, also check that the shade used as the top and bottom of a column are different. Think of it like a game of green block Sudoku, though since there are four shades of green and five spaces, you will always have shades repeat.

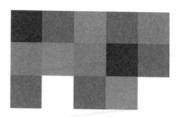

Figure 8.6   Two medium green
pixels are placed down at the
same time to save one green
shade switch per line.

You're done placing down pixels. Now it's time to replicate that base grass square.

To duplicate the square

1 Go to the Duplicator tool on the Side Toolbar of the Art Editor. It has a stamp icon, similar to the tool that exists in the Grey Toolbar.

Figure 8.7   The base 5-pixel-by-5-
pixel grass square. The same
shades of green never touch,
and the ends of rows and
columns are always different.

2 Draw a box around the base grass square, as in Step One of figure 8.8. You will see the highlighted tool jump from the Duplicator tool to the Select tool once the box is made.

3 Move the mouse to the dot in the center of the box and slide the copy (it's on top of the existing square) underneath the square so there is now a large rectangle. You can see the two squares in Step Two of figure 8.8.

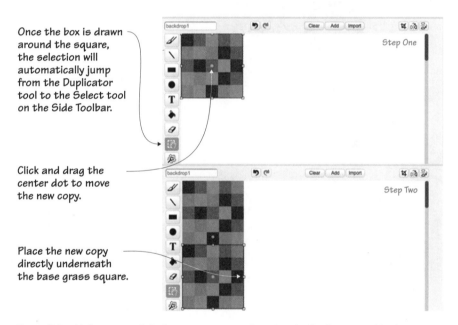

Once the box is drawn around the square, the selection will automatically jump from the Duplicator tool to the Select tool on the Side Toolbar.

Click and drag the center dot to move the new copy.

Place the new copy directly underneath the base grass square.

Figure 8.8   Make a copy of the base grass square by using the Duplicator tool in the Side Toolbar.

4 Zoom out to 400% and use the same Duplicator tool to draw a box around the new grass rectangle. Drag the new copy underneath the existing grass rectangle.

5 Repeat this copying method, expanding the selected pixels to include every pixel on the screen. As the line grows down the left side of the Art Editor, you'll need to zoom out to 200% and then 100% to see the canvas.

6 Using the same method, build the grass toward the right side of the screen, as in figure 8.9. The goal is to use this method, zooming in and out as necessary to see the selection, to fill the entire screen with the grass squares.

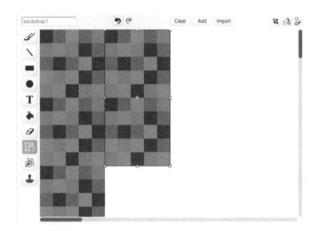

Figure 8.9   Once you have built a solid line of base grass squares down the left side of the canvas, begin building out toward the right.

FIX IT   MY BASE GRASS SQUARES AREN'T LINED UP!   You may zoom in and notice that there are white spaces between your base grass squares because they didn't align properly when you were zoomed out. Have no fear; you don't have to repeat your work. Instead fill in the empty white space by using the Duplicator tool to select a small portion of the base grass square and then drag it to fill in the space, as in figure 8.10.

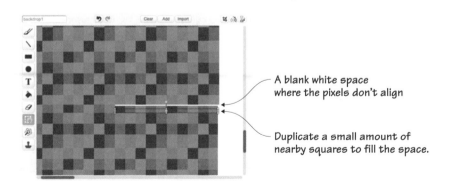

A blank white space where the pixels don't align

Duplicate a small amount of nearby squares to fill the space.

Figure 8.10   Fix missing pixels by copying nearby squares using the Duplicator tool.

Filling the backdrop so it looks
like the one in figure 8.11 takes
time and patience. If you get
frustrated, feel free to create a
plain green backdrop, filling the
canvas using the Paint Bucket
tool. It won't affect the game play
when you program the game,
though the backdrop will lack
texture.

Figure 8.11   The completed grass backdrop

Examining texture

How do you know if you're touching a dog or touching a table, assuming that your table doesn't pant and have a wet nose? The answer is texture. Dogs are soft and furry, and tables are hard and smooth.

Although a *drawing* of a dog and a *drawing* of a table will feel the same, the viewer needs to sense what that dog or table would feel like if they stepped into the picture. By including texture, you not only give the viewer sensory information, you add depth and interest to the image. The point is to make the viewer feel as if they can pick up the sprites in the game or run their hand over the ground. Texture can even change the mood in a picture! A blue ball with sunlight shining off of it is different from that same ball spotted with raindrops.

Take a sensory tour of your home by making your own texture treasure hunt. Find an object that fits each texture: smooth, soft, scratchy, fuzzy, slick, bumpy, silky, and slimy. Place these eight objects in front of you and start your observations.

How does the light reflect off of each object? How many shades of the same color do you see in the object? Do the transitions between shades look jagged or smooth? Incorporating that information into your drawings creates the illusion of texture. An *illusion* is a trick of the senses, making the eye believe that a two-dimensional blue circle is a ball and not a flat disc. You created an illusion of grass with your backdrop, using the fact that grass is not solidly one color but a blend of greens.

Even though the background and sprites you're making for your games are flat images on a screen, draw the objects so the viewer can sense how those backgrounds and sprites would feel if the game came to life.

Prepping the main sprites

Keep texture in the forefront of your mind as you make the sprites. If you own sneakers or a ball, place them in front of you as you make their pixelated counterparts. Seeing (and more importantly, feeling) those real items will help you make them on the screen. Before you begin making your sprites, get rid of the default cat sprite by clicking the scissors in the Grey Toolbar and clicking the cat on the Stage.

Making the shoe

The background is green, which means you want to create a red shoe because green and red are complementary colors. The sneaker in figure 8.12 has stylized shading on the side to show depth and a rubber sole like a real shoe.

Figure 8.12   The completed red shoe sprite uses a grey line on the bottom of the shoe for the rubber sole and stylized shading on the back of the shoe to add interest.

Look for the plus sign in the center of the canvas and start drawing your shoe sprite:

1 Select the black paint and the Paintbrush tool. Zoom in to 800%.

2 Make a three-pixel horizontal line on the canvas. Then go down one pixel on the far right side of the line, as in Step One in figure 8.13.

3 Move to the right of the single pixel and draw a four-pixel horizontal line, as in Step Two in figure 8.13.

4 Go up one pixel on the far right side of this new line and continue to string four more pixels until your line looks like Step Three in figure 8.13.

5 Draw five diagonal pixels, beginning in the bottom right corner of the last pixel. Your shoe should currently look like the shape in Step Four in figure 8.13.

6 Make a vertical line of four pixels extending from the last diagonal pixel.

7 Build a horizontal line that moves from right to left, stopping when it is parallel to the beginning of the shoe. Close off the shoe outline by connecting the bottom horizontal line to the top horizontal line, as in figure 8.14.

8 Add the rubber sole to the shoe by switching to a medium grey paint sample square and making a line across the bottom of the shoe, as in figure 8.15.

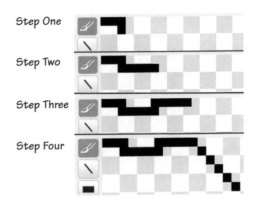

Figure 8.13   The shoe is formed pixel-by-pixel, beginning with these four steps.

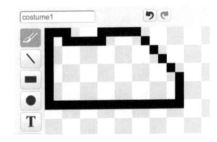

Figure 8.14   The black outline of the shoe

9 Switch back to black and make a broken line, stamping every other pixel, underneath the grey line for the spikes on the cleats, also seen in figure 8.15.

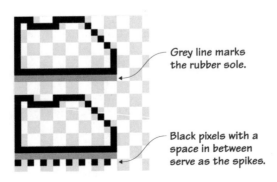

Grey line marks the rubber sole.

Black pixels with a space in between serve as the spikes.

Figure 8.15   Draw a simple line for the sole of the shoe, and a broken line for the cleats.

10 Choose the brightest shade of red from the paint sample squares. You will need to use multiple shades of red on the shoe to give the shoe texture, and you want the base color to be the bright red in the middle of the column of red paint options.

11 Use the Paint Bucket tool to fill the shoe with red paint. Then switch to the next darker shade of red. Starting at the opening of the shoe, staircase down toward the bottom left corner of the shoe. Compare your line to the staircase in Step One of figure 8.16.

12 Use the Paint Bucket tool to fill the area behind the staircase with the darker red paint, as in Step Two of figure 18.16.

13 Return to the Color Toolbar and choose the next darkest shade of red. Repeat the same staircasing line and color spill performed in the last steps. You can see this new section of the shoe in Steps Three and Four of figure 8.16.

14 Repeat this pattern one last time with the darkest red option in the paint sample squares. You can see the staircasing line and color spill in Steps Five and Six of figure 8.16.

Figure 8.16   Shade the back of the shoe by drawing a staircasing line and then filling the space behind it with a darker color.

You should now have the finished shoe, shown in figure 8.17. Make sure you go to the Sprite Zone and rename the sprite Shoe.

Figure 8.17   The completed shoe will be the paddle in this ball-and-paddle game.

Making the ball

You have a paddle (the shoe), but now you need to make the ball for this ball-and-paddle game. The blue ball in figure 8.18 uses a lot of shading in order to convey its roundness.

If you were painting, you'd blend many shades of blue with a brush. If you were using charcoals, you'd blend the shades with your finger. But you're drawing on a screen, which means you have to blend with

Figure 8.18   The finished blue ball will bounce against the net in this ball-and-paddle game.

pixels. Digitally blending two shades together is called *dithering*.

LEARN IT   DITHERING   The word *dithering* means wavering between two options. For example, if a person is trying to decide between chocolate and vanilla ice cream, they're dithering about the ice cream flavor. In pixel art, dithering is wavering between color options. By mixing up two or more shades of the same color, the eye is tricked into seeing simple shading on the sprite. Dithering is done by creating a pattern between the two *colors*. You started using this idea in chapter 4 when you created the yolk for the pixelated egg, and you can see another example of blending tones in Shading A in figure 8.19. But you can also blend pixel by pixel by using a

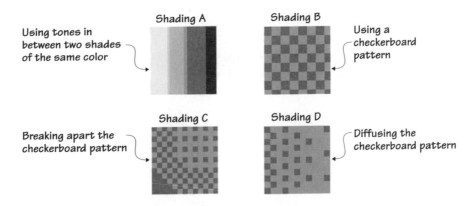

Figure 8.19   Pixelated shading uses a technique called dithering that creates a pattern out of two or more related colors.

checkerboard pattern (Shading B). Breaking apart the pattern (Shading C) by leaving spaces between pixels creates another layering of texture, and diffusing the pixels by leaving even bigger gaps (Shading D) can create subtle changes.

Let's learn how to dither in steps beginning with practicing that checkerboard pattern on the ball:

1 Select the darkest shade of blue and the Circle tool. Zoom in to 800%.

2 Draw a circle about 10 grey-and-white squares across. Fill the center if you used the outline option so you have a solid navy blue circle, as in figure 8.20.

Figure 8.20   A solid navy blue circle drawn using the Circle tool

3 Switch to the next lighter shade of blue and make another circle on the canvas, slightly smaller than the original circle. Drag the smaller, lighter circle inside the larger, darker circle, aligning the two circles on the top right side, as in Step One of figure 8.21.

Step One   Step Two   Step Three

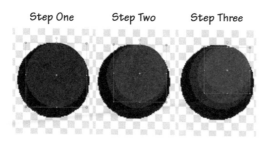

Figure 8.21   Place circles inside circles to create visual depth for the ball.

4 Repeat the last step again, choosing the next lighter shade of blue and drawing an even smaller circle. Drag the new circle inside the second circle, aligning them on the top right side, as in Step Two of figure 8.21.

5 Create one last layer by choosing a lighter shade of blue and drawing the smallest circle. Drag it inside the last circle. You should now have four layers of circles, as in Step Three of figure 8.21, all of them aligned on the top right side.

6 Shade the ball by returning to the darkest blue (the one you used for the first layer of circles) and using the magnifying glass to zoom in even more, to 1600%. You will need the circles enlarged because you will be carefully placing down pixels to create the checkerboard pattern in each layer.

7 Create a checkerboard pattern inside the neighboring shade of blue, as in Step One of figure 8.22. Don't worry if you cross the lines between shades of blue. Jumping over the border on occasion helps make the shading look more natural.

8 Switch to the shade of blue you used for the second circle and repeat this pattern in the third circle, as in Step Two of figure 8.22. Again, don't worry if you cross into the final circle with part of a pixel.

9 Choose the shade of blue you used for the third circle and repeat this pattern one last time, leaving a few open pixels near the top right edge, as in Step Three of figure 8.22.

10 Use the Eraser tool to shave off parts of pixels if you went outside the border when creating shading on the top circle. Remaining zoomed in at 1600% but using the slider to set the eraser on its smallest setting makes it easier to use the Eraser tool, as in figure 8.23.

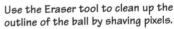

Use the Eraser tool to clean up the outline of the ball by shaving pixels.

Step One   Step Two   Step Three

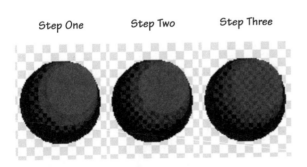

Figure 8.22 Create shading by mixing the neighboring shade of blue into each layer.

Figure 8.23 Use the Eraser tool to smooth out the edge of the circle.

You should now have the finished ball, as seen in figure 8.24. Make sure you go to the Sprite Zone and rename this sprite Ball.

Making the net

The net stretches across the top of the Stage when the game begins. The net is made by taking the black or white net sprite and cloning it dozens of times while giving the duplicated sprites instructions to line up in the formation seen in figure 8.25.

You will only need to make one solid rectangle sprite to make the net, but you'll give it two costumes.

Figure 8.24   **The finished, shaded blue ball**

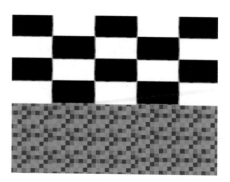

Figure 8.25   **The net is a checkerboard of black and white rectangles at the top of the Stage.**

To make the net

1 Click the Paintbrush tool and the black paint sample square. Zoom out to 200%.

2 Draw a small black rectangle, 19 pixels by 10 pixels. Fill in the center using the Paint Bucket tool, as in the top portion of figure 8.26.

3 Navigate to the Grey Toolbar and choose the Duplicator tool with the stamp icon.

4 Go to the Costumes tab and click your black rectangle on the tab. (The blue box should be around it.) You can see this in the middle portion of figure 8.26. A copy of the black rectangle will appear. Click the second black rectangle so the blue box is around that rectangle.

5 Switch to the white paint sample square and use the Paint Bucket tool to click anywhere on the black rectangle that is on the canvas (not the

tab). Look at the Costumes tab, as seen in the bottom portion of figure 8.26. There should be a black rectangle and a white rectangle.

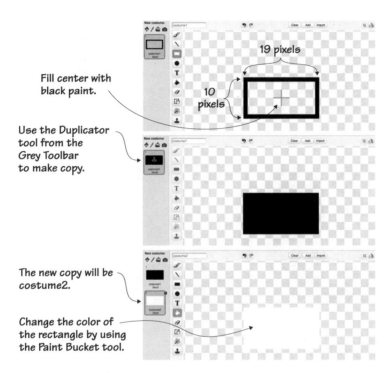

Fill center with black paint.

19 pixels

10 pixels

Use the Duplicator tool from the Grey Toolbar to make copy.

The new copy will be costume2.

Change the color of the rectangle by using the Paint Bucket tool.

Figure 8.26   Make sure the two rectangles are the same size by duplicating the first one and then changing the color using the Paint Bucket tool.

You will only see one rectangle on the Stage. That's because there *is* only one rectangle. Think of costumes as outfits or versions of sprites. There's only one sprite—a rectangle—but that rectangle may have a black appearance or a white appearance. This will be important later when you go to program your game and you make both costumes show, alternating between the two copies of the rectangle.

Make sure you go to the Sprite Zone and rename the rectangle Net. Again, you will only see one copy of the rectangle in the Sprite Zone, though when the blue box is around it, you will see both costumes in the Costumes tab of the Block Area.

LEARN IT   SETTING THE CONTRAST   The amount of contrast between shades of the same color affects the texture. Take the grass, for example. The paint sample squares make it easy to choose four distinctly different shades of green. But what if you used the rainbow box and its slider to make subtle changes to the shades of green? The block on the left side of figure 8.27 shows the original base grass square. The block on the right side of figure 8.27 shows a new base grass square using the slider on the rainbow box to make slight changes to the shade of green. Which option better conveys that the ground is made up of individual blades of grass? Think about how closely you make the shades of a color when you're adding texture to a solid shape or background.

 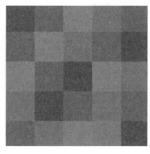

Figure 8.27   The amount of contrast between shades of the same color creates deeper texture.

Prepping the odds and ends

There are two more sprites you need to make before you can code the game. The first is a scoreboard and the second is your friend, the barrier line.

Making the scoreboard

The original *Breakout* had a scoreboard that flashed on the screen at the end, telling you how well you played the game. Dribble also has a scoreboard that will fill the screen when the game is over. The scoreboard in figure 8.28 gives a range of points, and players can look at their end score and judge how well they did.

What's Your Score?
0 – 19   Caught in the net
20 – 39   Almost ready for the World Cup
40 – 49   Bend it!
50+   GOAL!

Figure 8.28   The scoreboard pops onto the screen at the end of the game.

To make the scoreboard

1 Select the white paint and the Paint Bucket tool. Click anywhere on the canvas. You want to flood the background with the white paint before you begin typing your words.

2 Switch to the black paint sample square and click the Text tool (the T icon on the Side Toolbar).

3 Type the following:

What's Your Score?

  0 – 19 Caught in the net

20 – 39 Almost ready for the World Cup

40 – 49 Bend it!

50+   GOAL!

Congratulations! You now have a scoreboard that will flash at the end of the game. Go to the Sprite Zone and rename this sprite End of Game.

Making the barrier line

The barrier line seen in figure 8.29 is the same one that you've made in the last few chapters.

Figure 8.29
The barrier line at the bottom of the screen

To make the barrier line

1 Select the black paint sample square and Line tool. Zoom out to 100%.

2 Draw a line that starts at the bottom left corner of the canvas and ends at the bottom right corner. Hold down the Shift key on the keyboard as you drag your mouse to make the line completely straight.

Make sure you rename this last sprite Bottom Line in the Sprite Zone.

Preparing to code

This chapter builds on what you know about shading and gives you a few extra tricks to use in order to add texture to your sprites and backgrounds.

Play with the game

Although you may have already tried playing with the texture inside the shoe, attempt these other challenges to judge color choice and test your shading skills.

CHALLENGE   Create a new background and try choosing four shades of green that have subtle differences from one another. As the base grass squares begin duplicating on the screen, decide whether you like the new, less textured version or the old, highly textured version.

CHALLENGE   Put the highlight on a different part of the ball. How would you have to shift the circle layers and the way you add the checkerboard pattern to show that the light is shining from the left side of the screen instead of from the right?

What did you learn?

Texture isn't only part of art—it's an important consideration in every area of STEAM. How things feel affects how we interact with them. It's not just that we're grossed out by slimy, soggy things or prefer objects to be smooth and not spiky. Texture is something engineers keep in mind as they're designing objects for everyday use, such as mobile phones. They need to be easy to pick up and hold. Think about food science and how many of the foods we prefer to eat are tied to their texture, or think of soil scientists and how they judge the texture of the dirt to determine whether the fields are getting enough water. Texture is everywhere.

Pause for a moment and think about everything you learned in this chapter:

- How texture affects the visual qualities of the sprite and backdrop
- How to blend colors to create texture
- How to fill in large spaces and then go back in to change the texture with shading
- How to make two costumes for the same sprite

Even if you can't touch this digital field, it leaves an impression on the player's mind and gives the illusion of individual blades of grass, all slightly different colors. It will be a fun backdrop for your ball-and-paddle game. Ready to create Dribble?

9

Using variables to build your one-player ball-and-paddle game

The people who made the Atari game *Breakout* also started a brand that will be familiar to anyone with a Mac computer or an iPhone. Steve Jobs and Steve Wozniak, two of the three founders of Apple, made the game *Breakout* in four days.

Steve Wozniak includes the story of this game in his book, *iWoz*. He made his own version of *Pong* to play at home using a television set. It was about a year before Atari made their home version. Steve Jobs worked at Atari, and Wozniak showed them his television-based *Pong* while visiting Jobs. The people at Atari loved it so much that they offered Wozniak a job, but he turned it down.

Atari went on to develop its own version of *Pong* that could be played at home, and it was such a huge hit that Nolan Bushnell at Atari wanted to play with that ball-and-paddle format, making a different kind of game. Look at the difference between *Pong* and *Breakout*. In *Pong*, you're hoping your opponent misses the ball, similar to real Ping-Pong. In *Breakout*, you're aiming for the bricks, trying to clear the board by bouncing the ball against the wall. In one case, you want to miss the target, and in the other, you want to hit it.

Steve Jobs called Steve Wozniak and said that Bushnell wanted him to come help with this new game because he thought that Wozniak could design the game using the least amount of computer chips (something that would save Atari a lot of money!). What Wozniak didn't know was that Jobs didn't know how to make the game and desperately needed his help! Maybe Jobs could have figured it out if he'd had more than four days, but he had promised Bushnell that he could have the entire game made in that short amount of time. So Wozniak thought they were just having fun, but it was the start of the two friends each using his strengths to complete projects together. Wozniak designed the circuits, and Jobs wired the computer chips. They pulled it off, finishing *Breakout* in four days, an unbelievably short amount of time to design and build a video game. In 1976, Atari released the game, and yes, it was another big success.

Like *Breakout*, the goal of Dribble is to hit a ball off a paddle into a line of "bricks," though in this case, the paddle is a shoe, the ball is a blue rubber ball, and the bricks are black and white sections of a soccer net, as seen in figure 9.1.

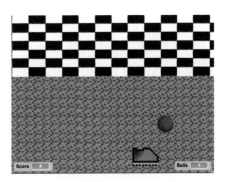

Variables are the star of this game. Up until this point, you've used variables to track numerical values, such as counting the number of points or chances. In this game, you'll start to use variables abstractly, such as by creating a variable that checks whether the ball has been served and stops generating new balls if one is already in action. You'll learn how to use true and false values with your variables, turning them on and off.

Figure 9.1 In Dribble, the player moves the shoe back and forth across the screen, positioning it under the ball in order to knock it into the black and white net. The player gains a point when the ball hits the net and removes that piece from the screen. The player loses one of the three balls if it misses the shoe.

In this chapter, you will learn

- How to detect whether a ball is in motion by using variables
- How to redesign two-player games into one-player games
- How to generate a pattern on the screen using code
- How to make a sprite switch between costumes
- How to add a *game over* score message

Here's a little secret before you start writing your own program. Google has a game of *Breakout* hidden in its image search! Go to Google and type "Atari Breakout." Then click Images. Wait for a moment, and all the images will start traveling upward, becoming the bricks. A paddle will appear at the bottom of the screen that you can control with a mouse or the arrows on your keyboard. Play a few rounds, but then let's get started coding Dribble.

Preparing to program

Most of these steps should feel familiar by now. Think of these tasks as your pre-coding ritual.

Missing sprites

If you skipped chapter 8 or part of chapter 8 (that background required a lot of patience!), either finish it now or go to the Manning site and download the background and sprites for Dribble. The directions for importing are the same as chapter 5. You should have a shoe, ball, net, end of game message, and bottom line, as well as the multi-hued grass background.

Preparing the Stage

If the end of game message is blocking the other sprites on the Stage, right-click (or control-click on a Mac) the End of Game sprite in the Sprite Zone and choose the Hide option for the moment. Drag the shoe toward the bottom of the Stage, leaving about a half a centimeter of space between the sneaker and the lower edge (see figure 9.1 for placement). Drag the ball slightly below the middle of the Stage. The other sprites will be positioned with code.

The shoe's size increased a lot—18 clicks using the Grow tool from the Grey Toolbar—while every other sprite remained the same size.

Programming the shoe

The shoe is the equivalent of the paddle in *Breakout*. It moves left and right using the arrow keys on the keyboard, and the ball will bounce against it in order to reach the sections of the net. A single movement script powers the shoe. Put the blue box around the shoe sprite in the Sprite Zone. Remember, the names or values on *your* blocks may differ slightly from time to time, so use the completed script images to make sure you chose the correct block.

Making a movement script

You have a shoe, but it's stuck in the grass, unable to move. How can it kick the ball into the net, shown in figure 9.2, if it can't move?

This script will look familiar because it's similar to the one in Wizards vs. Ghosts. In fact, before you dive into the directions below, see if you can figure out how to create this basic movement script on your own based on what you remember from the last game.

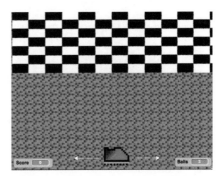

Figure 9.2 **The shoe moves back and forth along the bottom of the screen.**

In case you need the directions, to give the shoe the ability to move

1 Start with a When Flag Clicked (Motion) block.

2 Slide a Forever (Control) block onto the chain to start a loop.

3 Stack two If/Then (Control) blocks atop one another inside the Forever block.

4 Drag a Key Space Pressed (Sensing) block into each of the empty hexagonal spaces on the If/Then block. Change the top Key Space Pressed block to Left Arrow and the bottom Key Space Pressed block to Right Arrow using the drop-down menu in the block. This sets the condition so that the action will happen if the left or right arrow keys are pressed on the keyboard.

5 Slide a Change X by 10 (Motion) block inside each If/Then block. Change the number in the first Change X by 10 block to –7 and the second Change X by 10 block to 7. This will allow the shoe to move seven coordinate spaces to the left or right.

The first script is complete. Does your script match the one in figure 9.3?

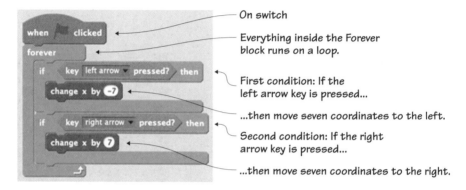

Figure 9.3   The movement script allows the player to move the shoe left and right across the field.

Wizards vs. Ghost's movement script has the wizard jump 10 coordinate spaces at a time. The shoe can only move seven coordinate spaces at a time, making it a slower movement script. Remember, the higher the coordinate number, the faster the sprite will move.

Programming the ball

Breakout has a dot, but Dribble has a blue rubber ball that the player "kicks" against the net to clear the board. The player is given three balls (or chances) to clear the screen, and a new ball is served by pressing the spacebar. The ball has six scripts: a setup script, a cloning script, a movement script, a shoe detection script, a net detection script, and a ball deduction script. Put the blue box around the ball in the Sprite Zone and don't move the blue box until you've written all six scripts.

Making a setup script

If you can see the ball, you know exactly where to position the shoe in order to catch it after it bounces off the net, as in figure 9.4. But *Breakout* (and Dribble) is full of surprises.

Before you start programming the ball to move, you need to set up a few variables and hide the ball's location so the player won't know where the ball is going to come from at the bottom of the screen.

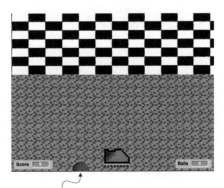

The ball will be served from random points at the bottom of the Stage.

Figure 9.4   The ball comes out randomly along the bottom of the Stage.

To hide the ball

1 Start with a When Flag Clicked (Motion) block.

2 Switch to Data and make two variables. The first is called HBS (which stands for *has been served*), and the other is called Score. Uncheck the box next to HBS because you do not want it to appear on the Stage, but leave the box next to Score checked because you want the player to be able to see how well they're doing. Position the Score variable in the lower left corner of the Stage.

3 Put two Set Score to 0 (Data) blocks under the When Flag Clicked block. Change the top block to HBS using the drop-down menu. Leave the other block untouched.

4 Place a Hide (Looks) block at the bottom of the script. This block will hide the ball on the Stage until it is in motion.

You can see the completed script in figure 9.5.

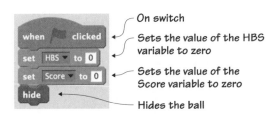

On switch

Sets the value of the HBS variable to zero

Sets the value of the Score variable to zero

Hides the ball

Figure 9.5   The completed setup script gets the ball ready to be used in the game.

LEARN IT   ZEROS AND ONES   Why are both variables set to zero (0)? In the first case, HBS, the number refers to "false" and is a Boolean (not a numerical) value. With Booleans, 0 is always used for false (or off), and 1 is used for true (or on). Because the variable is false—the ball has not been served—it's set to zero (0). The variable Score is also set to zero (0), but in that case it means that the player hasn't collected any points yet. Using 1 to represent true and zero (0) to represent false is a common practice in coding languages, and in this case, those are not numerical values but Boolean values. See chapter 3 if you need a refresher on Booleans.

Making a cloning script

Right now you have one ball sprite, seen in figure 9.6. But you're going to give the player three chances to clear the board, which means you need three balls.

This script will create a clone of the ball sprite and serve it from a random point along the bottom of the Stage.

To make the cloning script

1 Start with a When Space Key Pressed (Motion) block.

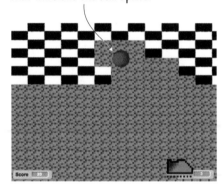

You need to write a script that will clone the ball sprite.

Figure 9.6   The ball becomes visible after it is cloned and served.

2 Move an If/Then (Control) block underneath the When Space Key Pressed block.

3 Place a Square = Square (Operators) block into the empty hexagonal space in the If/Then block. Slide an HBS (Data) variable block into the left square and type a zero (0) into the right square. The zero (0) stands for false, which means that the condition is "if the ball has been served is false..." Meaning, the ball *hasn't* been served.

4 Drag a Set X to 0 (Motion) block inside the If/Then block. You're not going to set the X position to a single number because you want the ball to clone in a random place along the bottom of the Stage

each time the ball is served. Instead, place a Pick Random 1 to 10 (Operators) block in the number bubble, as seen in figure 9.7.

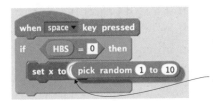

Place the Pick Random block into the number bubble. This will set the X position to a random number every time the ball is served, which means the ball could come from any point at the bottom of the Stage.

Figure 9.7   Placing the Pick Random 1 to 10 block inside the Set X to 0 block means the X position of the ball is randomly chosen.

5 Change the number in the left bubble of the Pick Random block to −240 and the number in the right bubble to 240. This will use every point along the bottom of the Stage.

6 Snap a Create Clone of Myself (Control) block under the Set X to Pick Random −240 to 240 block.

7 Place a Set Score to 0 (Data) block under the Create Clone of Myself block. Change the variable to HBS in the drop-down menu and the value to 1. Why 1? Because 1 is true, and this means the ball has now been served.

Look at the completed script in figure 9.8.

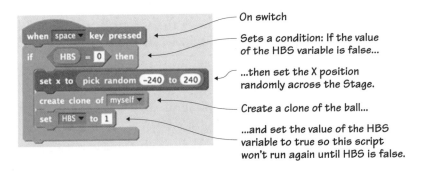

On switch

Sets a condition: If the value of the HBS variable is false...

...then set the X position randomly across the Stage.

Create a clone of the ball...

...and set the value of the HBS variable to true so this script won't run again until HBS is false.

Figure 9.8   The completed cloning script duplicates and serves the ball.

This script only runs if the value of the variable HBS is 0 (or false), meaning the ball hasn't been served. You wouldn't want it running when the ball has been served and on the screen. Can you imagine the field filling up with hundreds of blue rubber balls bouncing around? By designing the script to only run if a ball hasn't been served, it stops the game from generating a new clone of the ball sprite when the ball is in motion. You can hit the spacebar all you want when there is a ball on the screen and nothing will happen.

Making a movement script

The ball is served but...it can't go anywhere! You haven't told the ball how it moves; therefore it's paused on the screen, as in figure 9.9.

The ball will move from the bottom of the Stage toward the nets at the top.

To make the movement script

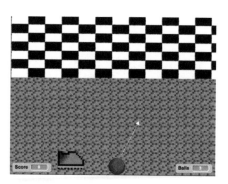

Figure 9.9 The ball will move from the bottom to the top of the Stage after it is served.

1 Start with putting a When I Start as a Clone (Control) block into the workspace.

2 Snap a Go to Front (Looks) block underneath. This sends the sprite to the top layer on the Stage. This block will ensure that the ball doesn't glitch because it will be the top layer, even if you don't click and move the ball last while setting up the Stage.

3 Slide a Show (Looks) block under the Go to Front block. This will reveal the previously invisible clone of the ball.

4 Place a Point in Direction 90 (Motion) block under the Show block. Change the 90 to 45. You will need to type the number, because 45 degrees is not in the drop-down menu. You want the ball to move on the diagonal, hence you're using 45 degrees. If you kept it at 90, the ball would move horizontally and never reach the net!

5 Slide a Forever (Control) block under the Point in Direction 45 block to set a loop.

6 Place a Move 10 Steps (Motion) block inside the Forever block. Change the 10 to a 7 to slow down the ball a little bit. It's now the same speed as the shoe.

7 Put an If on Edge, Bounce (Motion) block underneath the Move 7 Steps block.

Compare your script to the completed script in figure 9.10.

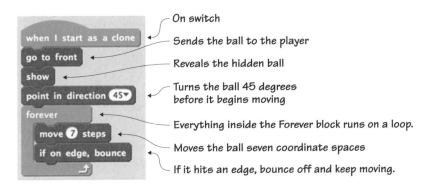

Figure 9.10   The completed movement script tells the ball how to bounce around the screen.

Making a shoe detection script

The ball can now hit the edge of the Stage and bounce back toward the shoe, but how does it know when it has reached the shoe sprite, as in figure 9.11?

This script will detect that the ball is touching the shoe and turn the ball by 90 degrees so it can move in a new direction. To make the detection script

1 Start with a When I Start as a Clone (Control) block.

2 Slide a Forever (Control) block onto the chain to start a loop.

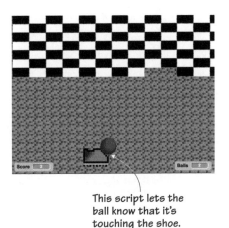

This script lets the ball know that it's touching the shoe.

Figure 9.11   The ball needs to bounce off the shoe, just as the ball bounces off the paddle in *Breakout*.

3 Put an If/Then (Control) block inside the Forever block to set a condition.

4 Place a Touching (Sensing) block in the empty hexagonal space in the If/Then block. Use the drop-down menu to choose Shoe.

5 Slide a Turn Clockwise 15 Degrees (Motion) block inside the If/Then block. The arrow should be moving in the same direction as a clock, as you can see in the completed script in figure 9.12. Change the 15 to a 90. This sets the condition: if the ball is touching the shoe, turn 90 degrees.

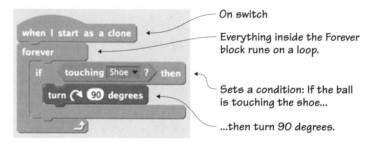

Figure 9.12   The completed detection script switches the direction of the ball when it bounces against the shoe.

This script changes the direction the ball is traveling. Because you're already thinking about clocks from that Turn Clockwise 90 Degrees block, imagine the ball in the center of a clock. It starts moving toward the 2 on the clock, hits the edge, and bounces back toward the center. Once it reaches the center, it encounters this script, which turns it 90 degrees. It's now going to move toward the 11 on the clock, as shown in figure 9.13. You need this to happen or the player will never be

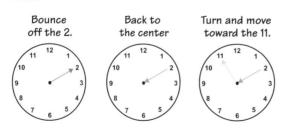

Figure 9.13   The ball needs to be able to twist and change direction.

able to clear the board because the ball will keep traveling in the same direction.

Making a net detection script

Right now the ball can touch the net, but nothing happens. In fact, it can keep going across it all the way until it hits the edge of the Stage, as shown in figure 9.14.

You need to create a script that will cause the ball to bounce off the net. When you program the net, you'll make a different script that removes the piece, but for now you want the ball to be able to return to the shoe.

The ball should bounce against the net and remove the black-and-white sections.

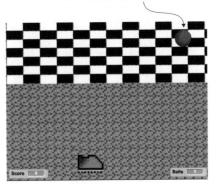

Figure 9.14   The ball is traveling over the net without stopping.

To make the net detection script

1 Start with a When I Receive (Events) block. Use the drop-down menu to choose New Message. Name this message Rebound. You will write the message sending script when you program the net, which means that you're writing the receiver script first that will catch that message and cause something to happen.

2 Snap a Turn Clockwise 15 Degrees (Motion) block underneath. If the ball receives the Rebound message from the net, it will turn 180 degrees.

This script turns the ball 180 degrees whenever it hits a black (or white) section of the net. This script is now complete. Does your script look like the one in figure 9.15?

On switch

Turns 180 degrees, clockwise

Figure 9.15   The completed net detection script makes the ball bounce off the net.

Making a ball deduction script

Right now the shoe can miss the ball and nothing happens, as in figure 9.16. The ball keeps bouncing around the Stage, and the game continues forever.

This script will check whether the ball is touching the line at the bottom of the Stage, and if it is, it will remove one of the player's three chances to clear the board:

1 Start with a When I Start as a Clone (Control) block.

2 Add a Forever (Control) block onto the chain to start a loop.

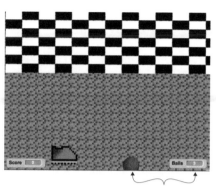

The ball is touching the line, but the clone isn't disappearing, and it's not deducting one of the chances in the game.

Figure 9.16   The ball is touching the line at the bottom of the Stage, but the game isn't deducting one of the player's three chances.

3 Slide an If/Then (Control) block inside the Forever block to set a condition.

4 Put a Touching (Sensing) block into the empty hexagonal space in the If/Then block. Use the drop-down menu to change the option to Bottom Line. This is the barrier line that you will soon position at the bottom of the Stage.

5 Drag a Set Score to 0 (Data) block inside the If/Then block. Use the drop-down menu to change Score to HBS. Keep the value at zero (0), since zero means false. If the ball is in motion, the variable HBS (or has been served) is true. This part of the script resets it to false so the ball can be served again.

6 Snap a Delete This Clone (Control) block under the Set HBS to 0 block. This will remove this copy of the ball sprite.

You're done programming the ball. You can see this final ball script in figure 9.17.

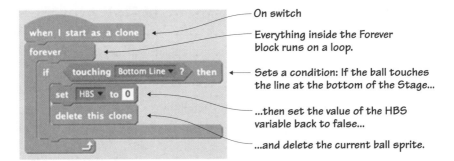

— On switch

— Everything inside the Forever
block runs on a loop.

— Sets a condition: If the ball touches
the line at the bottom of the Stage...

...then set the value of the HBS
variable back to false...

...and delete the current ball sprite.

Figure 9.17   *The completed ball deduction script removes a chance every time the player
misses the ball.*

Programming the net

The soccer net is the equivalent of the bricks in *Breakout*. The point of
the game is to bounce the ball off each section of net. If the ball hits the
net, that section of net disappears, giving the ball a chance to reach the
higher sections of net by the top of the Stage. The net has two scripts: a
cloning script that will generate all those sections of net from a single
rectangle and a ball detection script. Put the blue box around the net in
the Sprite Zone.

Making the cloning script

You currently have a single piece
of net. It wouldn't be an exciting
game if the net looked like the one
in figure 9.18—a lone rectangle in
the top corner of the screen.

This script is going to take that
single rectangle and turn it into a
black-and-white soccer net, alternating the two colors 11 sections
across and 7 sections down. You
may need to play with the numbers in this script to have the net

You currently only have one
piece of net. You need the net
to fill the top of the Stage.

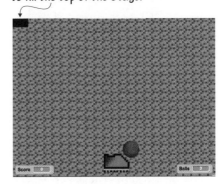

Figure 9.18   *If there was only one section of
net, it would be a difficult and boring game.*

fit your Stage if you didn't draw your rectangle 19 by 10 pixels (which were the instructions in chapter 8), but you'll play with these numbers once you get to the Troubleshooting section of this chapter.

To make this net-generating cloning script

1   Start with a When Flag Clicked (Events) block.

2   Snap a Show (Looks) block next in the chain to make the net appear on the screen.

3   Drag the single piece of net on the Stage into the top left corner.

4   Slide a Go to X/Y (Motion) block underneath the Show block. Scratch will automatically set these numbers to your sprite's position. Mine were X:–217 and Y:170, but yours may be different and that's okay.

5   Drag a first Repeat 10 (Control) block and snap it under the Go to X/Y block. Change the number from 10 to 7. Next, drag a second Repeat 10 (Control) block and place it inside the *first* Repeat 7 block. Change this 10 to an 11. You now have two loops—one that generates the number of sections in each row (11) and one that sets the number of total rows (7).

6   Drag a Create Clone of Myself (Control) block and place it inside the Repeat 11 block.

7   Place a Next Costume (Looks) block under the Create Clone of Myself block. This will make the next section black if the current section is white or vice versa.

8   Slide a Move 10 Steps (Motion) block under the Next Costume block and change the number to 46. This will start the next section of net 46 coordinate spaces over so the sections of net are touching but not running on top of one another. This will be a number you play with in the Troubleshooting section.

9   Place another Go to X/Y (Motion) block underneath the Repeat 11 block. Look at the placement in figure 9.19 if you're confused. Change the number for the X position to –217 again. You're going to do something a little different with the Y position because that will change each time the game starts a new row.

10 Put a Circle – Circle (Operators) block into the bubble for the Y position in the Go to X/Y block, as in figure 9.19.

11 Place a Y Position (Motion) block in the left circle. Type the number 24 in the right circle. This typed number will be another number you play with when you get to the Troubleshooting section if you don't like the way the net looks on the screen. This block is looking at the last Y position for the net and then starting the next row 24 coordinate spaces down.

12 Slide a Hide (Looks) block at the bottom of the script. This will hide that original net sprite once there are 7 rows of 11 sections of net.

Place the Circle - Circle block inside the space for the Y position.

Figure 9.19   This script uses some math on the go because the Y position will be different for each of the seven rows.

That's the end of this long, complicated script. Look at the completed script in figure 9.20. Does your script match the one shown here?

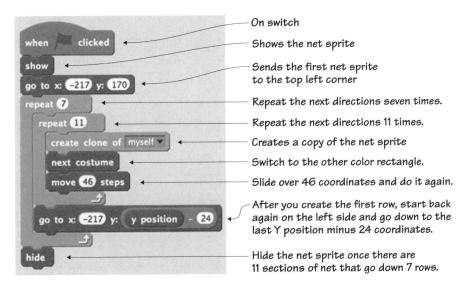

- On switch
- Shows the net sprite
- Sends the first net sprite to the top left corner
- Repeat the next directions seven times.
- Repeat the next directions 11 times.
- Creates a copy of the net sprite
- Switch to the other color rectangle.
- Slide over 46 coordinates and do it again.
- After you create the first row, start back again on the left side and go down to the last Y position minus 24 coordinates.
- Hide the net sprite once there are 11 sections of net that go down 7 rows.

Figure 9.20   This completed cloning script creates the soccer net.

The numbers in this script may change slightly when you're checking for bugs in your game. But they're a good starting point for now.

Making a ball detection script

The net is made, and the ball can even bounce off of it, but you want the net to start disappearing as the ball touches each section, as in figure 9.21.

Pieces of the net disappear when the ball bounces against it.

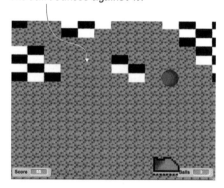

This script will check whether the ball is touching a section of net. If it is touching the net, it will remove that section and give the player one point.

Figure 9.21   The ball removes each section of the net that it touches.

To make the ball detection script

1 Start with a When I Start as a Clone (Control) block in the Script Area.

2 Add a Forever (Control) block onto the chain to start a loop.

3 Slide an If/Then (Control) block inside the Forever block to set a condition.

4 Place a Touching (Sensing) block inside the empty hexagonal space in the If/Then block. Use the drop-down menu to set the sprite to Ball. The condition will be if the net is touching the ball sprite.

5 Drag a Change Score by 1 (Data) block inside the If/Then block. Leave the number as 1 because you want the game to reward a point (increasing the value of the variable Score by 1) each time the ball touches a section of net.

6 Snap a Broadcast Rebound (Events) block underneath the Change Score by 1 block. This will send a message to the earlier Net Detection script, telling the ball that it's time to turn clockwise 180 degrees.

7 Put a Delete This Clone (Control) block under the Broadcast Rebound block.

Figure 9.22 shows the whole script.

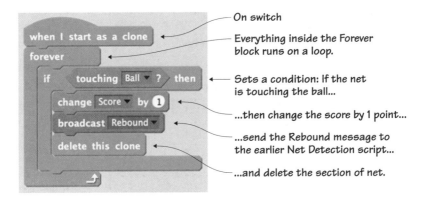

On switch

Everything inside the Forever block runs on a loop.

Sets a condition: If the net is touching the ball...

...then change the score by 1 point...

...send the Rebound message to the earlier Net Detection script...

...and delete the section of net.

Figure 9.22   The completed ball detection script gives a point as it removes a section of the net.

You've now programmed all the main sprites, but there are still five more small scripts to write for the odds and ends.

Programming the odds and ends

Dribble has five small scripts that apply to the scoreboard and the barrier line. These scripts help the game play, though they aren't sprites you'll interact with on the screen like the ball and the shoe. The first two scripts apply to the scoreboard, and the last three scripts apply to the line. Pay attention to where the programming switches from one sprite to the other so you'll place your script under the correct sprite.

Making a scoreboard hiding script

When your game begins, you don't want to see the end scoreboard, as in figure 9.23.

This script will hide the scoreboard at the beginning of the game so it is only

What's Your Score?

0 - 19   Caught in the net
20 - 39   Almost ready for the World Cup
40 - 49   Bend it!
50+   GOAL!

Compare the final score to the ranges on the score board.

Figure 9.23   The player achieves 67 points during the game: a score of GOAL!

seen when the game ends. Put the blue box around the End of Game sprite in the Sprite Zone.

To hide the scoreboard

1 Start with a When Flag Clicked (Events) block in the workspace.

2 Snap a Go to X/Y (Motion) block under the When Flag Clicked block. This will send the center of the sprite to the center of the Stage. Because your scoreboard sprite fills the Stage, the center of the scoreboard will be the center of the Stage.

3 Slide a Hide (Looks) block next to hide the scoreboard until you're ready for it to be revealed at the end of the game. You can see this small script in figure 9.24.

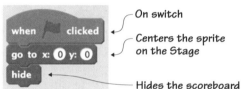

On switch

Centers the sprite on the Stage

Hides the scoreboard

Figure 9.24   The completed scoreboard hiding script makes the scoreboard invisible until the end of the game.

Making a scoreboard showing script

Intellivision's version of *Breakout* (called *Brickout*) teases the player at the end of the game with statements like "Try cards," but I wanted to make a kinder scoreboard. The scoreboard pops onto the screen after the player misses the third and final ball. This tiny script makes the board (which has been there the whole time) visible.

To make the script

1 Start with a When I Receive Message1 (Events) block.

2 Snap a Show (Looks) block under the When I Receive Message1 block.

Figure 9.25 shows the whole script! The script receives a message and reveals the scoreboard, which was hidden at the beginning of the game when the green flag was clicked.

When the sprite receives a broadcasted message...

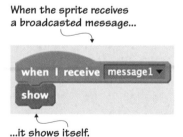

...it shows itself.

Figure 9.25   The completed scoreboard showing script reveals the scoreboard when the script receives a message.

This tiny script is waiting for a message that hasn't been sent yet. You will get to that when you program the other item in the odds and ends section: the bottom line.

Making a line positioning script

The final three scripts apply to the barrier line, so go put the blue box around it in the Sprite Zone for all three scripts. This bottom line helps keep score and sets up the terms of game over. Though you can't see the line in figure 9.26 because it's positioned at the bottom of the Stage, you can see the effects of the line because the player is out of chances and the scoreboard is on the screen.

What's Your Score?

0 - 19   Caught in the net
20 - 39   Almost ready for the World Cup
40 - 49   Bend it!
50+   GOAL!

The barrier line is positioned at the bottom of the Stage.

The deduction script and the game ending script look at how many chances the player has left.

Figure 9.26   The line will be positioned at the bottom of the Stage. It will remove a player's chance each time the ball hits the line, and when the player is out of chances, it will end the game.

This first script positions the line, and it is the same script you used in Wizards vs. Ghosts.

To make the line positioning script

1 Start with a When Flag Clicked (Events) block.

2 Add a Forever (Control) block underneath to start a loop.

3 Place a Go to X/Y (Motion) block inside the Forever block and change both numbers to zero (0). This will send the center of the sprite to the center of the Stage.

Figure 9.27 shows this familiar script.

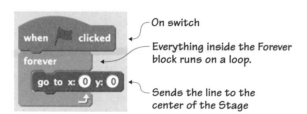

On switch

Everything inside the Forever
block runs on a loop.

Sends the line to the
center of the Stage

Figure 9.27   The completed positioning script sends the line to
the correct place on the screen.

Making a line deduction script

The line may not award points, but it certainly takes away chances. Each time the ball hits the barrier line, this script will deduct a chance. The player starts out with three chances to clear the board, and the game ends when those chances are gone.

To make the deduction script

1 Start with a When Flag Clicked (Events) block.

2 Navigate to Data and make a new variable called Balls. This will be the chances the player has to clear the board. Make sure the variable is checked because you want it to appear on the Stage. In fact, drag that new variable down to the bottom right corner of the Stage so the player can always see how many chances they have left.

3 Place a Set Balls to 0 (Data) block under the When Flag Clicked block. Change the zero (0) to a 3, to give the player three balls, or chances, to clear the board.

4 Add a Forever (Control) block underneath to start a loop.

5 Place an If/Then (Control) block inside the Forever block. You're setting a condition.

6 Put the Touching (Sensing) block into the empty hexagonal space on the If/Then block. Use the drop-down menu to set it to Ball. The condition will be if the line is touching the ball.

7 Slide a Change Balls by 1 (Data) block inside the If/Then block. Change the 1 to a –1 because you want to remove a ball (not give another ball) whenever the ball touches the line.

8 Snap a Wait 1 Secs (Control) block under the Change Balls by –1 block. This small pause will ensure that the game doesn't glitch and deduct more than one chance at a time.

Figure 9.28 shows the whole script.

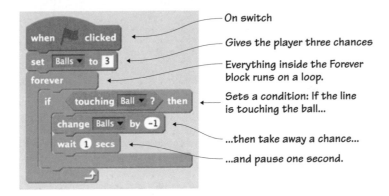

Figure 9.28   *The completed deduction script removes a chance every time the ball hits the line.*

The final script works with this script to set an end point for the game after all those chances are used up.

Making a line game ending script

Right now the game will continue, even if the player goes into negative chances. You need to set a stopping point for the game so the scoreboard will flash on the screen. This is the script that contains the broadcasted message the scoreboard is waiting for in order to reveal itself.

To make this game ending script

1 Start with a When Flag Clicked (Events) block.

2 Add a Forever (Control) block underneath to start a loop.

3 Place an If/Then (Control) block inside the Forever block to set a condition.

4 Slip a Square = Square (Operators) block into the empty hexagonal space in the If/Then block. Place a Balls (Data) variable in the left

square and type zero (0) in the right square because the condition should be "If the value of the Balls variable is zero then..."

5 Slide a Broadcast Message1 (Events) block inside the If/Then block. This will send the message to the earlier scoreboard script.

6 Place a Stop All (Control) block under the Broadcast Message1 block to stop all the scripts in the game. You can see the completed script in figure 9.29.

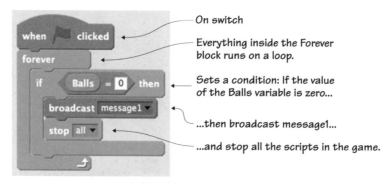

Figure 9.29   The completed game ending script sends a message to the scoreboard that the game is over.

Your game is now complete. Click the flag and watch the net generate across the Stage. If all goes according to plan, you should be ready to kick the ball with the shoe. But in case you run into some trouble, keep reading so you can tweak the code in the game.

Troubleshooting your game

This game, more than any other in the book, is difficult to get right on the first try. Read on to learn how to fix problems with your game.

Center your sprites

If your net is behaving oddly, make sure that the rectangle net sprite is centered. Click the rectangle in the Sprite Zone, go to the middle Costumes tab to return to the Art Editor, and navigate to the plus sign in the top right corner. After the cross appears on the screen, click the center of the rectangle, as in figure 9.30, to center the sprite.

First click the plus sign
in the top right corner.

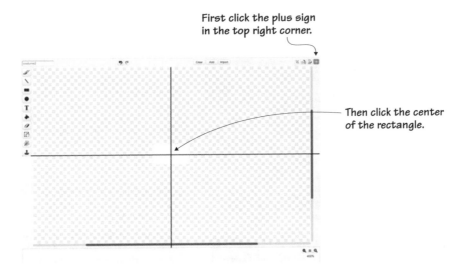

Then click the center
of the rectangle.

Figure 9.30   Center the sprites by clicking the plus sign in the top right corner of the Art Editor.

Make sure you also center the shoe and ball sprites or they won't work correctly.

Tweak the code

When the net first generated on our game, it looked like figure 9.31, with spaces between each section of net.

Remember the net cloning script? You need to return to this script and tweak the numbers marked in figure 9.32 until the net fills the screen. Change your numbers in small increments, maybe only one coordinate space

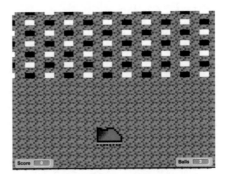

Figure 9.31   The net generates with big gaps when using the first trial numbers in the net cloning script.

or one additional base net rectangle at a time. Your end numbers may still be slightly different from the ones in figure 9.32 due to differences in the sprite's size.

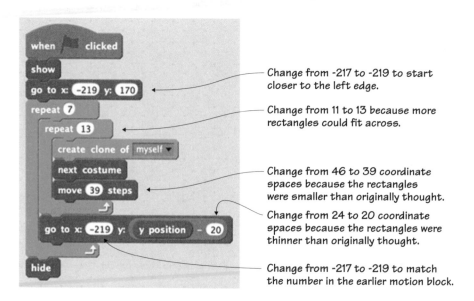

Change from -217 to -219 to start closer to the left edge.

Change from 11 to 13 because more rectangles could fit across.

Change from 46 to 39 coordinate spaces because the rectangles were smaller than originally thought.

Change from 24 to 20 coordinate spaces because the rectangles were thinner than originally thought.

Change from -217 to -219 to match the number in the earlier motion block.

Figure 9.32   Make small changes to the net cloning script, clicking the flag between each change to see how it affects the net.

Learning in action

Variables are the star of Dribble, being used to track points, check chances, and even determine whether the ball has been served. Sometimes the value is numerical, like giving the player three chances to clear the board, and sometimes the value is a Boolean (a true/false value), such as checking whether the ball has been served.

Play with the code

You already probably had a bit of a challenge troubleshooting the game, but in case you want to stretch more, try these challenges to change the game play.

CHALLENGE   Change the ball and shoe's movement speed to create a more challenging game. You can either keep the two sprites synchronized, changing each of them by the same amount, or you can make one go faster than the other. How difficult can you make the game and still get to the GOAL! level?

CHALLENGE   You saw from the net cloning script that sometimes you need to tweak the code in order to make all the rectangles fit. Want to make the game more challenging? Shrink down the base net rectangle even more, and go back to that script to generate even more cloned pieces of net. How many small black and white rectangles can you fit across the screen? How does this also change the scoring of the game if you don't change the ball size to match the smaller net pieces?

What did you learn?

Before you jump back into Dribble and score some goals, take a moment to reflect on which common computer science ideas from chapter 3 were used in this game:

- Using an on switch for every script in the game, including using the spacebar to clone and serve a ball mid-game
- Sending the scoreboard to the center of the screen with X and Y coordinates
- Writing conditional statements to detect whether the ball is touching the net
- Setting up a loop to keep the ball in motion
- Using a variable to keep track of how many sections of net have been removed
- Working with Booleans to check whether the ball has been served using the HBS variable
- Cloning all the sections of net from a single base net rectangle
- Broadcasting a message from the barrier line to the scoreboard so the scoreboard knows when the game is over

Eight out of eight common programming ideas! With three games under your belt (and two more to go), I hope you're feeling comfortable with these concepts and seeing how they can be applied differently depending on the game.

Additionally, in Dribble you learned

- How to use 1 and 0 to stand for true and false in programming
- How to use a variable to track whether or not something has happened
- How to switch back and forth between two costumes on the same sprite using code
- How to give meaning to a player's points with a scoreboard
- How to tweak your code on your own

Now that you have Dribble working, play a few more rounds and then take a deep breath. You're about to start making a simple platformer called Beach Blast that will have your sprites switching from screen to screen.

10

Designing a simple platformer

It's a beautiful summer day, not a cloud in the sky, which makes it the perfect time for a beach trip. But Buffy finds a mess when she finally gets on the sand. There are ditches filled with water, snapping crabs, and to top it off, some kid has left a city of sandcastles behind that makes walking impossible, as you can see in figure 10.1. There's a better patch of sand about a mile away, but how is she going to navigate that mile?

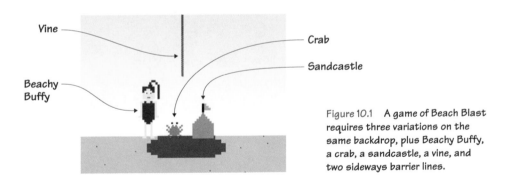

Figure 10.1   A game of Beach Blast requires three variations on the same backdrop, plus Beachy Buffy, a crab, a sandcastle, a vine, and two sideways barrier lines.

Beach Blast is a side-scrolling platformer like Activision's 1982 game *Pitfall*. *Pitfall* follows the adventures of Pitfall Harry as he leaps over scorpions, sails over tar pits, and dodges rolling barrels. Beach Blast takes the mechanics of *Pitfall* but sets the jumping and swinging on the beach, making the obstacles water, crabs, and sandcastles.

To draw those obstacles, you're going to learn an important art concept that you can use to tackle any problem in life: taking a large object and breaking it down into smaller parts.

In this chapter, you will learn

- How to look for basic shapes within an object
- How to break down a unique shape into smaller parts using the grid method to copy an object
- How to look at an image in segments

You'll start off by making a beach backdrop, only this time you're going to make three variations on the same setting in order to create a sense of movement.

Prepping the backgrounds

The games you've made so far have only required one backdrop. A side-scrolling platformer requires two or more backdrops to create the illusion of movement. Whenever Beachy Buffy touches the left or right side of the Stage, the backdrop will switch, making it look as if she is continuously running.

Making the open sand backdrop

The simple sandy backdrop in figure 10.2 can be tweaked to make the other two backdrops. This first one will be the backdrop you'll use

Figure 10.2   The open sand backdrop can be tweaked to build the other two backdrops.

when she's jumping over the sandcastle sprites that you'll make later in this chapter.

Open the Backdrop Art Editor and get ready to make the open sand backdrop:

1 Open the rainbow box and choose a shade of tan for the sand, such as the one shown in figure 10.3.

Shows the current color

Move the black bubble in the rainbow box to find a tan for the sand.

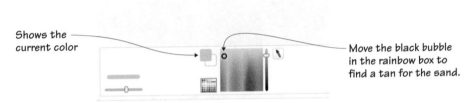

Figure 10.3   Choose a light tan for the sand.

2 Choose the Line tool and split the screen horizontally with a straight line across the Stage about one third of the way up from the bottom.

3 Use the Paint Bucket tool to fill the bottom of the canvas.

4 Look toward the boxes on the left side of the Color Toolbar where you'll see the four fill options, shown in figure 10.4.

Spills the color so it is dark near the top of the Stage and fades into white toward the bottom of the Stage

Figure 10.4   You'll find four gradient (or fading) options on the left side of the Color Toolbar.

5 Choose the bottom left gradient option, which concentrates the blue paint at the top of the screen and fades downward into white.

6 Switch to a pale blue paint sample square to make the sky. Make sure the blue box is around the gradient tool as it is in figure 10.5 to

make the sky darkest at the top of the Stage, fading to white. Click anywhere in the empty, top two-thirds of the canvas.

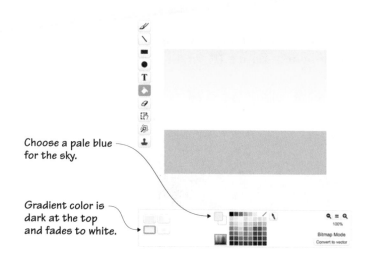

Choose a pale blue for the sky.

Gradient color is dark at the top and fades to white.

Figure 10.5   The gradient tool makes a more realistic sky that fades as it moves closer to the horizon line.

7 Select the dark brown paint sample square and click the Paintbrush tool. Make random dots across the sand to give the illusion of texture and graininess.

Your backdrop should look like the open sand background in figure 10.6.

Figure 10.6   The completed open sand backdrop is where Beachy Buffy will jump over sandcastles.

Making the hole in the sand backdrop

You need three backdrops to make Beach Blast, but you don't have to start each time from scratch. This second backdrop takes the open sand backdrop and cuts out a hole for Beachy Buffy to land in when she's trying to escape the crabs, as shown in figure 10.7.

To duplicate the open sand background, navigate to the Grey Toolbar, choose the Duplicator tool, and click the backdrop on the Costumes tab, as seen in figure 10.8.

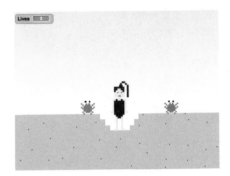

Figure 10.7   Cutting a hole into the sand in the previous backdrop creates a different background.

Figure 10.8   The Duplicator tool saves you from needing to draw the backdrop from scratch.

You should now see two backdrops on the Costumes tab. Make sure the blue box is around backdrop2 and get ready to remove part of this backdrop in order to create the hole in the sand:

1   Choose the Select tool and draw a small rectangle in the sand in the middle of the Stage, as in Step One in figure 10.9. If you're having trouble selecting a thin rectangle of sand, zoom in to 200% for a larger workspace.

2   Press the delete or backspace key on the keyboard to remove this section of sand.

3   Make a smaller rectangle underneath and touching the first rectangle, as in Step Two in figure 10.9. Repeat a second time, making an even smaller rectangle, like Step Three in figure 10.9.

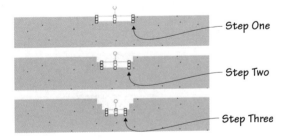

Figure 10.9   The hole in the sand is made out of three rectangles removed from the open sand backdrop.

You now have a safe space for Beachy Buffy to land when she's dodging the pinching crabs, as shown in figure 10.10.

Making the water ditch backdrop

Similar to the hole in the sand backdrop, the water ditch backdrop tweaks the original open sand backdrop, this time making the dark blue rectangles seen in figure 10.11 instead of removing sections of sand.

Figure 10.10   The completed hole in the sand backdrop

Once again, duplicate the original open sand backdrop on the Costumes tab and make sure the blue box is around the new backdrop3.

To make the water ditch

1 Choose a dark greenish-blue for the seawater that has pooled in the ditch.

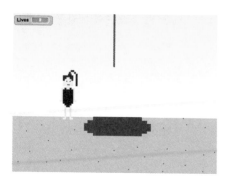

2 Select the Square tool and draw a fat rectangle touching the top of the sand in the middle of the Stage, as in Step One in figure 10.12.

Figure 10.11   The water obstacle is three blue rectangles drawn on top of one another. The vine sprite is drawn separately later in this chapter.

3 Draw a longer, thinner rectangle on top of the first rectangle, as in Step Two in figure 10.12. Repeat this step a second time, drawing an

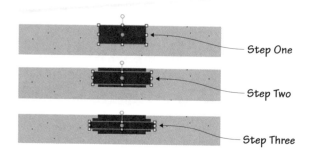

Step One

Step Two

Step Three

Figure 10.12   The three rectangles are drawn on top of one another.

even longer, thinner rectangle on top of the second rectangle, like Step Three in figure 10.12.

The three rectangles meld together to create the pool of water shown in figure 10.13.

You now have three backdrops. You'll be able to program the game to switch between the backdrops to make it look as if Beach Buffy is running across the sand, switching environments. Which means it's time to make Buffy.

Figure 10.13   **The completed water ditch backdrop**

Prepping the main sprites

There are four main sprites that you'll need to make for Beach Blast: Buffy, a crab, a sandcastle, and a vine. All of them can be broken down into a series of basic shapes. Once you can see the shapes inside a larger, irregularly shaped object, you can create...*anything*. Make sure to get rid of the default cat sprite before you begin making your other sprites.

Making Beachy Buffy

Buffy is the player character in this game, and you'll make her run and jump over obstacles. The best part about making Buffy, shown in figure 10.14, is that you'll quickly realize that she's a bunch of rectangles and squares.

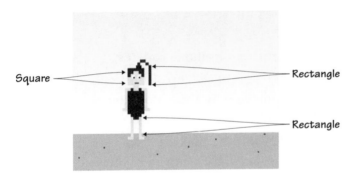

Figure 10.14   **Buffy is a series of squares and rectangles in different colors.**

Open the Art Editor to make Beachy Buffy:

1 Zoom in to 800% and get ready to start building Buffy near the light grey plus sign that marks the center of the canvas.

2 Select any skin tone color from the rainbow box.

3 Click the Paintbrush tool. Make a 6-by-6 square out of square dots. Fill the inside of the square using the Paint Bucket tool. (Make sure you're on the solid fill and not the gradient tool!)

4 Return to the Paintbrush tool and make two connecting horizontal square dots underneath the square for the neck.

5 Begin one pixel beyond the left side of the head and start making a line of horizontal pixels running parallel to the bottom of the head. (It should be eight pixels across.)

6 Make a thin vertical rectangle out of seven square dots extending off either end of the horizontal shoulder line. When you get to the end, make one pixel out to the left or right depending on the side. Buffy should now look like figure 10.15.

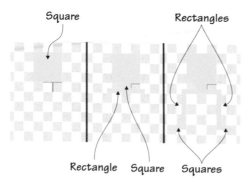

Figure 10.15 Every part of Buffy is either a square or rectangle.

7 Choose a dark purple from the paint sample squares.

8 Draw a letter H out of square dots at the top of Buffy's body to make the swimsuit straps. You can see how these dots touch the neck in Step One of figure 10.16.

9 Continue the side of the swimsuit, making two vertical lines of square dots that extend two pixels beneath the bottom of her arm.

Close off the bottom of the swimsuit with two square dots, as seen in Step Two of figure 10.16.

10 Fill the inside of the swimsuit using the Paint Bucket tool, as in Step Three of figure 10.16.

11 Switch back to the Paintbrush tool and fill in the space between the arm and the swimsuit with square dots, as seen in Step Four of figure 10.16.

12 Use the eyedropper to reselect the skin tone color.

13 Make two vertical lines out of eight square dots beginning on either side of the bottom of the swimsuit. When you get to the end, make one pixel out to the left or right depending on the side. Buffy now has legs, as seen in figure 10.17.

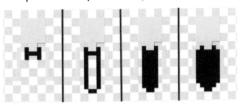

Step One   Step Two   Step Three   Step Four

Figure 10.16   Even Buffy's swimsuit can be broken down into squares and rectangles.

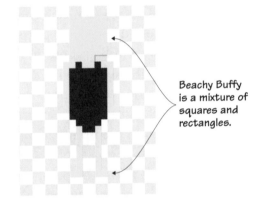

Beachy Buffy is a mixture of squares and rectangles.

Figure 10.17   Buffy's legs are made up of thin rectangles with square feet.

14 Choose a dark brown from the paint sample squares. Begin at the top of the head in the center of the skin-tone square. Draw two horizontal, brown, square dots to start the hairline. Make a two-pixel diagonal line from either end of the centered line, as in Step One of figure 10.18.

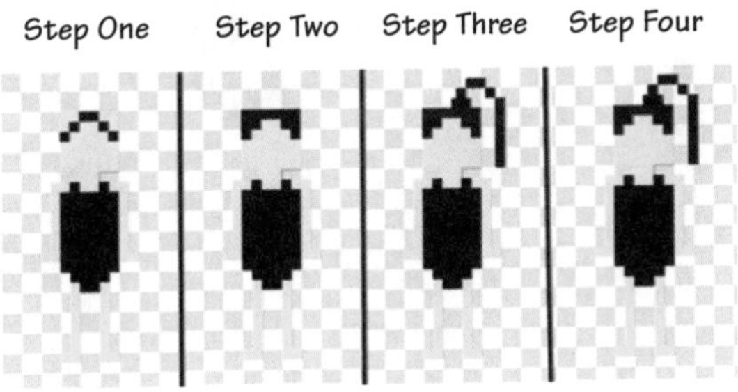

Step One   Step Two   Step Three   Step Four

Figure 10.18   Buffy's hair is built pixel-by-pixel.

15 Fill the three skin-tone pixels at the top of her head with the hair color, as shown in Step Two of figure 10.18.

16 Make two side-by-side pixels to the right of center. You can see the placement in Step Three of figure 10.18, where the ponytail attaches to the head. Draw a single square dot on top of the two-pixel line. Starting in the top right corner of the single square dot, make a two-pixel horizontal line toward the right. Draw two pixels diagonally from the bottom right corner. Continue drawing a vertical line of six more pixels until the end of the ponytail is level with the end of Buffy's head.

17 Switch to the swimsuit purple, use the slider to make a smaller pixel size, and draw a tiny purple line where the ponytail meets the head, as shown in Step Four of figure 10.18.

18 Select the white paint sample square. Keeping the Paintbrush tool on the thinnest setting, draw a square out of four pixels on the left side of Buffy's face. Repeat this step on the right side of her face.

19 Switch to the green paint sample square and draw a single pixel in one of the corners of the white square.

20 Change to the red paint sample square and draw two horizontal pixels side-by-side, as shown in figure 10.19.

Buffy is now complete. Look at her body in figure 10.20 and you'll notice that although you drew all of her body parts pixel-by-pixel, they

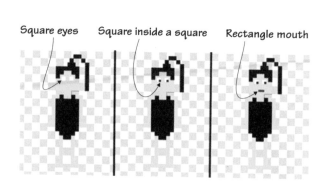

Figure 10.19   Squares and rectangles make Buffy's face.

Figure 10.20   The completed Beachy Buffy sprite

add up to a lot of rectangles and squares. Don't forget to name her Buffy in the Sprite Zone.

LEARN IT BREAKING DOWN AN OBJECT INTO SHAPES   Many budding artists have trouble drawing people. A person is an irregular shape, and it's hard to know where to begin. But once you start making Buffy, you can see that she breaks down into a series of rectangles and squares. The same can be said for every object you want to draw. You can replicate any irregularly shaped object by breaking down the larger shape into smaller basic shapes. Take, for example, the mouse in the sprite library. (See figure 10.21.) Look for the basic shapes that make up the irregularly shaped

mouse. There are a cluster of four circles that form its head, body, and ears. There are also three tiny circles inside the face for the eyes and nose. The legs are squares with three circles attached at the end, and the tail is a thick, curved line. Always look for the basic shapes to make drawing easier.

Figure 10.21   The mouse is a series of circles stuck together.

Making the sandcastle

Speaking of basic shapes, sandcastles are all about packing sand into square bricks or flying triangular seaweed flags. The sand castle in figure 10.22 will serve as an obstacle for Buffy to jump over as she runs down the beach.

Start a new sprite to make the sandcastle:

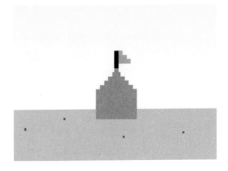

Figure 10.22   The sandcastle is also a series of squares and rectangles.

1 Keep the Art Editor zoomed in to 800%.

2 Open the rainbow box and click the Eyedropper tool. To pick up the color you used for the sand, click the thumbnail of the Stage in the Sprite Zone. This will open the backdrop so you can click anywhere on the sand to pick up the color using the Eyedropper tool. Switch back to the sandcastle sprite by clicking it in the Sprite Zone.

3 Move the slider to the right of the rainbow box to make the color slightly darker than the original sand to show that the sand is damp.

4 Go to the Paintbrush tool and make sure it's on its default size. Make a 10-by-7 horizontal rectangle out of square dots. Fill in the center using the Paint Bucket tool.

5 Switch back to the Paintbrush tool and staircase from the top sides of the rectangle toward the middle, connecting the square dots in the corner. Any dot you make on the left side, make on the right side too to keep it symmetrical. Top the sandcastle with a single pixel.

6 Fill the middle of the sandcastle using the Paint Bucket tool. It should look like figure 10.23.

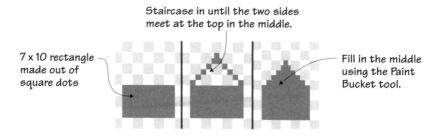

Figure 10.23   The symmetrical sandcastle is the same on the left and right side.

7 Switch to the black paint sample square and make a four-pixel vertical line extending from the top sand pixel.

8 Choose any color from the paint sample squares (I went with orange) to make the flag. At the top of the black line, make a single pixel to the right. Underneath that, starting at the black line again, make two side-by-side pixels to the right. Do this one more time, making a three-pixel line under the two-pixel line.

Figure 10.24   The completed sandcastle sprite

You can see the finished sandcastle in figure 10.24. Don't forget to go to the Sprite Zone and name this new sprite Castle.

Making the crab

The little red crab may look complicated to make, but it's once again basic squares and rectangles, with a few diagonal lines making its pincers.

The crab in figure 10.25 is a moving obstacle for Beachy Buffy to leap over on her way down the beach.

Start a new sprite to make the crab:

Figure 10.25   The crab is smaller than the sandcastle and the height of one of Buffy's legs.

1 Choose the bright red paint sample square and click the Paintbrush tool. Leave the Art Editor zoomed in to 800%.

2 Make a rectangle six pixels by four pixels and then place four pixels, centered, along the top of the rectangle, and three pixels, centered, along the bottom of the rectangle.

3 Make two pixels on top of the four-pixel line, leaving a space in between, as seen in figure 10.26.

4 Make six sets of two-pixel diagonal lines off the main rectangle: two in the top two corners, two in the center, and two in the bottom two corners, as seen in figure 10.27.

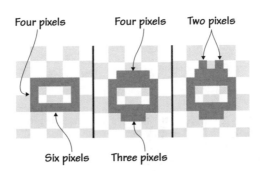

Figure 10.26   The body of the crab is drawn in three steps.

Figure 10.27   Diagonal lines of pixels extend off the body.

5   Switch to any dark paint sample square and spill paint to fill the background of the canvas. This step will make it easier to draw the white eyes because it's difficult to see white squares against the grey-and-white canvas.

6   Choose the white paint sample square and make a four-pixel white square on top of the two red pixels using the Paintbrush tool, as shown in figure 10.28.

7   Switch to the black and place a single pixel in the center of the white squares, also shown in figure 10.28.

8   Return to the red paint sample square and fill the center of the crab's body. Return the background to the clear, grey-and-white canvas by clicking the paint sample square with a line through it and then using the Paint Bucket to spill the clear paint.

Add a black square in
the center of the eyes.

The white square
eyes are easier
to see on the
grey background.

Fill the center of the
crab with red and
then make the
background clear.

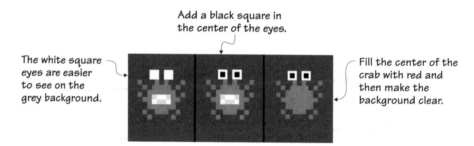

Figure 10.28   The temporary grey background makes it easier to draw the eyes on the crab.

9   Click the eraser and use the slider to set the eraser on its smallest setting. Click the outer top corner of the two claw pixels, as seen in figure 10.29. This removes a quarter of the pixel and completes the crab.

Eraser tool cuts out
the corner of the claw.

Claw begins as
a red square.

Place the eraser on
the square and click.

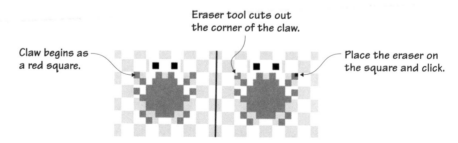

Figure 10.29   The Eraser tool removes a fraction of the pixel to make a pincer shape.

Don't forget to go to the Sprite Zone and rename the sprite Crab.

LEARN IT   THE GRID METHOD   Another way of reproducing an unusual shape is by using the grid method. Instead of looking for basic shapes inside the larger object, you turn each section of the image you're copying into a square, and then draw the contents of that square. The idea is to take a large object and to break it into small, manageable parts. Take a look at the crab in figure 10.30, which is broken down into smaller parts with a grid. The idea is that instead of trying to reproduce a crab—which could be overwhelming if you don't have step-by-step instructions—you try to copy everything inside the square on the grid. Don't add in those grid squares in *your* copy; only use them to help you break down the original object into smaller parts. As you draw, make each new section touch the existing sections.

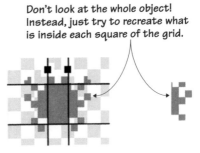

Don't look at the whole object! Instead, just try to recreate what is inside each square of the grid.

Figure 10.30   Draw the inside of each square in the grid rather than look at the whole crab.

Making the vine

The final sprite is the green vine that Buffy will use to sail over the water traps in the sand. You could make a simple green line, but the checkerboard pattern vine, seen in figure 10.31, adds depth and interest to a tool that Buffy will use to cross an obstacle.

Start a new sprite to make the vine:

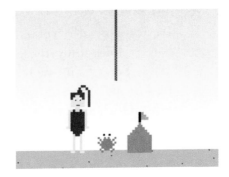

Figure 10.31   The checkerboard pattern on the vine makes it stand out on the screen.

1   Choose the darkest green paint sample square and click the Paintbrush tool. Leave the Art Editor zoomed in to 800%. Make sure the Paintbrush tool is back on its default size setting.

2   Make a 60-pixel checkerboard pattern down the Art Editor, leaving empty spaces, as seen in the far left section of figure 10.32.

3 Return to the top of the checkerboard. Choose the next lightest shade of green from the paint sample squares. Fill in the empty spaces in the top 20 pixels of the vine.

4 Go a step lighter and repeat this two more times with the remaining shades of green, going lighter each time. In the end, you should see the pattern in figure 10.32.

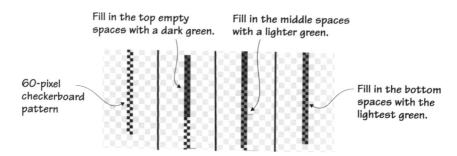

Figure 10.32   *The checkerboard pattern adds depth to the green line vine.*

Your final sprite is complete! Go to the Sprite Zone and rename it Vine.

Prepping the odds and ends

Platformers also sometimes need barrier lines, only these lines will allow Scratch to switch between backdrops instead of counting missed ghosts.

Making the side barrier lines

You have made a lot of barrier lines at the bottom of the Art Editor in order to track whether a sprite has hit the bottom of the Stage. This time you need the barrier lines to run up and down the sides of the Stage, as in figure 10.33. Each time Buffy touches the

Draw a straight line on the left (or right) side of the Stage to make the same type of barrier line you've made for each game.

Figure 10.33   *Side barrier lines are made the same way as bottom barrier lines, except they run vertically on the far left (or right) side of the Stage rather than horizontally across the bottom.*

left or right side of the Stage, the backdrop will switch, creating the illusion of running down the beach.

Start a new sprite to make the side barrier lines:

1 Zoom out until you're back at 100% so you can see the whole canvas.

2 Choose the black paint sample square and use the Line tool to draw a straight line up and down the left side of the canvas.

3 Go to the Sprite Zone and name this sprite Left Line.

4 Start another new sprite and repeat these steps, this time making the line on the right side. Name this sprite Right Line.

You should have two barrier lines in the Sprite Zone, a Left Line and a Right Line, along with Buffy, the sandcastle, the crab, and the vine. Your sprites are now complete, and you're almost ready to code.

Preparing to code

You've probably noticed that platformers require more sprites than ball-and-paddle or fixed shooter games. One sprite is the player character, and the rest of the sprites are obstacles or tools that the main sprite will use during the game. All will need to be programmed in chapter 11, which means there will be more scripts than the other games.

Play with the game

Currently you have three backdrops and three obstacles: the water, the sandcastles, and the crabs. But longer platformers contain many more boards and problems to solve.

CHALLENGE Make a fourth backdrop for Buffy to run past during the game. My brother will show you how to incorporate more boards into your game if you choose this challenge, so pause for a moment to duplicate that original beach scene and tweak it again to create a new scene for Buffy to encounter as she runs down the beach.

CHALLENGE Make another object to challenge or help Buffy as she makes her way down the beach. Think about other objects you may find on the beach, such as a loose umbrella that blows around the sand (and if it touches Buffy, she loses a life) or a seashell that she can collect to gain additional lives. Umbrellas and seashells are both irregular shapes. Look up a picture of an umbrella or seashell and then copy it using the grid method.

CHALLENGE   Can you tweak Buffy (or Bert, if you want to change her into a boy) to look like you? What are your defining features? Or can you work dithering into the sprite to show depth so that Buffy or Bert looks three-dimensional?

What did you learn?

Taking a problem and breaking it down into smaller parts will help you in every area of STEAM. When you encounter a long math problem, you break it down into smaller sections using PEMDAS (parentheses, exponents, multiplication, division, addition, subtraction). That order of operations not only makes you solve the problem in the correct order, but it simplifies a big, unruly equation into manageable parts. The same goes for all the programming you're doing in this book. You're not attempting to make the whole program at once. Instead, you're breaking down the program into smaller scripts so you can see how it fits together. That same idea is reflected in the concept of looking for basic shapes inside a large, irregular shape.

Pause for a moment and think about everything you learned in this chapter:

- How to copy a background and tweak it to make several backdrops
- How to look for shapes inside a larger object
- How to use a grid to break down an irregular shape into smaller parts for easier copying
- How to use the checkerboard pattern to add interest to a plain line

You have a player character. You have obstacles. You even have a vine that can help you get over those obstacles. It sounds like you're ready to make a simple platformer—Beach Blast.

11

Using X and Y coordinates to make a simple platformer

In 1982 the world met Pitfall Harry, and the great platformer tradition was born. Activision's game has a little pixel man jumping over rolling barrels, landing on crocodile heads to cross lakes, and climbing down ladders to get to a second, underground level that runs parallel to the main level of the game but contains scorpions that can stop Harry in his tracks.

Jumping, landing, racing, and collecting are the hallmarks of the platformer genre. Think of *Pitfall* as a jumping puzzle game or video obstacle course—one that would challenge even an American Ninja Warrior. Harry has to leap over rattlesnakes and land on the other side. He leaps over holes in the ground, leaps up to grab onto a vine, and leaps over the scorpions when he's underground. He's also racing against a clock to collect treasure. Harry only has 20 minutes to collect all the gold and silver bars or diamond rings scattered across the game.

Beach Blast is a simple platformer, so you're not going to focus on time limits or treasure collecting in this game (though you will in the next platformer, School Escape). Instead you'll focus on a single idea shared by every platformer on the market, from *Pitfall* to *Leo's Fortune* to *Geometry Dash*: simulated gravity.

What happens when *you* jump up? You don't hang out in the air, looking around until you force yourself back down. Gravity instantly starts pulling you back toward the ground after liftoff. You need to program gravity into video games so that what goes up will eventually come down, as seen in figure 11.1.

X and Y coordinates are the stars of Beach Blast, noting where Buffy is on the screen and bringing her back down to the ground every time she jumps. Beach Blast is also a side-scroller, which means Buffy can run to the side and she won't hit the end of the Stage.

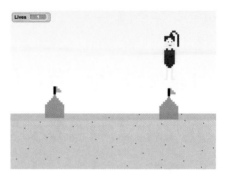

Figure 11.1   In Beach Blast, Buffy has to run down the beach, jumping over sandcastles and moving crabs and swinging over a water hazard on a vine.

Instead, she'll keep on going as the game scrolls out in that direction. You'll accomplish this by having the backdrop change every time Buffy touches the left or right side of the Stage.

One last thing to consider with *Pitfall*, which is a mark of any good game, is that the skills you'll need on the harder levels are all learned and practiced on the easier levels. Jumping, for instance, has lower stakes on the first *Pitfall* screen because the obstacles are rolling barrels, which remove points but don't remove lives. Once the player has gotten a chance to practice jumping over barrels, *Pitfall* ups the stakes by making Pitfall Harry have to sail over deadly obstacles. Finally, once players have gotten the hang of jumping, they'll have to jump and land precisely on the crocodiles to avoid being eaten or time their jumps to sail over the disappearing and reappearing sand pit.

As you make Beach Blast, think about that game design idea, allowing players to learn new skills on easier boards as you plan extra backdrops and obstacles into your game. For instance, programming Beach Blast follows this same step-by-step learning process, having players jump over sandcastles (stationary), crabs (moving), and finally onto the vine (definitely moving *and* the dismount needs to be well timed). If you insert new obstacles and backdrops, make sure to order them so the player can become comfortable with the mechanics of the game before the difficulty level goes up.

In this chapter, you will learn

- How to design a side-scrolling platformer
- How to switch between backdrops to give the illusion of continuous movement
- How to simulate gravity
- How to make enemies that move side-to-side

This simple platformer will teach you everything you need to know in order to make more complicated platformers in the future. Ready to start coding?

Preparing to program

It's time for your pre-coding ritual. Get your sprites and the Stage ready for Beach Blast.

Missing sprites

If you skipped chapter 10, either return to it and finish it or go to the Manning site and download the background and sprites for Beach Blast. The directions for importing are the same as chapter 5. You should have Buffy, a sandcastle, a crab, a vine, two side barrier lines, and three beach-themed backgrounds.

Preparing the Stage

I used the Grow tool in the Grey Toolbar to increase the size of Buffy (20 clicks), the castle (25 clicks), and the crab (12 clicks). Then we duplicated both the crab and the sandcastle, as shown in figure 11.2.

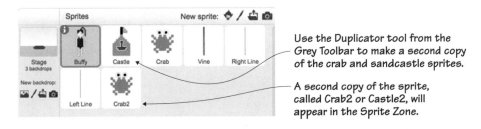

Use the Duplicator tool from the Grey Toolbar to make a second copy of the crab and sandcastle sprites.

A second copy of the sprite, called Crab2 or Castle2, will appear in the Sprite Zone.

Figure 11.2   You should have a second sprite called Crab2 and one called Castle2.

Switch the background to backdrop1 (the basic beach backdrop) by clicking the thumbnail in the Sprite Zone and making sure the blue box is around the first backdrop on the Costumes tab. Position the two sandcastles on either side of the Stage, about an inch from the left or right wall. Look at figure 11.3 to see the Stage layout.

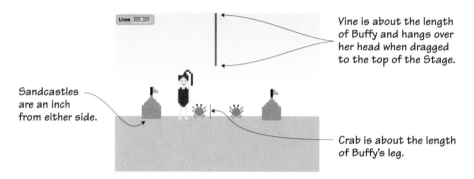

Figure 11.3   Only the sandcastles need to be positioned on backdrop1.

Programming Beachy Buffy

Beachy Buffy is the player character—the sprite on the screen controlled by the player. The player controls all of her actions using the arrow keys, and she has ten scripts to enable her to run, jump, fall, and grab the vine: a movement script, a falling velocity script, a falling script, a jumping script, a positioning script, a life deduction script, a background changing script, a zipline dismount script, and a two-part grabbing vine script. All scripts in this section are applied to Buffy, so go put the blue box around Buffy in the Sprite Zone and don't move the blue box until you program the sandcastles in the next section. Remember, the names or values on *your* blocks may differ slightly from time to time, so use the completed script images to make sure you chose the correct block.

Making a movement script

Buffy can't jump at the moment, but she also can't even run back and forth along the sand, as in figure 11.4.

Let's enable Buffy to run left and right:

1 Start with a When Flag Clicked (Events) block.

2 Snap a Forever (Control) block underneath to start a loop.

3 Place two If/Then (Control) blocks inside the Forever block.

4 Slide two Key Space Pressed (Sensing) blocks into the empty hexagonal spaces of the If/Then blocks to set the conditions.

Figure 11.4 **Buffy needs to be able to run left and right over the sand.**

5 Change the top Key Space Pressed block to Left Arrow using the drop-down menu. Change the bottom Key Space Pressed block to Right Arrow.

6 Slide a Change X by 10 (Motion) block inside each of the If/Then blocks. Change the first Change X by 10 block to –5. Change the second Change X by 10 block to 5.

Your script should look like the script in figure 11.5, and it will move Buffy five coordinate spaces to the left or right whenever the arrow

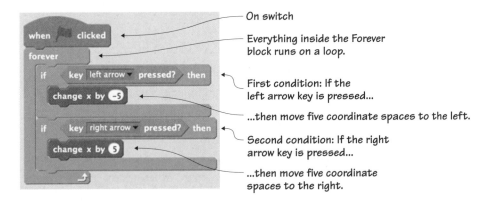

Figure 11.5 **The movement script allows Buffy to run left and right when the arrow keys are pressed.**

keys are pressed. You don't want Buffy to move too quickly and accidentally run into a sandcastle, so five coordinate spaces at a time is a perfect speed.

Making a falling velocity script

Simulating gravity is tricky. What happens to an object as it falls? It picks up speed. That includes people, like Beachy Buffy, as seen in figure 11.6.

 WHAT IS
VELOCITY?

Question: what is velocity?

Answer: what happens when you jump? Go ahead, get up from your chair and jump. Your feet leave the ground and now there is a Y coordinate marking your feet's location in the air. But wait, you don't hang in the air indefinitely. You start falling back toward the ground. You fall faster than you rise due to gravity. That is your *velocity*—the speed at which your body (or, in the case of a game, the sprite) is moving in a certain direction. Your Y velocity is how fast the person (or sprite) is falling within the Y coordinate, which is directionally up or down.

Buffy's speed increases the longer she falls.

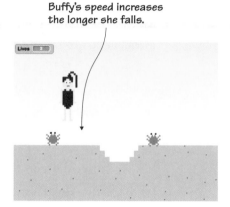

Figure 11.6   After a jump, Buffy's speed will increase the closer she gets to the sand.

This first of three simulated gravity scripts sets the changing rate at which Buffy will fall:

1 Start with a When Flag Clicked (Events) block.

2 Snap a Forever (Control) block underneath to start a loop.

3 Place an If/Then (Control) block inside the Forever block.

4 Slide a Not (Operators) block into the empty hexagonal space of the If/Then blocks to set a condition. This is what will happen if something is *not* true. If the statement is true, this script won't run. But if the statement is not true, whatever action you place inside the If/Then block will happen.

5 Drag a Touching Color (Sensing) block and place it inside the space on the Not block.

6 Change the color inside the Touching Color block square to the color of the sand. The condition is now if Beachy Buffy is not touching the sand.

7 Create a variable (Data) called yVelocity. Unclick the variable so it doesn't show up on the Stage.

ANSWER THIS   WHY USE STRANGE CAPITALIZATION FOR THE YVELOCITY VARIABLE?

Question: why make the y lowercase but the word *Velocity* uppercase?

Answer: programmers often write multi-word variables in something called *camelcase*, mostly because your words will start to resemble the humps of a camel. The first letter or word is always lowercase (in this example, *y*). The first letter of the next word is uppercase (in this example, *Velocity*). If there were more words smushed together to make this variable, all the other words would always start with an uppercase letter, too.

8 Drag a Change yVelocity by 1 (Data) block and place it inside the If/Then block. Change the number to –0.5.

If Buffy is not touching the sand—if her feet are in the air—then she will start to fall, with her speed increasing by half of a coordinate each loop. The script in figure 11.7 will work together with Buffy's falling script.

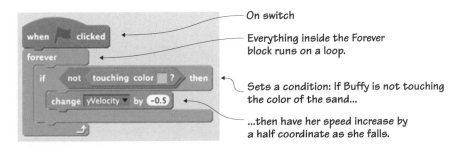

Figure 11.7   The falling velocity script mimics how gravity affects an object or a person, like Buffy.

Making a falling script

You now know how Buffy's speed will incrementally increase as she falls, but you haven't written a script that allows her to return to the sand, as in figure 11.8.

This script will allow Buffy to fall if she jumps up in the air:

1 Start with a When Flag Clicked (Events) block.

2 Snap a Forever (Control) block underneath to start a loop.

3 Place an If/Then/Else (Control) block inside the Forever block. This is a new type of conditional statement. It not only tells what will happen if a condition is met; it also states what will happen if a condition is not met, setting a second possible action.

4 Slide a Not (Operators) block inside the empty hexagonal space on the If/Then block.

5 Add a Touching Color (Sensing) block to the empty space on the Not block and once again change the color square to the color of the sand. The condition is if Buffy is not touching the sand.

6 Place a Change Y by 10 (Motion) block inside the If section of the If/Then/Else block.

7 Slide a yVelocity variable (Data) block into the number bubble on the Change Y by 10 block, as seen in figure 11.9. This will make the Y position change by the current value of the variable, which will always be increasing by a half coordi-

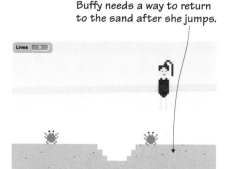

Buffy needs a way to return to the sand after she jumps.

Figure 11.8 Buffy needs to be able to get back down to the ground once she is in the air.

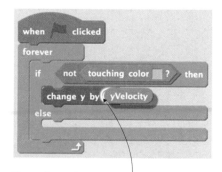

Place the yVelocity variable inside the number bubble on the Change Y by 10 block.

Figure 11.9 Put the variable inside the number bubble of the Change Y by 10 block.

nate each loop thanks to the Falling Velocity script. It means the longer Buffy falls, the faster she will fall, like in real life.

8   Add a Set yVelocity to 0 (Data) block inside the Else section of the If/Then/Else block. If Buffy is touching the sand, set the value of the variable yVelocity to zero (0) because she isn't falling.

That final instruction is true whether Buffy has stopped falling or hasn't fallen at all. Anytime Buffy is on the sand, the Else portion in figure 11.10 will be true, and anytime Buffy is in the air, the If portion is true.

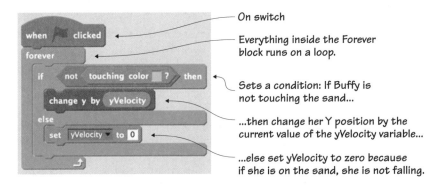

Figure 11.10   The falling script allows Buffy to fall back to the sand after she jumps in the air.

Making a jumping script

Buffy can return to the sand (falling script) and even have her body move in a realistic manner (falling velocity), but right now, her body can't get up in the air so those two other scripts can kick into action. She is stuck on the sand, as in figure 11.11.

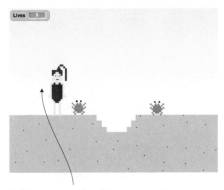

Figure 11.11   Buffy needs to be able to jump off the sand so she can sail over the obstacles.

Buffy needs to be able to go up in the air so she can jump over the crabs.

Make a script that will allow Buffy to jump off the sand.

1 Start with a When Space Key Pressed (Events) block. Change the key to Up Arrow using the drop-down menu on the block.

2 Place an If/Then (Control) block underneath to start a conditional.

3 Slide a Touching Color (Sensing) block to the empty space on the If/Then block. Change the color square to the color of the sand. The condition is if Buffy is touching the sand.

4 Position a Change Y by 10 (Motion) block inside the If/Then block. Change the number to 9 because you want Buffy to go nine coordinates into the air each time the up arrow is pressed.

FIX IT   BUFFY CAN'T JUMP OVER THE CRABS!   Until you run the game, you won't know whether the nine coordinates in Step Four will be enough to take Buffy over the crabs and sandcastles. In the future, you may need to increase this number if it's not high enough, or you can decrease it to make it even harder for Buffy to sail over obstacles.

5 Snap a Set yVelocity to 0 (Data) block underneath the Change Y by 9 block. This will change the value of the yVelocity variable to 9.

Check the script in figure 11.12. You'll notice that the yVelocity variable is now set to a positive number (9) rather than a negative number. This is because you want Buffy to have the ability to leave the sand and go up. It's working with the motion block to bring Buffy nine coordinate spaces into the air (because positive numbers go up), versus having Buffy receive conflicting information about where her body should go. This script works in harmony with the last two scripts to perform an action.

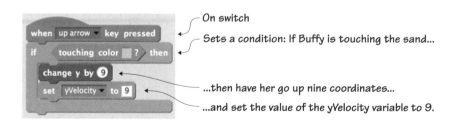

Figure 11.12   The jumping script gives Buffy a way to leave the ground.

LEARN IT   X AND Y COORDINATES   Geocaching is a game where people hide caches (usually a small box containing tiny toys or a log book) around the world and give the coordinates for the cache. Players can plug those coordinates into a GPS device and try to find the treasure. Similarly, Letterboxing is a game where people hide caches and write clues for the treasurer seeker, talking about things they'll see along the way such as a tree or a bridge. Using latitude and longitude coordinates is an exact way of giving directions; using landmarks is not because the landscape may change over time. Scratch likes exact directions, programmed into a game using X and Y coordinates. Scratch can't understand directions like "jump over the sandcastle," though it can understand "go up nine coordinates, go to the right five coordinates, and then go down nine coordinates." Going geocaching can help you to build better Scratch games because working with GPS coordinates will help you to think about the Stage in X and Y coordinates.

Making a positioning script

You have three backdrops, but which one will be on the screen when the game begins? Moreover, Buffy needs a starting point, a place to stand when the game begins, as in figure 11.13. Finally, you need to determine how many chances the player will get.

This script ensures that Buffy begins on the first backdrop and gets three chances:

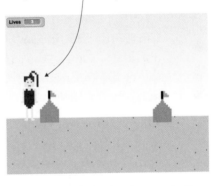

Buffy needs a starting point for the game.

Figure 11.13   Buffy begins the game to the left of the first sandcastle.

1 Start with a When Flag Clicked (Events) block.

2 Snap a Switch Backdrop to Backdrop3 (Looks) block underneath to set the proper backdrop to be on the screen when the game opens. Use the drop-down menu to change the option to backdrop1.

3 Add a Set X to 0 (Motion) block to the chain, changing the number to –180 to send Buffy to the left side of the Stage when the game opens. –240 is the left-most point on the Stage, so –180 is a centimeter or so from the edge.

4 Make a variable in Data called Lives. This will be the chances the player has to reach the end of the game. Move the variable bubble on the Stage to the top left corner.

5 Place a Set Lives to 0 (Data) block at the bottom. Change the number to 3 to give the player three chances.

The script in figure 11.14 sets three important elements at the beginning of the game: the backdrop, Buffy's position, and the number of chances.

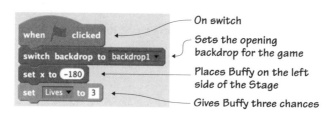

On switch

Sets the opening backdrop for the game

Places Buffy on the left side of the Stage

Gives Buffy three chances

Figure 11.14   The positioning script sets three elements of the game opening.

Making a life deduction script

Currently Buffy can touch the obstacles, such as the sandcastle or the crab, and nothing happens, as in figure 11.15.

This script removes a "life" every time Buffy touches a sandcastle, crab, or water obstacle. It's a long script, so check your work against the examples:

1 Start with a When Flag Clicked (Events) block.

2 Snap a Forever (Control) block underneath to start a loop.

3 Drag four If/Then (Control) blocks inside the Forever block to set up four conditionals.

4 Place a Touching Color (Sensing) block in the empty hexagonal space of the top If/Then block. Change the color square to the color

Buffy is touching the crab, but the game is not deducting a "life".

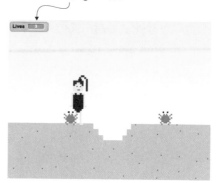

Figure 11.15   Buffy needs to lose a "life" every time she touches an obstacle.

of the water on backdrop3. Remember, you will need to switch to the backdrop if you're not currently on backdrop3 to grab the color and return to programming Buffy.

5 Slide a Hexagon or Hexagon (Operators) block into each of the empty hexagonal spaces in the second and third If/Then blocks.

6 Grab four Touching (Sensing) blocks and place them inside the four empty spaces of the Hexagon or Hexagon blocks. Use the drop-down menus to set the options in the first two Touching blocks to Crab and Crab2. Set the options in the second two Touching blocks to Castle and Castle2, as in figure 11.16.

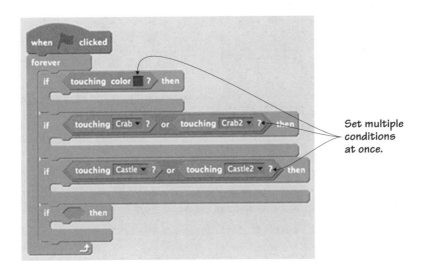

Figure 11.16 *Set three conditions at the same time.*

7 Place a Change Lives by 1 (Data) inside the first If/Then block. Change the number to –1 because you want to deduct a life if Buffy goes in the water.

8 Snap a Go to X/Y (Motion) block underneath, though still inside, the If/Then block. Change the X to –180 and the Y to 50. –180 sends Buffy back to the left side of the Stage, and 50 sends Buffy to the top of the sand, though you may need to play with those numbers.

9 Add a Wait 1 Secs (Control) block underneath the stack of blocks inside the If/Then block. This pause will ensure that only one life is removed.

10 Duplicate the three-block script inside the first If/Then block by right clicking (or Control + Clicking) the top Change Lives by –1 block. Choose Duplicate and drag the new three-block set inside the second If/Then block. Do this a second time and place the three-block set inside the third If/Then block, as in figure 11.17.

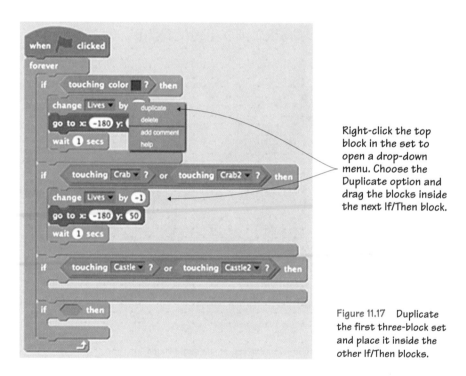

Right-click the top block in the set to open a drop-down menu. Choose the Duplicate option and drag the blocks inside the next If/Then block.

Figure 11.17   Duplicate the first three-block set and place it inside the other If/Then blocks.

11 Place a Square = Square (Operators) inside the final empty hexagonal space in the bottom If/Then block.

12 Slide a Lives (Data) variable into the left square and type the number zero (0) into the right square.

13 Drag a Stop All (Control) block inside the final If/Then block to stop all the scripts if the value of the Lives variable equals zero.

This long script is done! Look at figure 11.18 to make sure all your blocks are in the correct places.

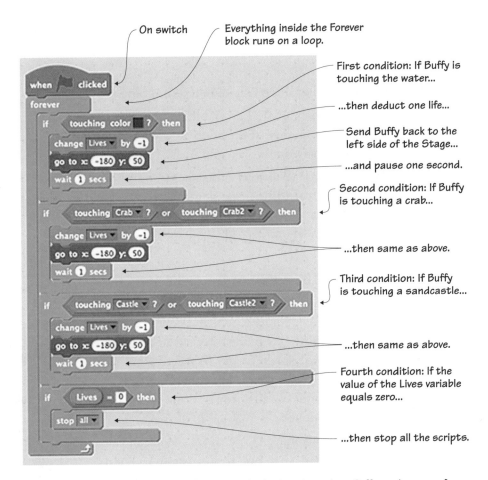

On switch

Everything inside the Forever block runs on a loop.

First condition: If Buffy is touching the water...

...then deduct one life...

Send Buffy back to the left side of the Stage...

...and pause one second.

Second condition: If Buffy is touching a crab...

...then same as above.

Third condition: If Buffy is touching a sandcastle...

...then same as above.

Fourth condition: If the value of the Lives variable equals zero...

...then stop all the scripts.

Figure 11.18 The life deduction script sets up multiple situations where Buffy can lose one of her lives.

Making the background changing script

Buffy can currently run to the left or right, but nothing happens when she touches a wall, as you can see in figure 11.19.

You need to make Buffy continue running along the next background when she reaches either side of the Stage.

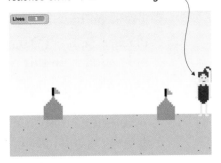

Figure 11.19 The backdrop needs to switch when Buffy touches either edge of the Stage.

This script will cause the backdrops to change whenever Buffy runs to the edge of the Stage. It's another long script, so check your work along the way:

1   Start with a When Flag Clicked (Events) block.

2   Place a Set Lives to 0 (Data) block underneath and use the drop-down menu to change the option to yVelocity. Keep the number at zero (0) because you don't want Buffy to begin the game falling!

3   Add a Set Y to 0 (Motion) block next and change the number to 50 to place Buffy on top of the sand. You may need to play with this number later.

4   Snap a Forever (Control) block next to start a loop.

5   Slide two If/Then (Control) blocks into the Forever block. Then place a third If/Then block inside the top If/Then block, as in figure 11.20.

6   Place a Touching (Sensing) block inside the empty hexagonal space of the first, external If/Then block. Use the drop-down menu to set it to the Right Line, because the actions will happen if Buffy touches the right side of the Stage.

7   Put a Square = Square (Operators) block in the empty hexagonal space of the internal If/Then block. (Look at figure 11.21 if you're confused about placement.)

Figure 11.20   Three conditions are set inside the Forever loop block.

8   Make a variable in Data called Zipline. This will track whether the vine is in use during the game. Uncheck the box because you don't want the variable to be visible on the Stage.

9   Place a Zipline (Data) variable in the left square and type a 1 in the right square. In this case, the value of 1 means true, or on.

10   Slide a Change Zipline by 1 (Data) block inside the internal If/Then block. Use the drop-down menu to change the option to Lives and change the number to –1, because you want the game to deduct a life if Buffy is still holding onto the vine when she reaches the right wall.

11 Add a Set X to 0 (Motion) block to the chain inside the If/Then block, changing the number to –180 to return Buffy to the left side of the Stage.

12 Snap a Set Zipline to 0 (Data) block to the chain and keep everything as is because you want the zipline to be turned off (or zero) if Buffy hits the right wall.

13 Complete this section with a Stop All (Control) block. Use the drop-down menu to set it to This Script, as in figure 11.21.

14 Place a Set X to 0 (Motion) block underneath the internal If/Then block but inside the top If/Then block. Change the number to –180 to send Buffy to the left side of the Stage.

15 Add a Set Y to 0 (Motion) block to the chain and change the number to 50 to place Buffy on top of the sand.

16 Put a Broadcast Message (Events) block at the bottom of the chain inside the If/Then block. Use the drop-down menu to choose New Message, as in figure 11.22. Call this message Right.

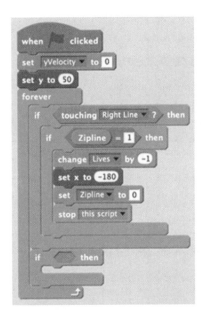

Figure 11.21   Certain actions will happen if Buffy hits the right wall while holding the vine.

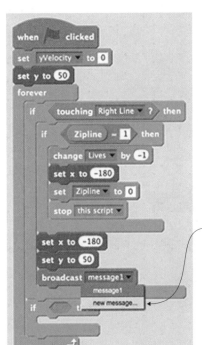

Set a new message to send to the other script.

Figure 11.22   Set a new message called Right that will broadcast if Buffy touches the right wall.

17 Fill in the final If/Then block by placing a Touching (Sensing) block in the empty hexagonal space. Use the drop-down menu to choose Left Line. This is what will happen if Buffy touches the left side of the Stage.

18 Place a Set X to 0 (Motion) block inside the If/Then block and change the number to 180 to send Buffy to the right side of the Stage.

19 Slide a Set Y to 0 (Motion) block underneath but still inside the If/Then block and change the number to 50 to send Buffy to the top of the sand.

20 Add a Broadcast Message (Events) block and use the drop-down menu to set a new message called Left.

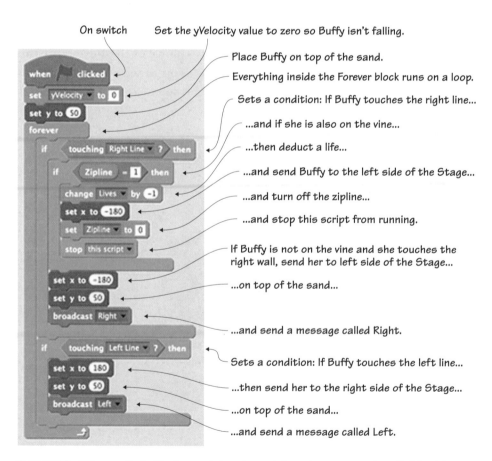

Figure 11.23   This complicated background changing script sends a message to switch backdrops.

Figure 11.23 shows the completed script. Because you are a seasoned Scratch programmer, you know that you still need to make a receiver script to catch the message that this script sends out to the game. That receiver script will change the backdrop once it receives this broadcasted message that Buffy has touched the left or right wall. Additionally, this script sets actions to occur if Buffy happens to touch the right wall while she's holding onto the vine. They're all negative actions because Buffy is supposed to drop off the vine when she reaches the other side of the water obstacle.

Making the zipline dismount script

Soon you'll code Buffy to jump up so she can catch the zipline or vine, as she's done in figure 11.24, but before that happens, you need to make it so she can drop off the zipline. You know from the last script that bad things happen if she's still holding onto the zipline when she touches the right wall.

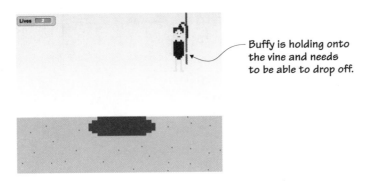

Figure 11.24   Buffy needs to drop off the vine once she is across the water.

This script will allow Buffy to release the vine after she is past the water obstacle:

1 Start with a When Space Key Pressed (Events) block. Change the key to Down Arrow using the drop-down menu on the block.

2 Snap a Set Y to 0 (Motion) block underneath. Change the number to 50 to send Buffy back to the sand after she drops off the vine.

3 Add a Set Zipline to 0 (Data) block. Keep it as is because you want the zipline to be set to off, or false, which is indicated by the zero (0) and means Buffy isn't on the vine.

Look at figure 11.25 to see if you have your blocks in the same order.

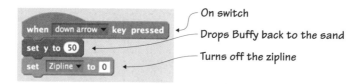

Figure 11.25   The completed zipline dismount script lets Buffy drop off the vine.

Making the two-part vine grabbing script

The last script gave Buffy the ability to drop off the vine after she gets over the water, but you also need to give Buffy the ability to grab onto the zipline when she jumps up. Currently, she can keep jumping and touching the zipline, but she isn't able to grab it as she can in figure 11.26.

The first part of this script detects whether Buffy has touched the vine. The second part allows Buffy to grab and remain on the zipline until you want her to drop off:

Buffy needs to be able to grab on when she jumps up and touches the vine.

Figure 11.26   Write a script that will allow Buffy to grab onto the vine.

1 Start with a When Flag Clicked (Events) block.

2 Slide a Forever (Control) block underneath to start a loop.

3 Place an If/Then (Control) block inside the Forever block to set up a condition.

4 Add a Touching (Sensing) block inside the empty hexagonal space on the If/Then block. Use the drop-down menu to set it to Vine.

5 Grab a Broadcast Message (Events) block and place it inside the If/Then block. Use the drop-down menu to make a new message called Zipline.

6 Place a Wait 1 Secs (Control) block underneath the Broadcast Zipline block inside the If/Then block. Change the number to .0001, because you only want it to be a fraction of a second.

The first part of this script checks if Buffy is on the vine. If she is touching the vine, it broadcasts a message to the second part of the script to keep her on the vine. Check the first part of the script in figure 11.27 and get ready to write the second part of the script.

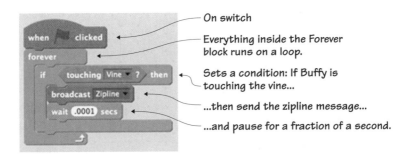

Figure 11.27   The first part of the grabbing vine script detects whether Buffy has touched the zipline.

The second part of the script is written separately as a new script, but these two parts work in tandem (together) with each other. The second script keeps Buffy on the vine until the player presses the down arrow to return to the sand:

1 Start with a When I Receive Left (Events) block. Use the drop-down menu to change the message to Zipline. This script receives the message sent by the last script and knows that Buffy has touched the vine. It is ready to spring into action.

2 Snap a Go to X/Y (Motion) block underneath.

3 Go to Data and make two variables, one called zipX and one called zipY. These two variables will allow the vine to continuously change its X and Y position and move over the water. Uncheck both variables so they don't show up on the Stage.

4 Slide a zipX (Data) variable into the number bubble for the X coordinate on the Go to X/Y block. Place a Circle – Circle (Operators) block in the number bubble for the Y coordinate, as shown in figure 11.28. Add a zipY (Data) variable in the left circle, and type the number 10 in the right circle so Buffy will be holding the vine a little under its center.

Place the Circle - Circle block inside the number bubble for the Y coordinate.

Figure 11.28   Place a Circle – Circle block in the number bubble for the Y coordinate so Buffy is dangling 10 coordinates under the current value of the zipY variable, which will be set when you program the vine.

5 Add two Set zipY to 0 (Data) blocks to the chain, one on top of the other. Use the drop-down menu to change the first block to yVelocity. Keep the number at zero (0) because you do not want Buffy to start falling. Use the drop-down menu to change the second block to Zipline. Change the number to 1, which means that the zipline is true, or on, because it's in use.

The second part of the vine grabbing script is complete. Check your work against figure 11.29 and breathe a huge sigh of relief. You've finished programming Beachy Buffy.

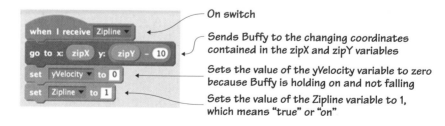

— On switch

— Sends Buffy to the changing coordinates contained in the zipX and zipY variables

Sets the value of the yVelocity variable to zero because Buffy is holding on and not falling

Sets the value of the Zipline variable to 1, which means "true" or "on"

Figure 11.29   The completed second part of the vine grabbing script keeps Buffy on the zipline.

Programming the sandcastle

Beach Blast has stationary sandcastle obstacles, which are like *Pitfall*'s flickering fires. Buffy has to jump over them to get to the next backdrop. A single script powers the sandcastles. To program them, make sure the blue box is around the first sandcastle in the Sprite Zone.

Making a show or hide script

The sandcastles are always on the screen, though you can only see them on certain backdrops. They appear when Buffy is running on the basic beach backdrop, and they disappear when Buffy runs into the other two scenes. They are still technically on the screen, though they are hidden, as you can see from the empty squares that appear on the Stage in figure 11.30 whenever I click the sandcastles in the Sprite Zone.

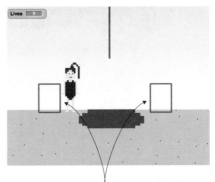

The sandcastles are always on the Stage, though Show and Hide blocks determine whether they are seen. On this backdrop, the sandcastles are present but hidden.

Figure 11.30   The sandcastles are always there, though you can only see them on certain backdrops.

This script will cause them to appear or disappear depending on the backdrop:

1 Start with a When Flag Clicked (Events) block.

2 Place a Forever (Control) block underneath to start a loop.

3 Position an If/Then/Else (Control) block inside the Forever block.

4 Slide a Square = Square (Operators) into the empty hexagonal space on the If/Then block. Place a Backdrop Name (Looks) block in the left square, and type *backdrop1* (lowercase and without spaces) in the right square. The condition is if backdrop1 is on the screen.

5 Place a Show (Looks) block inside the If section of the If/Then block.

6 Slip a Hide (Looks) block inside the Else section of the If/Then block.

The script in figure 11.31 sets up a simple condition: if backdrop1 is on the screen, the sandcastles will be visible, or else if it's any other backdrop, the sandcastles will be hidden.

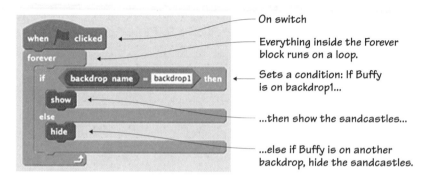

Figure 11.31   **The completed show or hide script makes the sandcastles appear and disappear.**

Duplicating the show or hide script

There are two sandcastles in the game, but you don't need to build the script a second time. Instead, apply the script to the other sandcastle by clicking the When Flag Clicked block and dragging all the blocks (they should move as a set) to the Sprite Zone. Hover over the other sandcastle sprite, as in figure 11.32, and release the mouse button.

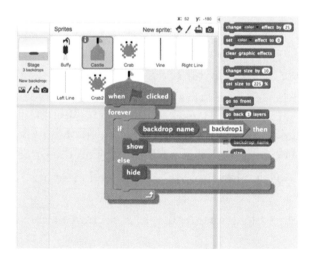

Figure 11.32   **Drag the script and hover over the other sandcastle in the Sprite Zone.**

The script should now appear in both sandcastle sprites' Script Areas. Click back and forth between the two sprites in the Sprite Zone and check the Script Area to make sure the same script is in both places.

Programming the crabs

Beach Blast has two snapping crabs that run back and forth along the sand, similar to the scorpions in *Pitfall*. You only need to write these scripts for one crab, and then you will transfer them to the other crab using the hover method. Make sure the blue box is around the first crab in the Sprite Zone, and keep it on the crab for both scripts in this section. The crab requires two scripts: a similar show or hide script as used with the sandcastles and a movement script.

Tweaking the show or hide script

The same script that you used to show or hide the sandcastles also works with the crabs, which remain on the screen but are only seen on backdrop2 (as opposed to the sandcastles which are seen on backdrop1). Rather than remake the script, go to either sandcastle sprite and drag the script into the first crab in the Sprite Zone.

The script needs to be tweaked in order to show the crabs at the correct time. Change backdrop1 to backdrop2, as in figure 11.33.

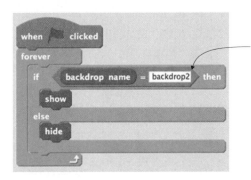

Change the backdrop name after you drag it into the crab's Script Area. This single change is all you need to make the crabs appear at the correct time.

Figure 11.33 Changing backdrop1 to backdrop2 makes the crabs appear at the correct time.

Once you've made this change, drag this tweaked script and hover over the second crab in the Sprite Zone. Release and check that both crabs have the same script, showing backdrop2 as the condition.

Making a movement script

Now that Buffy can jump over stationary sandcastles, it's time to give her a harder obstacle—moving crabs, as seen in figure 11.34.

The crabs move back and forth on either side of the hole. Remember, the crabs are technically on the screen at all times, though you can only see them on backdrop2. This script will program the crabs to only move when you are on the crab's backdrop. You can code either crab sprite because you will duplicate and tweak the code for the other sprite:

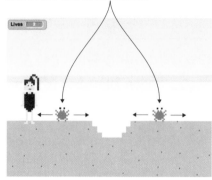

The crabs run back and forth on either side of the hole in the center.

Figure 11.34   The crabs move back and forth next to the hole.

1 Start with a When Flag Clicked (Events) block.

2 Snap a Forever (Control) block underneath to start a loop.

3 Place an If/Then (Control) block inside the Forever block.

4 Slide a Square = Square (Operators) block into the empty hexagonal space of the If/Then block. Put a Backdrop Name (Looks) block in the left square, and type backdrop2 in the right square.

5 Put a Go to X/Y (Motion) block inside the Forever block *above* the If/Then block, as in figure 11.35. You will need to play with these numbers later, but for now, set the X position to –148 and the Y position to –40 so the crab is on top of the sand to the left of the hole.

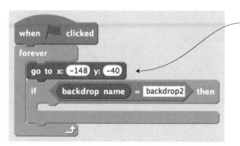

Place the Motion block inside the Forever block but above the If/Then block. You want the crab to always go to the same place, though you only want the crab to move if it is on the correct backdrop.

Figure 11.35   Place the Go to X/Y block above the condition so it happens all the time.

6 Stack two Repeat 10 (Control) blocks inside the If/Then block. Change both values to 20 so the action repeats 20 times.

7 Place a Move 10 Steps (Motion) block inside each Repeat 20 block. Change the top Move 10 Steps block to 5 and the bottom Move 10 Steps block to –5. This will make the crab move 20 five-step increments to the right and then switch and move 20 five-step increments to the left, over and over again.

That's the entire script. Check your work against figure 11.36.

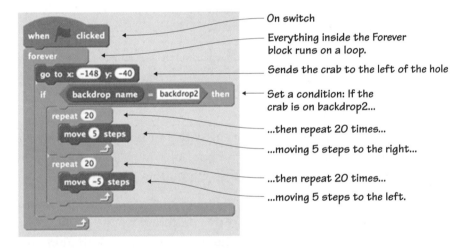

Figure 11.36   The completed movement script makes the crabs a difficult obstacle.

One crab is now to the left of the hole, moving back and forth when Buffy is on backdrop2. But what about the second crab? You're going to use the hover method to drop the script into the second crab's Script Area and then tweak a single number to place it on the right side of the hole.

By turning the –148 into a 48, as seen in figure 11.37, the second crab turns up to the right of the hole, making a true obstacle course for Buffy. You may need to tweak that number again when you start troubleshooting the game, but for now, you should have the two scripts in both crabs in the Sprite Zone.

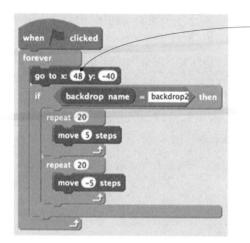

Play with the X position of the crab to have the second crab on the right side of the hole.

Figure 11.37   Tweak the X position of the crab to send the second crab to the right of the hole.

Programming the vine

The obstacle sprites are out of the way, but now you need to program a tool that will take you over the pool of water. The water is drawn on the backdrop, but the vine is a sprite that moves.

According to David Crane, the maker of *Pitfall*, the vine is a one-pixel sprite that has its angle constantly computed by the game. The position of that sprite keeps changing due to some fancy math going on behind the scenes in the game. To simplify the code, *your* vine for Beach Blast is not going to swing back and forth diagonally. Instead it will move horizontally the moment Beachy Buffy jumps out and grabs it.

Make sure the blue box is around the vine in the Sprite Zone, and keep it on the vine for all scripts in this section. The vine requires three scripts: a starter script, a positioning script, and a movement script.

Making a starter script

Like the sandcastles and crabs, the vine is always on the screen, but you can only see it on the water backdrop (backdrop3), as shown in figure 11.38.

This script hides the vine if Buffy is not on backdrop3, and shows the vine dangling from the top center of the Stage if she is on the water background:

1 Start with a When Flag Clicked (Events) block.

2 Snap a Set zipY to 0 (Data) block underneath and use the drop-down menu to change the option to Zipline. Leave the number at zero (0), because you are setting the zipline to false, or off.

3 Add a Hide (Looks) block to the chain to make the vine invisible on the screen.

4 Place a Forever (Control) block underneath to start a loop.

5 Slide an If/Then/Else (Control) block and an If/Then (Control) block inside the Forever block, one on top of the other, as in figure 11.39.

6 Drag a Square = Square (Operators) block into each of the conditional blocks' empty hexagonal spaces.

7 Place a Backdrop Name (Looks) block into the left square of the Square = Square block on the If/Then/Else block and type backdrop3 in the right square. The first condition is if Buffy is on backdrop3.

The vine hangs from the top center of the Stage, but is only visible on backdrop3.

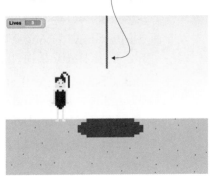

Figure 11.38 The vine dangles from the top center of the Stage and is visible on backdrop3.

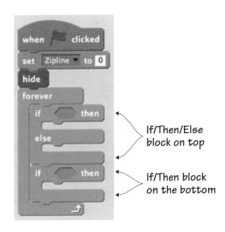

If/Then/Else block on top

If/Then block on the bottom

Figure 11.39 Add two conditional blocks inside the loop block.

8 Place a Zipline (Data) block in the left square of the Square = Square block on the If/Then block and type 0 in the right square. The second condition is if the zipline is off, or false.

9 Slip a Show (Looks) block inside the If section of the If/Then/Else block. If Buffy is on backdrop3, you want the vine to be visible.

10 Put a Set zipY to 0 (Data) block in the Else section of the If/Then/Else block. Use the drop-down menu to change the option to Zipline and keep the number at 0, which in this case means off, or false.

11 Snap a Hide (Looks) block underneath the Set Zipline to 0 block, because if Buffy is not on backdrop3, you want the vine to continue to hide.

12 Put a Set X to 0 (Motion) block inside the If/Then block. This sends the vine to the center of the Stage.

Check your script against figure 11.40 before you move on to positioning the vine.

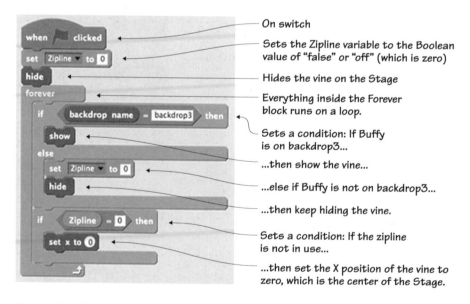

Figure 11.40   The completed starter script either shows or hides the vine.

Making a positioning script

The last script sent the vine to the center of the Stage, over the water, but the vine isn't a stationary object like the sandcastles. The vine moves during the game, as shown in figure 11.41.

This script will track where the vine is on the screen and make that X position or Y position the value of the zipX or zipY variable. For instance, when the vine is at X:55, the value of zipX is 55:

The position of the vine keeps changing as it travels across the screen, and the zipX and zipY variables keep track of where the vine is at all times.

Figure 11.41   The vine moves over the water, changing its position.

1 Start with a When Flag Clicked (Events) block.

2 Snap a Set Y to 0 (Motion) block underneath and change the number to 120 to place the vine near the top of the Stage. You may need to tweak this number later.

3 Place a Forever (Control) block next to start a loop.

4 Slide two Set zipY to 0 (Data) blocks inside the Forever block. Use the drop-down menu to change the top block to zipX.

5 Put an X Position (Motion) block inside the number space on the Set zipX to 0 block, as shown in figure 11.42. Put a Y Position block in the number space on the Set zipY to 0 block.

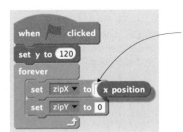

Place the variable block in the number space so the zipX variable's value is the location of the vine on the screen.

Figure 11.42   You can always place blocks inside any space where you can type a number.

The script in figure 11.43 is now complete and will keep checking the position of the vine and setting the value of the zipX and zipY variables according to where it is on the screen. This is important to know because Buffy needs to move *with* the vine, so the value of those variables will affect where Buffy is on the screen, too.

On switch

Set the vine's Y position to 120 near the top of the Stage.

Everything in the Forever block runs on a loop.

Set the value of zipX to the current X position of the vine.

Set the value of zipY to the current Y position of the vine.

Figure 11.43   The completed positioning script tracks where the vine is on the screen.

Making a movement script

But wait! The vine can't move yet as it's doing in figure 11.44, so that last script has nothing to track.

This script will make the vine move over the water hazard and keep going until it reaches the right side of the Stage or Buffy jumps off:

1 Start with a When I Receive Left (Events) block. Use the drop-down menu to change the option to Zipline. This script kicks into action when it receives the Zipline message.

The vine moves over the water hazard.

Figure 11.44   The vine needs to be able to move over the water when Buffy turns it on by touching it.

2 Snap an If/Then/Else (Control) block underneath to set a condition.

3 Place a Square = Square (Operators) block in the empty hexagonal space of the If/Then/Else block. Put a Zipline (Data) variable in the

left square and type 1 in the right square to indicate that the value is on, or true.

4 Slide a Repeat 10 (Control) block inside the If section of the If/Then/Else block.

5 Put a Change X by 10 (Motion) block inside the Repeat 10 block. Change the 10 to a 5 because 10 will move too quickly for Buffy to drop off once she is across the water.

6 Slide a Set zipY to 0 (Data) block into the Else section and use the drop-down menu to change the option to Zipline. Keep the number at zero (0) to indicate off, or false.

7 Put a Go to X/Y (Motion) block under the Set Zipline to 0 block. Make the X:0 and the Y:120. This will send the vine back to the top center of the Stage when it is not in use.

Does your script look like the one in figure 11.45?

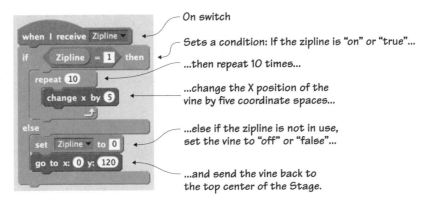

Figure 11.45   *The completed movement script allows the vine to slide to the right.*

All the sprites have been programmed, but you still have a few odds and ends to cover before you can begin troubleshooting the game.

Programming the odds and ends

Although you're accustomed to having a barrier line at the bottom of the Stage, this game uses barrier lines on the left and right sides of the

Stage to help the background change as Buffy runs across the screen. Additionally, you'll need to write two short programs for the backdrops themselves to ensure the correct one pops up when Buffy runs to the left or right side of the Stage.

Making a line positioning script

The left and right lines need to be placed on the left and right sides of the Stage to ensure that they're in the correct positions, as seen in figure 11.46. Start with the Left Line (and make sure the blue box is around it in the Sprite Zone).

Touching the left line on this screen will switch the backdrop to backdrop3.

Touching the right line on this screen will switch the backdrop to backdrop2.

Figure 11.46   The lines are against the far left and far right sides of the Stage.

Make the usual, brief positioning script in order to send the left line (that was drawn on the far left side of the canvas) into the proper position:

1 Start with a When Flag Clicked (Events) block.

2 Add a Forever (Control) block underneath to start a loop.

3 Snap a Go to X/Y (Motion) block and make sure both numbers are set to zero (0), as in figure 11.47, to send the center of the sprite to the center of the Stage.

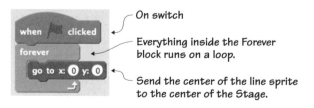

On switch

Everything inside the Forever block runs on a loop.

Send the center of the line sprite to the center of the Stage.

Figure 11.47   The completed positioning script sends the line to the correct place.

You need to use the hover method to send this script to the other line, too. Drop this script into the Right Line sprite in the Sprite Zone and check that this tiny script appears in both places before you move on to programming the backdrops. Both values should still be set to zero (0).

Making a previous backdrop script

Although you've tucked code into the backdrop before, these two scripts will be a little different. In order to write a program that applies to all the backdrops, navigate to the Sprite Zone and make sure the blue box is around the thumbnail of the backdrop (marked Stage) on the far left side of the Sprite Zone. You should see a blank Script Area open up on the right side of the screen. This is where you'll be dragging your blocks.

You need to write a program that allows Buffy to return to the previous backdrop if she runs to the left. If she's on the crab backdrop (backdrop2) and she runs to the left, she will find herself again on the sandcastle backdrop (backdrop1):

1 Start with a When I Receive Left (Events) block. This script kicks into gear when it receives the Left message.

2 Snap a Switch Backdrop to Backdrop3 (Looks) block.

3 Place a Circle – Circle (Operators) block into the drop-down menu space on the Switch Backdrop block, as in figure 11.48.

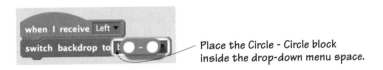
Place the Circle - Circle block inside the drop-down menu space.

Figure 11.48   Place the Operators block into the drop-down menu space.

4 Slide a Backdrop # (Looks) block into the left circle. Type a 1 into the right circle. This means that Scratch will check the number of the backdrop Buffy is currently on and subtract one backdrop. If she's on backdrop3, she'll go to backdrop2.

The script in figure 11.49 switches the backdrop if Buffy goes to the left. But what happens if she goes to the right?

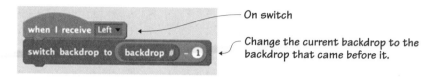

Figure 11.49   **This previous backdrop script changes the backdrop if Buffy runs to the left.**

Making a next backdrop script

Making the backdrop switch when Buffy goes to the left required a little workaround script with a real-time subtraction problem. Making the backdrop switch when Buffy goes to the right is a little easier due to an included Scratch block that allows for backdrop switches:

1 Start with a When I Receive Left (Events) block. Use the drop-down menu to change the option to Right. This script kicks into gear when it receives the Right message.

2 Snap a Next Backdrop (Looks) block underneath.

That's it! Figure 11.50 shows the final script. It's time to play Beach Blast.

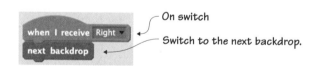

Figure 11.50   **Use Scratch's built-in backdrop switching block to move forward.**

LEARN IT   TYPES OF PLATFORMERS   There are two types of platformers: multi-screen platformers and single-screen platformers. *Pitfall* is a multi-screen platformer. When you move Pitfall Harry, he switches screens—256 of them, to be exact. Making a game like *Pitfall* on Scratch means making a lot of backgrounds. Super Mario Bros is a single-screen platformer. When you move Mario, he's running in place and the screen is moving. Don't worry, you'll get a chance to try your hand at a single-screen platformer with School Escape.

Troubleshooting your game

The first time I played my version of the game, the crabs were floating in the sky! It's difficult to know the exact X and Y positions of sprites, especially if you didn't draw your crabs in the center of the canvas. The first step will be to center both of your crabs. Turn back to chapter 9 if you need a reminder of how to center sprites. If your crabs are still above the sand, tweak their Y position so they can be running along the surface. Any sprite positioned with code can be helped by centering.

The second problem encountered was a layering issue with the vine. Buffy could grab on, but she couldn't drop off. If you run into this problem, navigate Buffy to backdrop3 by running to the left after starting the game. Click the stop sign above the Stage to stop the game, and click the vine, moving it slightly so it becomes the top layer.

The third possible issue is tweaking the values in various blocks, such as the Y-position of Buffy's feet on the sand at 50, or the placement of the vine at 120. Look back at all the times you were told to play with the value and adjust the numbers. Although I didn't need to adjust any values, you may want Buffy to jump higher or for the vine to hang lower.

Learning in action

X and Y coordinates featured heavily in Beach Blast. You even made variables that will track the X and Y coordinates of the vine, ensuring that Buffy can travel with the vine, over the water. You can always check a sprite's X and Y by touching your mouse pointer to the sprite and looking at the X and Y position listed under the Stage.

Play with the code

Pitfall has 256 screens. Beach Blast only has 3. Expanding the game means hours of play.

CHALLENGE   Create new backdrops. You won't need to write any additional code, though you will need to add obstacles to these backdrops for Buffy to jump over. You can either use the same obstacles or create other objects or animals found on the beach.

CHALLENGE   Right now, Buffy always regenerates on the left side of the current backdrop. Can you figure out a way to use a variable that will have Buffy start from the left side or the right side depending upon where she lost a turn on the Stage?

CHALLENGE   Create another character, either by drawing them on the backdrop or making a sprite. Have Buffy win the game by reaching this character on the last screen.

CHALLENGE   Add a points system to the game. Make shell sprites and scatter them through the game. Every time Buffy collects one, it adds to her overall score. You can also make obstacles that will remove points, such as stepping on a towel or running into a beach umbrella.

CHALLENGE   Play with the difficulty level of the game. You can change the height that Buffy can jump to make getting over sandcastles harder or easier. You can place obstacles such as the sandcastles closer together, and you can play with the speed at which the vine moves or Buffy runs to make the game more challenging. If you add more levels by adding more backdrops, you may also want to make the obstacles more difficult, such as increasing the speed or range of the crabs.

What did you learn?

Before you jump back to running down the beach, take a moment to reflect which common computer science ideas from chapter 3 were used in this game:

- Using an on switch for every script in the game, including using receiver hat blocks to kick into gear when they get a broadcasted message
- Setting X and Y coordinates to simulate gravity and enable Buffy to jump
- Writing If/Then/Else conditional statements to account for two possible situations
- Creating loops to have the crabs run back and forth
- Building variables to track the location of the vine

- Using Booleans to make true or false statements to detect whether Buffy is on the zipline
- Broadcasting messages between scripts to switch backdrops

Another seven out of eight common programming ideas! Additionally, in Beach Blast you learned

- How to simulate gravity so jumping and falling looks realistic
- How to make enemies or obstacles that move back and forth
- How to turn true or false statements into ones or zeros
- How to use variables to track a moving sprite
- How to make a multi-screen platformer

Pitfall influenced *Super Mario Bros*, so it's fitting that you will use everything you learned in this platformer to make a single-screen platformer called School Escape. If you're ready to start making your player character teacher jump onto desks and over kindergarteners, turn the page.

12

Making a single-screen platformer

Ms. Finebean is late for her brother's wedding. This teacher knew it would be a tight squeeze to get from her school to the ceremony on time, so she came to school already dressed up. Now she needs to navigate her way out of the school, except there are 30 clingy kindergarteners, shown in figure 12.1, in her way.

School Escape is a single-screen side-scrolling platformer. Although it will look as if Ms. Finebean is racing across the screen, leaping onto her desk and over students, the main sprite will be running in place while the other sprites move toward her.

Figure 12.1 A game of School Escape requires a single backdrop, a teacher, four variations of kindergarteners, a clock, a desk, and a door to the outside world.

This is how Nintendo's 1985 hit *Super Mario Bros* operates. Mario looks as if he is running forward to jump onto the brick platforms in order to collect coins and flowers and move over the Goombas (which are, strangely enough, mushrooms with legs), but it's really the platforms, backgrounds, and sprites coming at Mario, who can only jump up and down.

Drawing the sprites for this game means thinking about shadows and how they add realism to even cartoonish drawings. Although you've worked on adding shading *to* objects, for this game you're going to think about the way light interacts with objects *beyond* the surface.

In this chapter, you will learn

- How to add shadows to make objects look more realistic
- How to tweak a single sprite so it looks like multiple sprites
- How to use shadows to show the direction of the light source

You'll start off making a simple backdrop because you want the focus to be on the sprites in the foreground and not the background scene.

Prepping the backgrounds

You're back to making a single game backdrop. The goal is to make the background simple so that it doesn't distract from the sprites, such as the desk and kindergarteners.

Making the school backdrop

This backdrop will not technically move like the sprites in front of it, so it's important not to put decorations on the walls, such as school posters or windows, that would break the illusion. You're looking for something simple, such as figure 12.2.

Figure 12.2   The brown floor and grey wall keep the focus on the sprites in the foreground.

Open the Backdrop Art Editor and get ready to make the school backdrop:

1 Select the medium brown paint sample square and click the Line tool.

2 Draw a horizontal line about one-third up from the bottom. Use the Paint Bucket tool to fill the bottom of the Stage.

3 Switch to a medium grey paint sample square and fill the top portion of the Stage.

Your backdrop should look like the empty school hallway background in figure 12.3.

Prepping the main sprites

There are five main sprites you need to make for School Escape: a clock, a door, a desk, Ms. Fine-

Figure 12.3   The completed school backdrop is a drab, empty hallway.

bean, and a single kindergartener who will be tweaked to turn into at least four students. Delete the default cat sprite before you begin.

Making the clock

Super Mario Bros has its fireball power-up, and School Escape its clock, shown in figure 12.4, which buys the player more time.

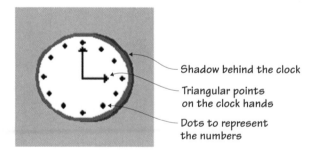

Shadow behind the clock

Triangular points on the clock hands

Dots to represent the numbers

Figure 12.4   The clock stands out from the wall due to the shadow behind it.

Open the Art Editor to make the clock:

1 Zoom in to 400%. Choose the darkest brown paint sample square and the Circle tool.

2 Draw a circle on the canvas that is 12 grey-and-white squares across.

3 Switch to a lighter shade of brown in the paint sample squares and draw a second circle above and to the left of the first circle.

4 Use the dot in the center of the second circle to drag it until it is touching the *inside* line of the first circle on the right side, as in figure 12.5.

12 grey-and-white squares across

Draw a light brown circle near the dark brown circle.

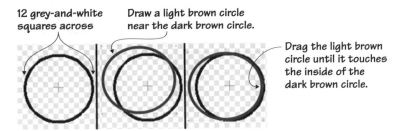

Drag the light brown circle until it touches the inside of the dark brown circle.

Figure 12.5   The darker circle should be visible on the right side after the second circle is moved into place.

5 Select the white paint sample square and fill in the inside of the light brown circle using the Paint Bucket tool, erasing the curved line from the dark brown circle with the white paint.

6 Switch to the black paint sample square and make four dots in the spaces for 12, 3, 6, and 9 on a clock.

7 Fill in the remaining dots, placing two in between the anchor dots already on the clock face, as shown in figure 12.6.

Fill center with white paint, erasing the dark brown line with paint, too.

Make four anchor dots.

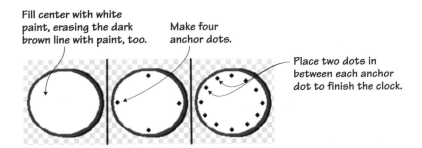

Place two dots in between each anchor dot to finish the clock.

Figure 12.6   Using anchor dots makes it easier to space the "numbers" on the clock.

8 Click the Line tool and draw two lines, one shorter than the other, extending in two directions from the center of the clock.

9 Return to the Paintbrush tool and make a triangle on the end of each line by making a line of five dots, topped by a line of three dots, topped by a line of one dot, like figure 12.7.

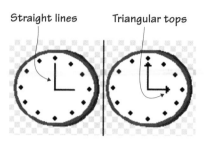

Figure 12.7   The clock is completed with two hands topped by triangular pointers.

The clock is now complete, as shown in figure 12.8. The technique of drawing double circles and erasing part of the line is an easy way to produce a drawing that looks three-dimensional due to the shadow. Go to the Sprite Zone and rename this sprite Clock.

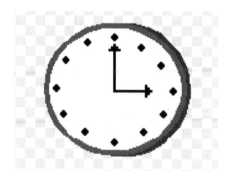

Figure 12.8   The completed clock sprite

LEARN IT   SHADOWS   Shadow is what happens when a ray of light meets a solid object. It can't go through it, so it makes a darker version of the object on the surface it couldn't reach. Look around the room you're in and note a shadow. This shouldn't be difficult unless you're sitting in the dark! Now examine the shadow. It's not one solid shade, is it? There are darker parts to the shadow and lighter parts. That's because light isn't hitting the object only in one place, which means there are multiple shadows that overlap. A two-dimensional object can't cast a shadow because it isn't a solid shape. By adding a shadow behind an object in a drawing, you're telling the viewer they should consider it a three-dimensional shape. The shadows you'll make for this game will all be a single shade, but if you want to add even more realism, make the color fade slightly on the edges.

Making the door

The door in figure 12.9 only appears at the end of the game, and it's Ms. Finebean's escape hatch. Reach that door and the game ends.

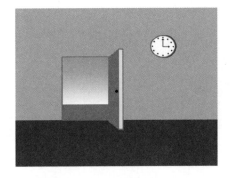

Figure 12.9 **The door provides high contrast with the boring hallway.**

Start a new sprite to make the door:

1 Keep the Art Editor zoomed in to 400%.

2 Choose a dark grey paint sample square and the Square tool.

3 Draw a vertical rectangle outline about 11 grey-and-white squares across, and then make two diagonal lines from the top and bottom right corners of the rectangle.

4 Connect the two diagonal lines with a vertical line, and finally make two tiny horizontal lines to extend the ends of the diagonal lines, connecting these horizontal lines with another vertical line, as in figure 12.10.

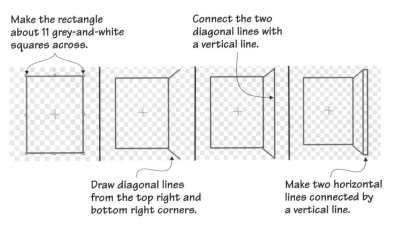

Make the rectangle about 11 grey-and-white squares across.

Connect the two diagonal lines with a vertical line.

Draw diagonal lines from the top right and bottom right corners.

Make two horizontal lines connected by a vertical line.

Figure 12.10 **Build the outline for the door in four steps.**

5 Fill the sideways trapezoid door with dark grey paint using the Paint Bucket tool.

6 Switch to a light grey and fill the outer edge of the door. The two greys used on the door should straddle the medium grey used for the wall (see figure 12.11).

7 Add a single black pixel with the Paintbrush tool for the knob.

8 Choose a bright green paint sample square and draw a line across the door opening, a quarter of the way up from the bottom. Fill the bottom section with the green paint using the Paint Bucket tool.

9 Fill the top section of the door opening with a blue, using the gradient tool so the color fades as it moves closer to the "grass," as shown in figure 12.11.

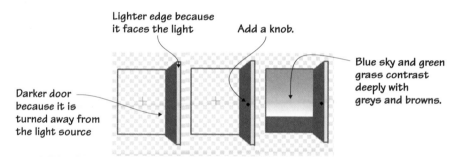

Figure 12.11   The inside of the door is dark because it's away from the interior light. The edge of the door is light because it's facing the interior light.

The finished door in figure 12.12 visually pops because it contains bright colors compared to the drab hallway. Make sure you go to the Sprite Zone and rename this sprite Door.

Making the desk

The desk shown in figure 12.13 serves as the actual platform in School Escape. Ms. Finebean can

Figure 12.12   The completed door sprite

jump onto and hang out on the desk. This is your first multilevel game where the player character can either be on the ground or standing on a platform off the floor.

Start a new sprite to make the desk:

1 Keep the Art Editor zoomed in to 400%.

2 Choose the black paint sample square and click the Line tool.

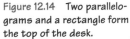

Figure 12.13   *The desk is a platform that Ms. Finebean can use to sail over the kindergarteners' heads.*

3 Draw a parallelogram, about 22-by-8 grey-and-white canvas squares.

4 Use the Paint Bucket tool to fill the center of the parallelogram.

5 Return to the Line tool and pick a dark grey from the paint sample squares. Draw a second parallelogram on the right side of the desk by drawing two vertical lines downward from either corner and connecting them along the open edge.

6 Draw a rectangle against the bottom edge of the parallelogram, as shown in the bottom picture of figure 12.14.

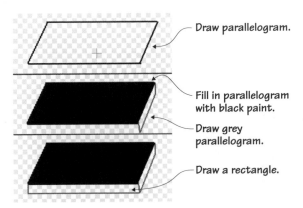

Figure 12.14   *Two parallelograms and a rectangle form the top of the desk.*

7 Fill the grey parallelogram and rectangle using the Paint Bucket tool.

8 Return to the black paint sample square and click the Square tool. Make sure the Square tool is on its solid and not outline setting. You're going to draw three rectangles, as shown in figure 12.15. The first one extends down from the front left corner (and is about 12 grey-and-white squares long). The second one extends down from the front right corner. The third one is smaller and is positioned slightly in from the left side.

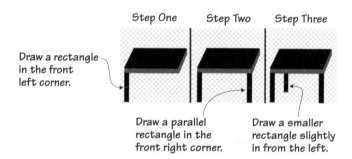

Step One   **Step Two**   **Step Three**

Draw a rectangle in the front left corner.

Draw a parallel rectangle in the front right corner.

Draw a smaller rectangle slightly in from the left.

Figure 12.15   The legs of the desk are carefully positioned rectangles.

9 Draw the final leg of the desk (another black rectangle) so that the top right corner of the rectangle touches the edge of the grey side of the desk, as shown in figure 12.16. This leg currently blocks the grey

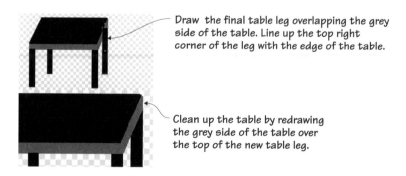

Draw the final table leg overlapping the grey side of the table. Line up the top right corner of the leg with the edge of the table.

Clean up the table by redrawing the grey side of the table over the top of the new table leg.

Figure 12.16   Add the final leg and clean up the side of the desk.

area, but you will switch back to the Line tool and the grey paint sample square to cover up the part that overlaps with the grey section. You may need to temporarily zoom in to 800% to see the space clearly.

10 Begin the chair to the right of the desk with a grey parallelogram. Make a second, black parallelogram overlapping the grey parallelogram by using the right edge of the first parallelogram.

11 Fill in the black parallelogram first, covering up the short, grey line that runs through it. Fill in the grey parallelogram second, including the black section on the left side that is part of the desk.

12 Draw four vertical black lines extending down from the four corners of the chair, much in the same way that you made the desk legs. Check your work against figure 12.17.

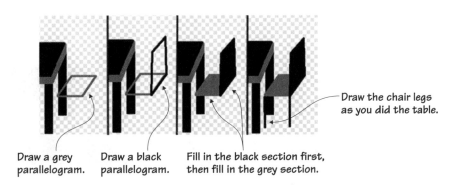

Draw a grey parallelogram.

Draw a black parallelogram.

Fill in the black section first, then fill in the grey section.

Draw the chair legs as you did the table.

Figure 12.17   The chair is a series of parallelograms and lines.

13 Move to the bottom of the desk and choose the darkest brown paint sample square. Use the Paintbrush tool to make a single pixel anywhere on the canvas. Because you used the darkest brown to make the floor, you need the shadow to be slightly darker to be visible. You will use this single dot of paint to set the color for the darker shadow.

14 Open the rainbow box and use the Eyedropper tool to set the color to that single, dark brown pixel on the canvas. Use the slider on the right side to slightly darken the brown, as shown in figure 12.18.

15 Using the Paintbrush tool, make an outline of brown square dots, starting with the back right leg of the chair, as shown in figure 12.18.

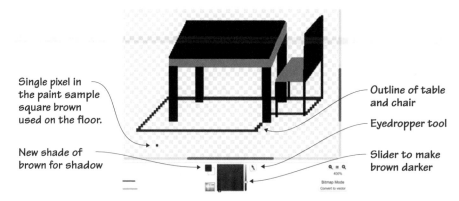

Single pixel in the paint sample square brown used on the floor.

New shade of brown for shadow

Outline of table and chair

Eyedropper tool

Slider to make brown darker

Figure 12.18   Place a single brown pixel on the canvas so you can use the Eyedropper tool to set the base brown before using the slider to make it darker.

16 Fill in the center using the Paint Bucket tool.

You now have a shadow under the desk, as shown in figure 12.19. You can erase the single pixel you placed on the canvas to set the shade of brown and rename the sprite Desk in the Sprite Zone.

Figure 12.19   The dark brown shadow under the desk will appear on the lighter brown floor.

Making the teacher

Ms. Finebean, shown in figure 12.20, is your Mario, jumping up on desks, collecting clocks, and sailing over the heads of kindergarteners, all while wearing a fancy dress and high heels because she's headed to her brother's wedding.

Figure 12.20   Ms. Finebean is the "Mario" in this *Super Mario*-like game.

Start a new sprite to make the teacher:

1 Choose a skin tone and click the Paintbrush tool. Make an eight-by-eight-pixel square and fill the center using the Paint Bucket tool.

2 Return to the Paintbrush tool and navigate to the right side of the square. Make a two-pixel horizontal line about midway down the side of the square. Top it with one pixel to make the nose. Navigate to the bottom of the square and center a two-by-four-pixel rectangle underneath the square for the neck, as shown in figure 12.21.

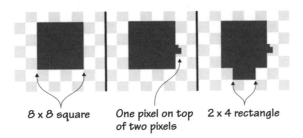

8 x 8 square   One pixel on top   2 x 4 rectangle   Figure 12.21   Ms. Finebean
                   of two pixels   is shown in profile.

3 Select a color for Ms. Finebean's dress. (I went with orange. Choose any color except brown or black.) Make the sleeve of the dress using the Paintbrush tool. Extending from the base of the neck, make two-pixel vertical lines on either side and connect them with a two-pixel horizontal line at the neck. Make the horizontal line slightly higher than the top of the vertical line, as shown in figure 12.22.

4 Return to the skin tone color and draw the arm. The top of the arm is two pixels thick and three pixels down until you get to the elbow.

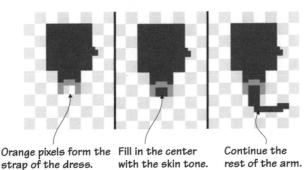

Orange pixels form the   Fill in the center   Continue the   Figure 12.22   Because Ms.
strap of the dress.   with the skin tone.   rest of the arm.   Finebean is in profile, you only
                                                                     need to draw the strap of the
                                                                     dress right now.

Once the arm changes direction, it's only one pixel thick and five pixels across. Stagger the line above to make the two-pixel hand, as shown in figure 12.22.

5 Select the dress color again and move back to the strap. Extend the dress down another two pixels. To make the dress fan out, add a diagonal pixel (the pixel in the front may be blocked by the arm, so imagine where it would be and continue the dress as if it is there) and then continue the dress as vertical lines, in both the back and front of the dress, for 11 pixels.

6 Make a diagonal pixel at the bottom of the dress on either side followed by a pixel underneath it. Connect those two lines with a horizontal line that runs along the bottom of the dress. Fill in the center of the dress with the Paint Bucket tool. You can see the finished dress in figure 12.23.

7 Draw the shoes by using the Paintbrush tool. Again, choose any color except brown or black. Draw a three-pixel vertical line at the bottom of the shoe. At the top of the line, make a single pixel to the right. Make a diagonal pixel and follow that with a second pixel to the right. Finish the shoe by making a three-pixel line underneath the two-pixel line, aligning them on the left side. You can close off the single empty pixel between the shoe and the bottom of the dress with the skin tone color.

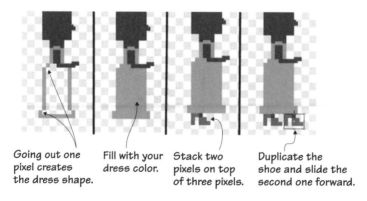

Going out one pixel creates the dress shape.

Fill with your dress color.

Stack two pixels on top of three pixels.

Duplicate the shoe and slide the second one forward.

Figure 12.23 The bell-shaped dress can be any color.

8 Use the Duplicator tool to make a copy of the shoe. Once it is outlined and copied, slide the new version forward so it's in front of the original shoe. Zoom in and make sure you only copied the shoe and didn't accidentally copy the bottom of the dress with it. See figure 12.23.

9 Choose a hair color and begin at the top right side of the head. Make seven diagonal pixel dots using the Paintbrush tool. Start a verticle line with a single pixel down to touch the bottom of the head.

10 Extend the vertical line three more pixels until you reach the strap of the dress. Continue the line diagonally three more pixels.

11 Switch directions and make a two-pixel diagonal line moving up (to form a V shape at the end of her hair) and then start moving back toward the skull, drawing three more pixels to get to the base of the head, and then outlining the head until you reach the front again. Fill in the hair using the Paint Bucket tool. See figure 12.24.

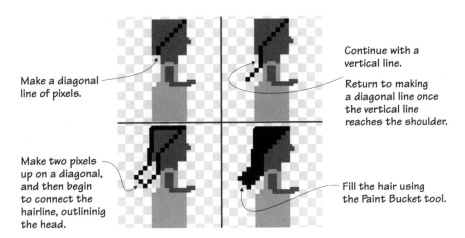

Make a diagonal line of pixels.

Continue with a vertical line.

Return to making a diagonal line once the vertical line reaches the shoulder.

Make two pixels up on a diagonal, and then begin to connect the hairline, outlininig the head.

Fill the hair using the Paint Bucket tool.

Figure 12.24   The hair can be any style, but this simple design adds to the illusion of movement when Ms. Finebean begins running.

12 Make a small dome at the top of her head, as in figure 12.25, using two diagonal pixels connected by a horizontal line. Fill in the space inside the dome using the Paint Bucket tool. Return to the Paintbrush tool to make the four-pixel white of her eye, a one-pixel dot for

the color of her eye, and a two-pixel line for the mouth, turning up at the end with a single pixel, also shown in figure 12.25.

Ms. Finebean, shown in figure 12.26, is complete! Make sure you rename her Teacher in the Sprite Zone to make coding her easier in the next chapter.

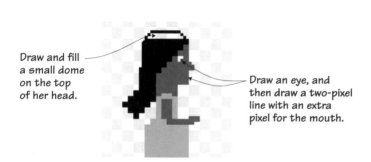

Draw and fill a small dome on the top of her head.

Draw an eye, and then draw a two-pixel line with an extra pixel for the mouth.

Figure 12.25   Doming the top of the head makes Ms. Finebean look more realistic.

Figure 12.26   The completed teacher sprite

Making the kindergarteners

Ms. Finebean has a large class of kindergarteners blocking her path, but you're not going to have to draw each individual one. Instead, you're going to make one and then make a few small tweaks to the "costume" in order to make it look like many different students. The students in figure 12.27 are all the same sprite, with changes to hair, clothing, and skin tone to make it look like lots of different students. Part of the duplicating will take place in this chapter, though you'll also use a coding technique so a random kindergartener pops up each time a new clone is generated.

Figure 12.27   Ms. Finebean will need to jump over the kindergarteners to get out of the building.

Start a new sprite to make the first kindergartener. Remember, you're making many students, so the color choices you make for the original sprite can be changed with each new "costume" you make for the sprite:

1 Select a skin tone color and click the Paintbrush tool. Make an eight-by-eight-pixel square and fill in the center using the Paint Bucket tool. Additionally, make a two-by-two-pixel square centered at the bottom of the head.

2 Choose a shirt color and draw a two-pixel horizontal line underneath the neck. Make a single diagonal pixel up from either side of the horizontal line.

3 Extend the single pixel to the left (or right on the right side of the neck) by three more pixels. Continue the lines vertically from the end on either side, three more pixels, as shown in figure 12.28.

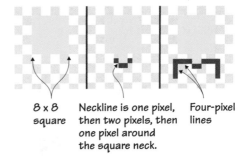

8 x 8 square   Neckline is one pixel, then two pixels, then one pixel around the square neck.   Four-pixel lines

Figure 12.28   The head and sleeves of the shirt come together with a few pixels.

4 Continue the shirt, as shown in figure 12.29, making the sleeve opening a three-pixel vertical line followed by two pixels to the right and five pixels down. Fill the center of the shirt using the Paint Bucket tool.

5 Choose a new color for the pants. The top of the pants are a 6-by-2-pixel horizontal line, and the legs of the pants are a 12-by-2-pixel vertical line, as shown in figure 12.29.

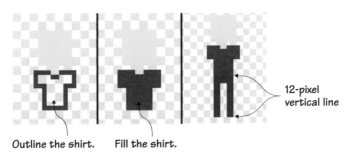

12-pixel vertical line

Outline the shirt.   Fill the shirt.

Figure 12.29   A boxy shirt and pants complete the student's body.

6 Switch back to the skin tone color and draw arms extending out of each sleeve. You can make these arms in any position and should change them with each student.

7 Pick a hair color and add a simple hairline to the top of the head. Again, you will change the style and hair color with each "costume," so keep it simple and have fun.

8 Draw a white pixel for each eye and then use the slider to set the brush on the smallest setting. Fill in one corner of the square with an eye color. Similarly, make a two-pixel line for the mouth (still on the smallest setting), as shown in figure 12.30. Additionally, give your sprite a pair of shoes by making a horizontal line at the bottom of the pants, or go fancy and construct shoes out of diagonal pixels.

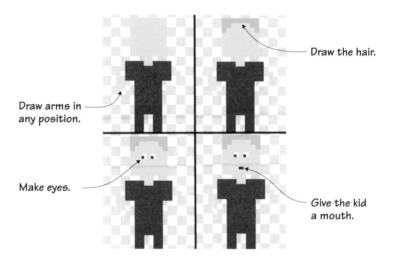

Figure 12.30   Be creative with the student. You can choose any hair and eye colors you want.

You now have a single student, but you need many students. Start by renaming the sprite Student in the Sprite Zone.

Duplicate the sprite by using the Duplicator tool from the Grey Toolbar and open this new version of the sprite in the Art Editor. It's time to use the Paint Bucket tool to change the colors.

You can see in figure 12.31 that the student on the left and the student on the right are essentially the same sprite. All I did was change the t-shirt, pants, shoe, eye, and hair color using the Paint Bucket tool. I added a few extra pixels of hair to give her a different style, as well as two pixelated hair bows.

Use the Paint Bucket tool to change the color and the Paintbrush tool to add pixels.

Change the hair color.

Change the eye color.

Change the shirt.

Change the pants.

Change the shoes.

The finished boy

Figure 12.31   The single sprite will look like four different students with small tweaks.

Feel free to change the position of the arms, draw designs on the clothes, and change everything from skin tone to hair color. In fact, do this two more times until you have four students, named Student, Student2, Student3, and Student4, in the Sprite Zone. In the next chapter, you'll combine them into a single sprite.

Preparing the code

Like your last platformer, this game requires a lot of sprites (even though it doesn't contain any odds and ends). You need obstacles (kindergarteners), power-ups (clocks), and platforms (desks) in order to give the teacher a virtual obstacle course to face between the start of the game and the end of the game: the door.

Play with the game

You already did a lot of creative thinking with this game because you got to set everything from dress colors to hairstyles. But there are still more things you can do to make your game unique.

> **CHALLENGE**   The desk and clock both have shadows, but the kindergar-
> teners and Ms. Finebean are shadowless. Can you add shad-
> ows to the wall behind the students (hint: the shadow will be attached to the
> sprite) or on the floor behind Ms. Finebean?

> **CHALLENGE**   The door also doesn't contain a shadow. Walk to the nearest
> door in your home or school and look for the shadow. Can
> you recreate that shadow on the screen and make it part of the sprite?

> **CHALLENGE**   Can you add dithering to Ms. Finebean's hair to make it look
> as if it's reflecting the light? How can you show that the
> teacher's hair is made up of individual strands instead of one clump?

What did you learn?

If you've taken geometry, you know that shadows play a big role in the measurement of every shape. A shadow shows the *volume*—or internal space—of an object, cast on the wall behind it as the solid object gets in the way of the light beam. Think about it this way: measuring how much liquid can fit inside a glass is finding out its volume. If you shine a light on that same cup, you're going to see the volume of the cup in shadow form behind it. Many times when you're studying geometry, you'll see the shape in your textbook drawn with the shadow behind it to show that it is a three-dimensional (as opposed to flat, two-dimensional) object.

Pause for a moment and think about everything you learned in this chapter:

- How to take a single student sprite and tweak it to make it look like multiple, unique kindergarteners
- How to add shadows to show that an object has volume or is three-dimensional
- How to show the direction of the light by using shadows

All your kindergarteners are currently their own sprites. In the next chapter, you're going to learn how to combine all these sprites into a single sprite, code the game so it randomly chooses one of those students to throw onto the teacher's path, and even get the teacher to be able to jump up and land on a surface. At the end of the chapter, you'll have a fun, single-screen platformer called School Escape.

13

Using arrays and simulating gravity in a single-screen platformer

Before *Donkey Kong*, games had goals, but the player didn't know their motivation or how they had ended up in the situation. *Donkey Kong* changed that by giving the player a story with a beginning, middle, and end that unfolded as the player moved from level to level, usually in the form of *cutscenes*, videos that occur before or after a level to pause the gameplay and give information. That story starred a little plumber known as Mario.

Yes, our friend, Mario, that you know from *Super Mario Bros*, started out as a carpenter at a construction site, climbing ladders in *Donkey Kong* to save his girlfriend who was stolen by a giant gorilla. Nintendo brought back Mario for *Mario Bros* and then *Super Mario Bros*, turning him into a plumber who needs to jump up on brick platforms or slide down pipes in order to save Princess Toadstool from the evil Bowser. Mario can only run to the right. That's because *Super Mario Bros* is a single-screen platformer.

Single-screen platformers may look and perform similarly to multiscreen platformers like *Pitfall*, but there is a key difference. In *Pitfall* or Beach Blast, the player character (Pitfall Harry or Beachy Buffy) is moving from

Figure 13.1   In School Escape, Ms. Finebean needs to sail over the heads of students, jumping off of desks and grabbing clocks as she runs out of school.

screen to screen, interacting with the other sprites on each screen. In *Super Mario Bros* or School Escape, seen in figure 13.1, the player character remains in the same X position, though they can jump up and down to change their Y position. The sprites in the game roll toward them whenever the player presses the right arrow. It looks as if Mario or the teacher is running, but the player character is staying in place while the objects move toward them.

To understand the mechanics of a single-screen platformer, it may help to imagine the character standing at the end of a conveyer belt. The belt only moves when the person marches in place. If the person stops moving, all the objects on the conveyer belt (as well as the belt itself) stop moving, and if the person marches in place, the items on the conveyer belt move toward them.

In School Escape, the teacher's X position is on the left side of the Stage. As the player presses the right arrow to "move" the teacher, the desk sprites (platforms) and kindergarteners (obstacles) generate and slide toward the teacher. It looks as if the teacher is moving, but it's the other sprites that are sliding across the screen, moving toward the left when the player presses the right arrow and stopping whenever the teacher pauses.

This game also introduces a common video game item: a power-up. Power-ups are items in games that the player can use to increase their chance of success or give them additional abilities. In School Escape, the power-up is a clock that players can jump up and grab in order to buy more time to reach the exit door because, yes, School Escape is also your first timed game.

To accomplish all this, School Escape uses lists, which are also known in coding as *arrays*. Lists allow the game to track multiple values for a single variable. It helps that Scratch calls them *lists* instead of *arrays* because you can think of them as you would any list: it's a place to write down information you want to remember and use later. In this case, the lists contain the X-positions for where we want students and desks to appear.

In this chapter, you will learn

- How to design a single-screen scrolling platformer
- How to add power-ups into a game
- How to set a timer to affect gameplay
- How to store values in a list
- How to jump up and land on objects using simulated gravity

With fewer scripts, you're going to make a much more complicated platformer. Take everything you learned in Beach Blast and apply it forward to create your own *Super Mario*-like School Escape.

Preparing to program

It's time for your pre-coding ritual. Get your sprites and the Stage ready for School Escape.

Missing sprites

If you skipped chapter 12, either go back and complete it or go to the Manning site and download the background and sprites for School Escape. The directions for importing are the same as in chapter 5. You should have Ms. Finebean, four students, the clock, the desk, the door, and the hallway background.

Combining the kindergarteners

You need to combine all your students into a single kindergartener. Navigate to the Sprite Zone and click Student2. Open the Costumes tab in the Block Menu and drag the sprite from the Costumes tab into the Student sprite in the Sprite Zone. Make sure that Student2 transferred into the Student sprite by clicking the Student sprite and looking at the Costumes tab. You should see two costumes, as in figure 13.2.

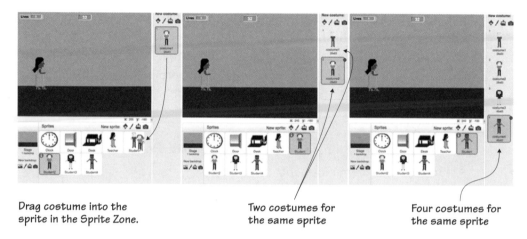

Drag costume into the
sprite in the Sprite Zone.

Two costumes for
the same sprite

Four costumes for
the same sprite

Figure 13.2   The steps to take to combine multiple "costumes" into a single sprite. There is a single student sprite, but it can look four different ways.

Repeat this step two more times for Student3 and Student4 until all four versions of the student are seen in the Costumes sidebar when you click the Student sprite. Once all the sprites are combined into a single sprite, you can delete the original copies of the Student2, Student3, and Student4 sprites.

> **FIX IT**   I ACCIDENTALLY DELETED A SPRITE!   What happens if you delete a sprite by accident? Don't worry, you can get it back. Navigate to the Edit menu in the Grey Toolbar and choose the Undelete option. You'll see the sprite you deleted return to the Sprite Zone.

Preparing the Stage

You'll need to resize a few sprites to have your code match our code. Use the Grow tool in the Grey Toolbar to enlarge the door (29 clicks), teacher (14 clicks), and student (4 clicks). The clock and desk are already the correct size.

Drag Ms. Finebean to the left side of the Stage, a centimeter from the edge. Place the clock sprite near the top third of the Stage on the far right side, around the X:200 and Y:80 position. (Check the bottom of the Stage as you move the clock to see the position. The clock doesn't need to be perfectly on those numbers; they're just a guide.)

Place the desk on the right side of the Stage, lining up the shadow with the top of the floor, and place the student sprite in the same place as the desk. Make sure neither sprite touches the wall. Finally, position the door in the middle of the Stage, also lining up the bottom of the door with the wall. All sprites should be in the same places as the ones in figure 13.3.

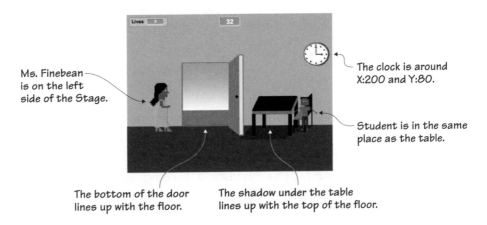

Ms. Finebean is on the left side of the Stage.

The clock is around X:200 and Y:80.

Student is in the same place as the table.

The bottom of the door lines up with the floor.

The shadow under the table lines up with the top of the floor.

Figure 13.3   Position the sprites on the Stage.

Download the list

Even if you made your own sprites, you will need to download two lists from the Manning site, https://www.manning.com/books/hello -scratch. These lists tell Scratch all the times you want the desk or kindergarteners to appear in the game. The lists are long, and instead of asking you to type in these values, we've made lists that you can import into your game.

Go to the Manning site and download the two .txt files (deskpositions.txt and kindergarteners.txt). You now need to create two blank lists in Scratch in order to import these .txt files into your game.

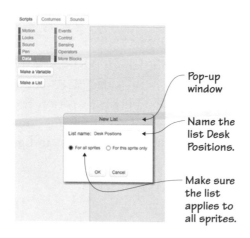

Figure 13.4   Make an empty, new list and name it Desk Positions.

Go to Data and click Make a List. Name this list Desk Positions, as seen in figure 13.4, and create it For All Sprites.

Make a second list and call it Kindergarteners. Keep both lists checked for the time being so you can see them on the Stage. Right-click (or control-click if you're on a Mac) the Desk Positions list on the Stage. A pop-up window will give you a few options, including Import, as seen in figure 13.5. Choose Import and navigate to where you've saved the deskpositions.txt file on your computer.

You should see 14 values appear in the previously empty Desk Positions list. Do the same thing for the Kindergarteners list, importing the kindergartener.txt file into the empty list. You should see 30 values appear in the previously empty Kindergarteners list, as in figure 13.6. Leave the lists on the screen for the time being, through you can uncheck the lists before you play so they're not visible on the Stage.

Right click to open the pop-up window. Choose the import option. Navigate to where the deskpositions.txt file is saved on your computer.

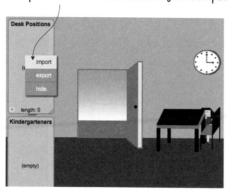

Figure 13.5   Right-click the empty list and import the .txt file.

The values from the .txt files fill the empty lists.

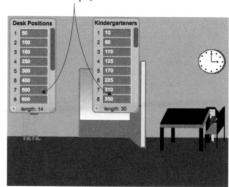

Figure 13.6   The values on the list will fill once you import the .txt files.

You're now ready to code.

Programming Ms. Finebean

The teacher, Ms. Finebean, is the equivalent of Mario in *Super Mario Bros.* She's the player character that the player controls, making her jump over students and onto desks, grabbing clocks along the way. She has five scripts: a movement script, jumping script, falling velocity script, falling script, and desk detection script. All scripts in this section are applied to Ms. Finebean, so go put the blue box around the Teacher sprite in the Sprite Zone and don't move the blue box until you program the kindergarteners in the next section. Remember, the names or values on *your* blocks may differ slightly from time to time, so use the completed script images to make sure you chose the correct block.

Making a movement script

Ms. Finebean needs to escape from school, but she can't move forward, as shown in figure 13.7.

This script will make it look as if Ms. Finebean is running toward the right whenever the right arrow is pressed. In reality, Ms. Finebean will be remaining in the same place, and this script sends the desks and kindergarteners toward her to give the illusion of movement:

Figure 13.7 Even though Ms. Finebean won't be moving, it will look as if she is running toward the right when you press the right arrow key.

1 Start with a When Flag Clicked (Events) block.

2 Click Data and make two variables. The first is called scrollX, and the second is called Lives. scrollX will track Ms. Finebean's X-position, and Lives will set the number of chances Ms. Finebean has to reach the door without running into a kindergartener. Uncheck the scrollX variable, but leave the Lives variable checked, and drag the box to the top left side of the Stage.

3 Drag two Set Lives to 0 (Data) blocks and set them underneath the When Flag Clicked block. Change the top option to scrollX using the drop-down menu, but keep the number at 0 because zero is the variable's starting point. Leave the bottom option as Lives but change the number to 3 to give Ms. Finebean 3 chances.

4 Snap a Forever (Control) block underneath to start a loop.

5 Place an If/Then (Control) block inside the Forever block.

6 Slide a Key Space Pressed (Sensing) block into the empty hexagonal space on the If/Then block to set the condition.

7 Change the option in the Key Space Pressed block to Right Arrow using the drop-down menu so the game emulates Ms. Finebean moving right when the arrow is pressed.

8 Slide a Change Lives by 1 (Data) block and place it inside the If/Then block. Use the drop-down menu to change the option to scrollX, but keep the number at 1, because you want the value of scrollX to go up by one every time the right arrow is pressed.

9 Add a Wait 1 Secs (Control) block under the Change scrollX by 1 block. Change the number to a small number such as .001. You want to ensure that the game doesn't glitch and increase the value of scrollX by more than 1 each time, which would make the sprites in the game move too quickly.

Check your script against the one in figure 13.8.

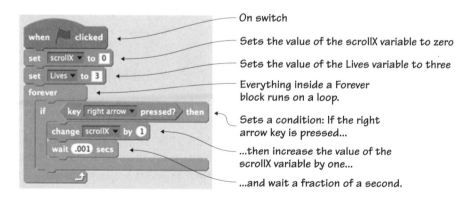

Figure 13.8   The completed movement script makes it look as if Ms. Finebean is moving.

Ms. Finebean's X-position isn't going to change, but you'll make it look like it's changing using the scrollX variable. This variable is tracking her *virtual* position, imagining her X-position increasing by 1 every time the right arrow is pressed. Get it? Ms. Finebean is always on the left side of the screen, but this value pretends her X-position is 1, 2, 3, and so on until she hits the thousands. When she reaches a certain X-position, different things will happen, such as a desk spawning or the door appearing. In this way, Ms. Finebean can technically run infinitely to the right, even though there are only 480 X-coordinate points (–240 to 240) if she is moving across the Stage. And different things happen, such as a student moving toward her, when she reaches a certain virtual point, because the value of scrollX has increased from the right arrow being pressed.

ANSWER THIS   WHY DOES SCROLLX NEED TO CHANGE BY 1?

Question: could you play with the number and make scrollX change by 2 or 3 each time to make Ms. Finebean run faster?

Answer: technically, yes, but you need to hit every value on the list, and that can only happen if scrollX increases one digit at a time. For instance, what if you set the desk to spawn when scrollX is 303, which means that Ms. Finebean is at her virtual X:303? If the value of scrollX jumps two "coordinates" at a time, she'll move from 302 to 304 without ever hitting that 303 value. Keep the number at 1 in order to use every value on the list.

Making the jumping script

Ms. Finebean needs to be able to go over the kindergarteners instead of mowing them down while she runs down the hall. She also needs to be able to jump up and grab the clocks, as in figure 13.9, to gain more time.

Figure 13.9   Ms. Finebean jumps up in order to grab the clocks, land on desks, and leap over students.

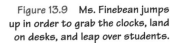

Ms. Finebean needs to be able to go up in the air to grab the clocks or get over the kindergarteners.

This script will enable Ms. Finebean to leave the ground and jump into the air:

1 Start with a When Space Key Pressed (Events) block. Use the drop-down menu to change the option to Up Arrow.

2 Snap an If/Then (Control) block underneath to set a condition.

3 Place a Hexagon or Hexagon (Operators) block inside the empty hexagonal space. Fill each of those hexagons with two Touching Color (Sensing) blocks.

4 Change the left Touching Color block to the brown you used for the floor. Change the right Touching Color block to the black you used for the top of the desk. The condition is if the teacher is touching the floor or the desk.

5 Slide a Change Y by 10 (Motion) block inside the If/Then block. Change the number to 100 so she will go up 100 coordinates each time the up arrow is pressed.

6 Make a new variable in Data. Call it yVelocity and uncheck the variable so it isn't visible on the Stage.

7 Snap a Set yVelocity to 0 (Data) block underneath the Change Y by 100 block inside the If/Then block. Change the zero (0) to a 7.

If the up arrow is pressed and Ms. Finebean is either on the floor or on a desk (meaning, she's not already up in the air), she will go up 100 coordinates, and at the same time the velocity variable will kick in so she starts falling a tiny bit as she's rising. This will give her a smooth arc. Look at the completed script in figure 13.10.

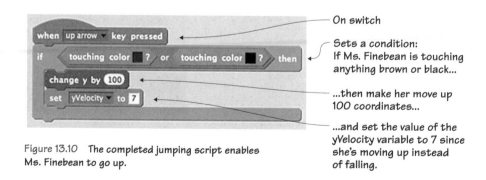

Figure 13.10   The completed jumping script enables Ms. Finebean to go up.

On switch

Sets a condition:
If Ms. Finebean is touching anything brown or black...

...then make her move up 100 coordinates...

...and set the value of the yVelocity variable to 7 since she's moving up instead of falling.

Making a falling velocity script

Once Ms. Finebean is in the air, she needs to fall realistically, floating back down to the ground smoothly, as she is doing in figure 13.11. This script will mimic a falling person's velocity, having her speed up the closer she gets to the ground so she floats back down instead of dropping like a dead weight.

To make the falling velocity script

1 Start with a When Flag Clicked (Events) block.

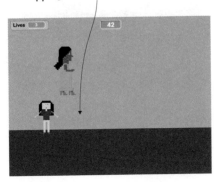

Ms. Finebean needs to gently fall instead of dropping to the floor like a dead weight.

Figure 13.11   Ms. Finebean needs to fall realistically.

2 Snap a Forever (Control) block under the When Flag Clicked block to start a loop.

3 Place an If/Then (Control) block inside the Forever block to set a condition.

4 Slide a Not (Operators) block into the empty hexagonal space on the If/Then block. Place a Hexagon or Hexagon (Operators) block into the empty hexagonal space on the Not block.

5 Fill the two empty hexagons with two Touching Color (Sensing) blocks. Change the left block color to the brown you used for the floor. Change the right block color to the black you used for the desk.

6 Place a Change yVelocity by 0 (Data) block inside the If/Then block. Change the number to –0.5 in order to have the rate of falling slowly increase over time.

You've set a condition in the script in figure 13.12: if the teacher is not touching the floor or the desk—meaning, she's in the air—then change the value of the yVelocity variable to –0.5. This means that Ms. Finebean's speed will increase by a half a coordinate as she falls.

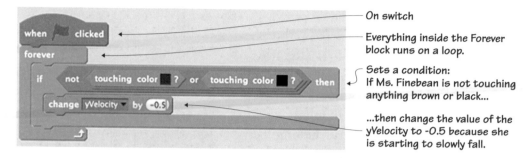

On switch

Everything inside the Forever block runs on a loop.

Sets a condition: If Ms. Finebean is not touching anything brown or black...

...then change the value of the yVelocity to -0.5 because she is starting to slowly fall.

Figure 13.12   The completed falling velocity script creates realistic movement.

Making a falling script

Ms. Finebean can go up, and you've set how she'll fall when she starts moving downward. Now it's time to make a script that will allow Ms. Finebean to fall, as in figure 13.13.

This script will allow Ms. Finebean to start falling when she reaches the peak height:

If Ms. Finebean is not touching anything brown (for example, the floor), she will start the process of falling.

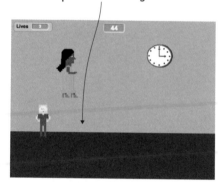

Figure 13.13   Ms. Finebean needs to start falling back down if her feet are not touching the brown floor.

1 Start with a When Flag Clicked (Events) block.

2 Snap a Forever (Control) block under the When Flag Clicked block to start a loop.

3 Place an If/Then/Else (Control) block inside the Forever block to set a condition.

4 Slide a Not (Operators) block into the empty hexagonal space on the If/Then block, and then place a Touching Color (Sensing) block inside the Not block. Change the color to the brown you used for the floor. The condition is if Ms. Finebean is not touching the floor.

5 Place a Change Y by 10 (Motion) block inside the If/Then portion of the If/Then/Else block. Add a yVelocity variable (Data) into the

number bubble on the Change Y by 10 block. This means the Y-position of Ms. Finebean will change based on the current value of the yVelocity variable.

6 Put a Set yVelocity to 0 (Data) block inside the Else portion of the If/Then/Else block. The other possibility is that if Ms. Finebean is *not* not touching the floor (meaning, she *is* touching), then the value of the yVelocity variable will be set to zero (0), because Ms. Finebean is on the ground and not falling.

Look at the script in figure 13.14. Does your work match the image?

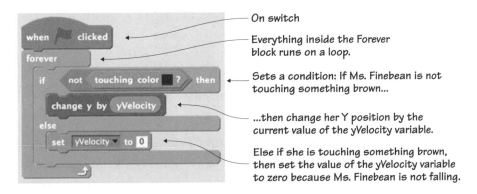

Figure 13.14   **The completed falling script allows Ms. Finebean to fall if her feet have left the ground.**

Making a desk detection script

Currently, if Ms. Finebean tries to jump on a desk, she'll go straight through it. You want the teacher to be able to land on the desk and run across it in order to use the height to leap over nearby kindergarteners, as in figure 13.15.

Ms. Finebean needs to be able to land on top of the desk. The desk is your platform in this multi-level platformer.

Figure 13.15   **You want Ms. Finebean to land on—and not go through—the desks.**

This script will recognize when Ms. Finebean has landed on the desk:

1 Start with a When Flag Clicked (Events) block.

2 Snap a Forever (Control) block under the When Flag Clicked block to start a loop.

3 Slide a Go to Front (Looks) block inside the Forever block to send the teacher to the top layer on the Stage.

4 Place an If/Then (Control) block under the Go to Front block (also inside the Forever block) to set a condition.

5 Put a Color is Touching (Sensing) block inside the empty hexagonal space of the If/Then block. Notice that this is a little different from the usual Touching Color block. Change the color in the first square to the color of Ms. Finebean's shoes (in my case, orange), and change the color in the second square to the top of the desk (in my case, black).

6 Grab a Set yVelocity to 0 block and put it inside the If/Then block.

The condition is if the teacher's shoe is touching the top of the desk, set the yVelocity variable to zero (0). This is an important script because you created a script earlier that said that if Ms. Finebean wasn't touching the ground, then she should be falling. This script changes that by creating a condition—standing on the desk—where Ms. Finebean isn't touching the ground, but you don't want her falling. Look at figure 13.16 to check your script.

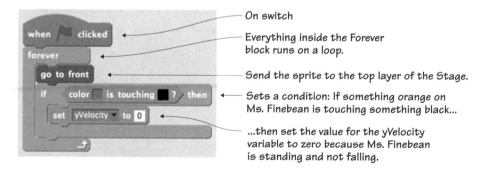

Figure 13.16 The desk detection script knows when Ms. Finebean has landed on top of the desk.

Ms. Finebean is ready to go. It's now time to code the students.

Programming the kindergarteners

The kindergarteners are the obstacle in School Escape, similar to the Goombas and Koopa Troopas in *Super Mario Bros*. Unlike those obstacles, you'll want to jump over the students rather than land on the students and squash them. The students have five scripts: a list adding script, cloning script, movement script, game stopping script, and pause movement script. Make sure the blue box is around the student in the Sprite Zone, and keep it on the student for all five scripts. It doesn't matter which costume is showing in the Sprite Zone thumbnail.

LEARN IT   LISTS   As mentioned earlier, a list is Scratch's name for an array, which is a collection of data. Think about lists as actual shopping lists. When you go to the store, you write down all the items you want to remember to purchase, one item on each line. For example, you may name your list Grocery Items and then start listing out what you need: (1) Apples, (2) Bread, (3) Milk. When you go to the store, you look down the list and put each item in your basket. A Scratch list works the same way. You give it a name (for instance, Kindergarteners) and then write out the information you want to remember and track in an ordered list. In the case of the Kindergarteners list, you're tracking a list of numbers: 10, 60, 110, and so on. Those numbers are virtual points in the game—times when you want a kindergartener to appear on the Stage. Scratch will know that it's time to throw a student in Ms. Finebean's path because it will keep checking to see whether the value of the scrollX variable (which goes up by one every time the right arrow is pressed) matches one of the items on the list. When they match, it will spawn a clone of the student sprite. You'll see a student when the scrollX variable equals 10, 60, 110, and so on.

Making a list adding script

You currently have your imported list that states when each kindergartener should spawn. Yet when you go to play the game, the values will begin deleting off the list after they're used. To solve this problem, you need to generate a second, identical list, as seen in figure 13.17, at the beginning of every game so the values will be deleted from the list copy instead of the original list.

This script enables you to play round after round of the game because the original list will always be intact, even though other scripts will delete values from the duplicate list:

The two lists are identical.

Figure 13.17   **The original list will remain untouched, and values will be deleted from the copy.**

1   Start with a When Flag Clicked (Events) block.

2   Go to Data and create a new variable called #ofKindergar-teners. You will use this variable to refer to an item on the list. When the value of #ofKin-dergarteners is 1, it will be looking at the first value on the list. Uncheck the variable.

3   Click Make a List and make a new list called Kindergarteners2. This will be your list copy of the original Kindergarteners list. You can uncheck this new list.

4   Snap a Set #ofKindergarteners to 0 (Data) block under the When Flag Clicked block. Change the value to 1 so this variable will line up with the first item on the Kindergarteners2 list.

5   Slide a Delete 1 of Kindergartener2 (Data) block under the Set #ofKindergarteners to 1 block and use the drop-down menu to change 1 to All. This will remove the values from the Kindergarteners2 list while keeping the identical, original Kinder-garteners list intact.

6   Grab a Repeat 10 (Control) block and add it to the chain of blocks. Change the number to 30 because you have 30 items on your list.

7   Place an Add Thing to Kindergarteners2 (Data) block inside the Repeat 30 block. Next slide an Item 1 of Kindergarteners2 block inside the space that says *Thing* on the Add Thing to Kindergarteners2 block, as seen in figure 13.18.

8   Slip a #ofKindergarteners (Data) variable into the number bubble on the Item 1 of Kindergarteners2 block. Now you need to tackle the

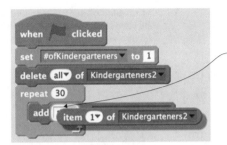

Place the Item 1 of Kindergarteners2 block inside the space on the other block.

Figure 13.18 Add the block inside the drop-down menu space on the Add Thing to Kindergarteners2 block.

drop-down menus. Change the line so it reads Add Item #ofKindergarteners of Kindergarteners to Kindergarteners2.

9 Drag a Change #ofKindergarteners by 1 (Data) block underneath that long block, inside the Repeat 30 block.

There will be 30 loops, one for each item on the original list, and in each loop the script will add an item from the Kindergarteners list to the Kindergarteners2 list. It knows to move to the second, third, and fourth item (and so on) due to that #ofKindergarteners variable. When that variable equals 2, it copies the second item on the list. When that variable equals 3, it copies the third item on the list, and so on. The script in figure 13.19 stops running once all the items are duplicated from the original list onto the list copy.

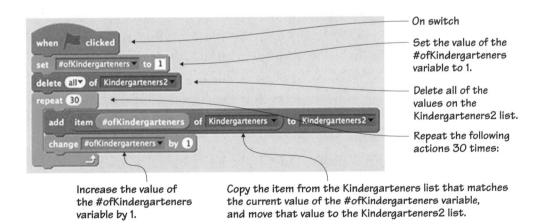

On switch

Set the value of the #ofKindergarteners variable to 1.

Delete all of the values on the Kindergarteners2 list.

Repeat the following actions 30 times:

Increase the value of the #ofKindergarteners variable by 1.

Copy the item from the Kindergarteners list that matches the current value of the #ofKindergarteners variable, and move that value to the Kindergarteners2 list.

Figure 13.19 The completed list adding script creates a copy of the original list.

Making a cloning script

You have a duplicate of your list, but it's currently hanging out as a group of numbers. It's time to put those numbers into action and have a kindergartener generate, as in figure 13.20, every time a number on the list matches up with the value of the scrollX variable, which marks the virtual location of Ms. Finebean.

If the value of scrollX is 60, and a value on the Kindergarteners2 list is 60, a student will spawn on the Stage, becoming an obstacle for Ms. Finebean to encounter on her way to the door.

Figure 13.20   The game looks at the values on the list and clones a student every time one of those values matches the value of the scrollX variable.

To make the cloning script

1 Start with a When Flag Clicked (Events) block.

2 Snap a Hide (Looks) block underneath the starter block.

3 Place a Forever (Control) block next to form a loop.

4 Slide an If/Then (Control) block inside the Forever block to set a condition.

5 Put a Square = Square (Operators) block inside the empty hexagonal space on the If/Then block. In the left square, place a scrollX (Data) variable block. In the right square, place an Item 1 of Kindergarteners2 (Data) block. So the condition is if the value of scrollX equals the value of the item on the Kindergarteners2 list.

6 Put a Go to X/Y (Motion) block inside the If/Then block. You don't need to change the values (even if they differ a bit from the ones in figure 13.21), because you want them to be the current position of the student on the Stage.

7 Drag a Switch Costume to Costume4 (Looks) block and place it underneath the Motion block.

8 Slide a Pick Random 1 to 10 (Operators) block inside the drop-down menu currently stating Costume4, as in figure 13.21. Change those numbers to 1 to 4 to stand for the four versions of the student

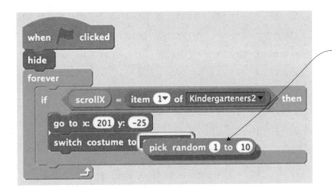

Place the Pick Random 1 to 10 block inside the drop-down menu space on the Switch Costume block to have the student randomly generate.

Figure 13.21 The Pick Random block goes inside the Switch Costume block in order to have it randomly choose one of the four options each time.

sprite. This means Scratch will randomly use one of the four options each time it spawns a kindergartener on the Stage.

9 Add a Create Clone of Myself (Control) block next (still inside the If/Then block), to generate the student.

10 Place a Delete 1 of Kindergartener2 (Data) block to complete that chain, which removes each individual value from the Kindergartener2 list after it's been used.

Four things will happen if the value of the scrollX variable matches an item on the Kindergartener2 list, as seen in the completed script in figure 13.22: (1) a student will appear on the Stage, (2) the student will be

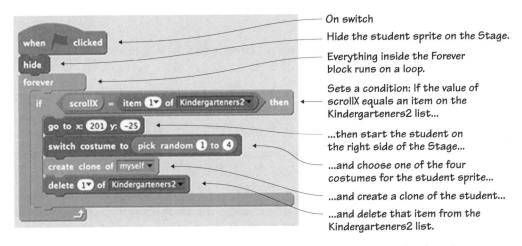

On switch

Hide the student sprite on the Stage.

Everything inside the Forever block runs on a loop.

Sets a condition: If the value of scrollX equals an item on the Kindergarteners2 list...

...then start the student on the right side of the Stage...

...and choose one of the four costumes for the student sprite...

...and create a clone of the student...

...and delete that item from the Kindergarteners2 list.

Figure 13.22 The completed cloning script puts a random kindergartener in Ms. Finebean's path.

standing where you positioned her when setting up the Stage, (3) the student will take the form of one of four possible options, and (4) that item will be deleted off the Kindergartener2 list.

Making a movement script

There are students on the Stage, but they need to move toward Ms. Finebean (even though it will look as if it's Ms. Finebean moving forward to reach the students). See figure 13.23.

This script will make the students move, but it will also tell Scratch what should happen when the students reach the edge of the Stage or if a student touches the teacher:

1 Start with a When I Start as a Clone (Control) block.

2 Snap a Show (Looks) block underneath, to make the sprite visible on the Stage.

3 Add a Forever (Control) block to form a loop.

It looks like Ms. Finebean is moving forward to jump over the student, but it's really the student moving toward Ms. Finebean. Watch out! She's about to touch him and lose a life!

Figure 13.23   The students move toward Ms. Finebean when the right arrow is pressed.

4 Stack three If/Then (Control) blocks inside the Forever block to set three conditions.

5 Add a Key Space Pressed (Sensing) block to the empty space on the first If/Then block. Change the option to Right Arrow using the drop-down menu. Add a Touching Mouse-Pointer (Sensing) block to the empty space on the second If/Then block. Change the option to Edge using the drop-down menu. Add a Touching Mouse-Pointer (Sensing) block to the empty space on the third If/Then block. Change the option to Teacher using the drop-down menu. You now have three possible conditions.

6 Put a Change X by 10 (Motion) block inside the first If/Then block. Change the number to –5 because you want the student to move 5 coordinates to the left.

7 Place a Delete This Clone (Control) block inside the second If/Then block to remove the sprite when it reaches the far left side of the Stage.

8 Place a Change #ofKindergarteners by 1 (Data) block inside the third If/Then block. Use the drop-down menu to change the option to Lives, and type –1 in the bubble, because you want to remove a chance each time the teacher lands on a student.

9 Add a Delete This Clone (Control) block underneath the Changes Lives by –1 block inside the third If/Then block.

The completed movement script in figure 13.24 states what will happen if the right arrow is pressed (the student will move to the left), the student reaches the end of the Stage (they'll disappear), or if the student touches the teacher (the player will lose one of their three chances, and the sprite will disappear).

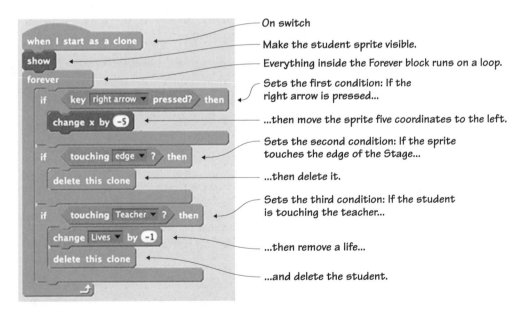

Figure 13.24 The completed movement script makes it look as if Ms. Finebean is moving toward the student when it's the student moving toward Ms. Finebean!

Making a game stopping script

School Escape would be an easy game if you had unlimited chances to reach the door. Giving Ms. Finebean three chances, as seen in figure 13.25, makes it harder to get to that ultimate goal.

This script ends the game when Ms. Finebean runs out of lives because she has landed on three kindergarteners:

On no! Ms. Finebean is about to land on the student, but she's using her last life.

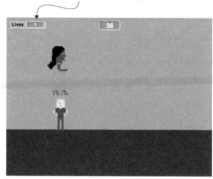

Figure 13.25   Ms. Finebean gets three chances to reach the door and escape.

1. Start with a When Flag Clicked (Events) block.

2. Add a Forever (Control) block underneath to start a loop.

3. Slide an If/Then (Control) block inside the Forever block to set a condition.

4. Put a Square = Square (Operators) block into the empty hexagonal space on the If/Then block. Place a Lives (Data) variable in the left square and type zero (0) in the right square.

5. Slide a Stop All (Control) block inside the If/Then block.

In figure 13.26, if the value of the Lives variable equals zero (0), all scripts stop.

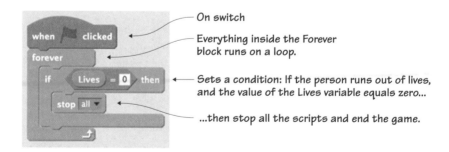

On switch

Everything inside the Forever block runs on a loop.

Sets a condition: If the person runs out of lives, and the value of the Lives variable equals zero...

...then stop all the scripts and end the game.

Figure 13.26   The completed game stopping script ends the game when you run out of chances.

Making a pause movement script

When Ms. Finebean runs up against a desk, she stops moving as if she has hit a solid object. But the kindergarteners keep coming, as in figure 13.27. This ruins the illusion that it's Ms. Finebean running across the Stage instead of moving in place while everything comes to her.

This script tells the kindergarteners to stop moving if Ms. Finebean is touching the side of the desk:

1 Start with a When I Receive Message1 (Events) block. Name this message Move Back using the New Message options from the drop-down menu. This script only runs if it receives the Move Back message that you'll broadcast when you write your desk scripts.

2 Add a Change X by 10 (Motion) block underneath. Change the number to 5. Because the kindergartener is normally moving 5 coordinates to the left (–5), you'll counter that with 5 coordinates to the right (5) to keep it in the same spot.

3 Snap a Change #ofKindergarteners by 1 (Data) block. Use the drop-down menu to choose scrollX and change the number to –1. Since scrollX increases by 1 each time, you're countering it by changing it by –1 to keep the scrollX value in the same place.

Figure 13.28 shows the completed touching desk script.

The desk stops moving toward Ms. Finebean when she touches the side, but the kindergarteners need to stop moving, too.

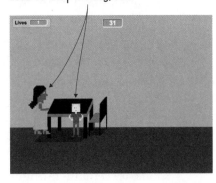

Figure 13.27 **This script troubleshoots a potential problem of having kindergarteners continue to move even when Ms. Finebean is up against the desk.**

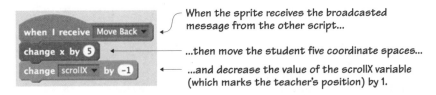

When the sprite receives the broadcasted message from the other script...

...then move the student five coordinate spaces...

...and decrease the value of the scrollX variable (which marks the teacher's position) by 1.

Figure 13.28 **The completed pause movement script keeps the kindergarteners from moving.**

Programming the desks

Super Mario Bros has brick walls that Mario can walk on to get over the Goombas below. School Escape has desks. Ms. Finebean can jump up on the desks and use them to launch herself over the kindergarteners. The desks have three scripts: a list adding script, cloning script, and movement script—all similar to the kindergarteners. Keep the blue box around the desk for all three scripts in this section.

Making a list adding script

Like the Kindergarteners list, you want the original list of desk positions to remain untouched so you can play this game over and over again. This script will generate a second copy of the Desk Positions list by importing the items into the second list, as seen in figure 13.29.

This script enables you to play round after round of the game because the original list will always be intact and other scripts will delete values from the duplicate list:

Figure 13.29   Scratch will delete values from the list copy rather than the original list.

1 Start with a When Flag Clicked (Events) block.

2 Go to Data and create a new variable called #ofDesks. You will use this variable to refer to an item on the list. When the value of #ofDesks is 1, it will be looking at the first value on the list. Uncheck the variable.

3 Click Make a List and make a new list called Desk Positions2. This will be your list copy of the original Desk Positions list. You can uncheck this new list.

4 Snap a Set #ofDesks to 0 (Data) block under the When Flag Clicked block. Change the value to 1 so this variable will line up with the first item on the Desk Positions2 list.

5 Slide a Delete 1 of Desk Positions2 (Data) block under the Set #ofDesks to 1 block and use the drop-down menu to change the 1 to All. This will remove the values from the Desk Positions2 list while keeping the identical, original Desk Positions list intact.

6 Grab a Repeat 10 (Control) block and add it to the chain of blocks. Change the number to 14 because you have 14 items on your list.

7 Place an Add Thing to Desk Positions2 (Data) block inside the Repeat 14 block. Next, slide an Item 1 of Desk Positions2 block inside the space that says *Thing* on the Add Thing to Desk Positions2 block.

8 Slip a #ofDesks (Data) variable into the number bubble on the Item 1 of Desk Positions2 block. Now you need to tackle the drop-down menus. Change the line so it reads: Add Item #ofDesks of Desk Positions to Desk Positions2.

9 Drag a Change #ofDesks by 1 (Data) block underneath that long block, inside the Repeat 14 block.

This time there will be 14 loops, one for each item on the original list. The script in figure 13.30 operates in the exact same way as the list adding script for the kindergarteners.

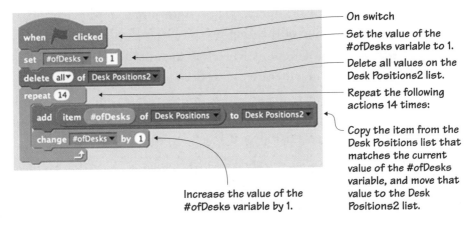

Figure 13.30 The completed list adding script keeps the original list intact while creating a second version that will be used during the game.

Making a cloning script

The desk continues to operate like the kindergarteners, spawning— as seen in figure 13.31—whenever the value of scrollX matches one of the items on the Desk Positions2 list.

If the value of scrollX is 190, and a value on the Desk Positions2 list is 190, a desk will spawn on the Stage.

Figure 13.31 Exactly like the Kindergarteners list, the game compares the value of scrollX with the items on the list and spawns a sprite when the two numbers match.

To make the cloning script

1 Start with a When Flag Clicked (Events) block.

2 Snap a Hide (Looks) block underneath the starter block.

3 Place a Forever (Control) block next to form a loop.

4 Slide an If/Then (Control) block inside the Forever block to set a condition.

5 Put a Square = Square (Operators) block inside the empty hexagonal space on the If/Then block. In the left square, place a scrollX (Data) variable block. In the right square, place an Item 1 of Desk Positions2 (Data) block. The condition is if the value of scrollX equals the value of the item on the Desk Positions2 list.

6 Add a Create Clone of Myself (Control) block next (inside the If/Then block) to generate the desk.

7 Place a Delete 1 of Desk Positions2 (Data) block to complete that chain, which removes each individual value from the Kindergartener2 list after it has been used.

The script in figure 13.32 is a little shorter than the kindergartener cloning script because there's only one desk, whereas there are four possible students who can show up on the Stage.

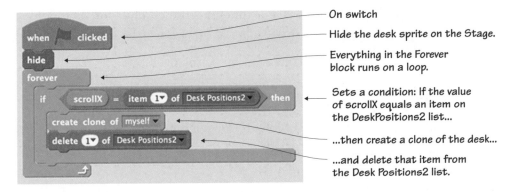

On switch

Hide the desk sprite on the Stage.

Everything in the Forever block runs on a loop.

Sets a condition: If the value of scrollX equals an item on the DeskPositions2 list...

...then create a clone of the desk...

...and delete that item from the Desk Positions2 list.

Figure 13.32 *The completed cloning script puts a desk in Ms. Finebean's path.*

ANSWER THIS   WHY DO YOU NEED TO DELETE ITEMS FROM THE LIST?

Question: it makes sense to create a clone of the list in order to make the game playable again and again, but why do you also need to delete the values from the duplicate list?

Answer: if you don't delete the values, every time a person plays the game, it will generate a new list, growing it from 14 items to 28 items to 42 items until later players are dealing with hundreds of desks at a time! By deleting values, you're not only playing the current game but you're setting up another game to be able to begin after the current game is done.

Making a movement script

Like the kindergarteners, the desks will also move toward Ms. Finebean, starting near the right side of the Stage and moving toward the left. Desks, like the one in figure 13.33, will also create the illusion that it's Ms. Finebean running to the desks rather than the other way around.

This script will make the desk move, plus it will tell Scratch what

The desk moves toward Ms. Finebean, but it looks like it's Ms. Finebean who is running toward the desk.

Figure 13.33 *The desk moves toward Ms. Finebean when the right arrow is pressed.*

should happen if the desk is *not* touching the teacher but *is* touching the side of the Stage, or if the teacher is up against the side of the desk:

1 Start with a When I Start as a Clone (Control) block.

2 Snap a Show (Looks) block underneath to make the sprite visible on the Stage.

3 Add a Forever (Control) block to form a loop.

4 Stack three If/Then (Control) blocks inside the Forever block to set three conditions.

5 Add a Key Space Pressed (Sensing) block to the empty space on the first If/Then block. Change the option to Right Arrow using the drop-down menu.

6 Put a Change X by 10 (Motion) block inside the first If/Then block. Change the number to –5 because you want the desk to move 5 coordinates to the left.

7 Add a Hexagon and Hexagon (Operators) block to the empty space on the second If/Then block. Place a Not (Operators) block in the left hexagon. Put a Touching Mouse-Pointer (Sensing) block into both of the currently empty hexagons. Change the first option to Teacher using the drop-down menu. Change the second option to Edge using the drop-down menu.

8 Place a Delete This Clone (Control) block inside the second If/Then block to remove the sprite when it reaches the far left side of the Stage as long as the teacher isn't currently standing on top of the desk.

9 Add a Touching Color (Sensing) block to the empty space on the third If/Then block. Change the color to the shade you used for the teacher's dress. You now have three possible conditions.

10 Place a Change X by 10 (Motion) block inside the third If/Then block. Change the number to 5. Remember, the desk is currently moving five coordinates to the left, so this will move it five coordinates to the right and keep it in the same place.

11 Add a Broadcast Move Back (Events) block underneath the motion block while still inside the third If/Then block.

The completed movement script in figure 13.34 states what will happen if the right arrow is pressed (the desk moves to the left), if the desk reaches the edge of the Stage as long as the teacher isn't currently on top of the desk (the desk disappears), or if the teacher is standing against the desk (stop moving and send a message to the other script).

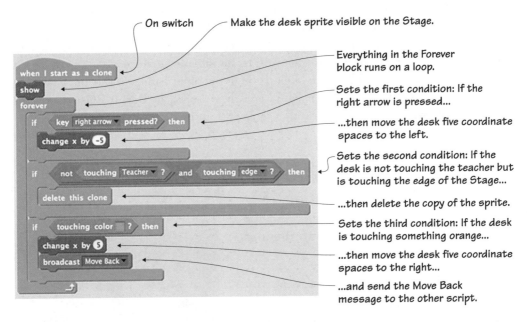

Figure 13.34   The completed movement script makes it look as if Ms. Finebean is moving toward the desk when it's the desk moving toward Ms. Finebean!

Programming the clocks

The clocks are the power-ups in your game—the collectable sprites that make the player character better able to tackle the obstacles in the game. In this case, the clocks add 10 additional seconds onto the timer, buying the player more time to reach the door. The clocks have four scripts: a cloning script, timer script, movement script, and pause movement script. Place the blue box around the clock sprite in the Sprite Zone and keep it there for all four scripts.

LEARN IT   POWER-UPS   The first power-up came in the game *Pac-Man*. The little yellow guy travels around the board eating up the dots and trying to avoid the ghosts. But in all four corners of the board are white circles that make Pac-Man invincible for a few seconds when he gobbles one of the power-up pellets. He can travel through ghosts and eat them instead of the other way around. Power-ups are items in a game that give the player a super ability, add time on a clock, or restore health. These items are usually collectable, like the mushrooms that cause Mario to grow or the flowers that give him firepower. Some can be used indefinitely through multiple levels of the game, and others expire after a set amount of time. Think about ways to work power-ups into your games to make the games more exciting. In fact, a fun exercise would be to go back through the older games in this book and see if there are power-ups you could add, like a shell in Beach Blast that gives Buffy the ability to run through crabs without being pinched.

Making a cloning script

Like the kindergarteners and desks, the clocks in figure 13.35 need to pop up at the correct time so Ms. Finebean can grab them as she runs down the hall.

Unlike obstacles or platforms, you want the appearance of power-ups to be special. You'll make it a rare occurrence by programming that fact into the script. This script contains a cool new block: the mod block.

The clock is School Escape's power-up, adding seconds onto the timer whenever Ms. Finebean grabs one off the wall.

Figure 13.35   The clocks add seconds on to the timer.

The mod block divides the two numbers you give it and prints out the remainder. In the script below, you will give it the current value of scrollX (which is always changing) and divide it by 100. Scratch will do that math problem on the fly and determine the remainder. You're going to use that remainder to set a condition: when the remainder equals zero, something will happen. If the math problem yields any remainder other than zero, nothing will happen:

1. Start with a When Flag Clicked (Events) block.

2. Slide a Hide (Looks) block underneath so the sprite is invisible on the Stage.

3. Snap a Forever (Control) block next to start a loop.

4. Add a Go to X/Y (Motion) block inside the Forever block. Even if your values are different slightly from the ones in figure 13.36, you don't need to change the values because they should be automatically set for where you originally dragged the clock on the Stage.

5. Place an If/Then (Control) block under the Go to X/Y block (still inside the Forever block), and then place another If/Then (Control) block inside the first If/Then block.

6. Slide a Square = Square (Operators) block into the empty hexagonal space on the outer If/Then block. Put a Circle Mod Circle (Operators) block into the left square. Type 0 (zero) in the right square. But wait! You need to fill the mod block. Place a scrollX variable (Data) in the left circle and type 100 in the right circle. The condition is if the value of scrollX is divided by 100 and yields no remainder.

7. Place a Square = Square (Operators) block in the empty hexagonal space of the inner If/Then block. Add a Pick Random 1 to 10 (Operators) block in the left square and type 1 in the right square. If the first condition is true, this second condition kicks in: a random number between 1 and 10 is chosen, and if that number matches 1, something happens.

8. Slide a Create Clone of Myself (Control) block inside the inner If/Then block. Add a Wait 1 Secs (Control) block underneath it (still inside the same If/Then block). Change the number to 2 to give a slightly longer delay.

If the first and second conditions are both true, the clock will spawn on the wall. This means that it will be a rare, random occurrence because the two conditions in figure 13.36 need to line up for this event to happen.

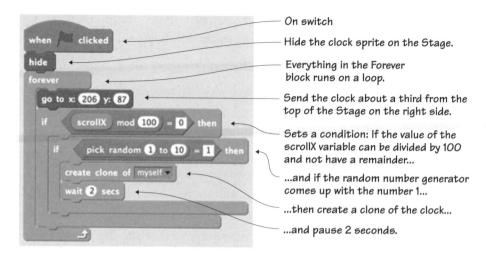

On switch

Hide the clock sprite on the Stage.

Everything in the Forever block runs on a loop.

Send the clock about a third from the top of the Stage on the right side.

Sets a condition: If the value of the scrollX variable can be divided by 100 and not have a remainder...

...and if the random number generator comes up with the number 1...

...then create a clone of the clock...

...and pause 2 seconds.

Figure 13.36   The completed cloning script places a clock on the screen at a random moment.

Making a timer script

Currently Ms. Finebean can run forever, which means that if she can get her jumps right, she will always reach the door. You can make the game harder by giving her a limited amount of time by placing a timer on the screen, like the one in figure 13.37, that counts down how many seconds she has to reach the door or have the game end.

The timer counts down how many seconds Ms. Finebean has to reach the door. The game ends when the time runs out, even if Ms. Finebean still has lives left.

Figure 13.37   The counter at the top of the screen allows the player to know how much time they have left.

To make the timer script

1 Start with a When Flag Clicked (Events) block.

2 Go to Data and make a new variable. Name it Timer. Drag the box to the top center of the Stage and right-click (or Control-click) it, choosing the large readout. Drag a Set Timer to 0 (Data)

block and snap it under the When Flag Clicked block. Change the number to 90 to give the player 90 seconds.

3 Add a Repeat Until (Control) block. Place a Square < Square (Operators) block in the empty hexagonal space. Put a Timer variable (Data) in the left square. Type a zero (0) in the right square. The actions you place inside this block will repeat until the value of the Timer variable is less than 0.

4 Put a Change Timer by 1 (Data) block inside the Repeat Until block. Change the number to –1 to deduct a number each time.

5 Slide a Wait 1 Secs (Control) block under the Change Timer by –1 block (still inside the Repeat Until block). For the first time, the Wait 1 Secs block isn't providing a delay to troubleshoot a possible glitch. You want the timer amount to go down one number every second. This time-based block is serving as an actual timer in this script.

6 Place a Stop All (Control) block at the bottom of the script, underneath the Repeat Until block. This means that all scripts will stop and the game will end when the value of the Timer variable is less than zero (0).

Check your script against the one in figure 13.38.

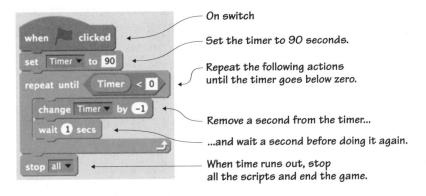

Figure 13.38   **The completed timer script places a time obstacle into the game.**

Creating a movement script

Like the kindergarteners and desks, the clock needs to move toward the teacher (as it is doing in figure 13.39), though it will look as though the teacher is running toward the clock.

This script is similar to the one you used for the kindergarteners, and it will move the clock as well as tell Scratch what should happen when the clock reaches the edge of the Stage or if the teacher touches the clock:

The clock starts on the far right side of the Stage, but this script will make it move toward Ms. Finebean, even though it will look as though it's the teacher running to the clock.

Figure 13.39   The movement script makes the clock move toward Ms. Finebean.

1 Start with a When I Start as a Clone (Control) block.

2 Snap a Show (Looks) block underneath to make the sprite visible on the Stage.

3 Add a Forever (Control) block to form a loop.

4 Stack three If/Then (Control) blocks inside the Forever block to set three conditions.

5 Add a Key Space Pressed (Sensing) block to the empty space on the first If/Then block. Change the option to Right Arrow using the drop-down menu. Add a Touching Mouse-Pointer (Sensing) block to the empty space on the second If/Then block. Change the option to Edge using the drop-down menu. Add a Touching Mouse-Pointer (Sensing) block to the empty space on the third If/Then block. Change the option to Teacher using the drop-down menu. You again have three possible conditions.

6 Put a Change X by 10 (Motion) block inside the first If/Then block. Change the number to –5 because you want the clock to move 5 coordinates to the left.

7 Place a Delete This Clone (Control) block inside the second If/Then block to remove the sprite when it reaches the far left side of the Stage.

8 Place a Change Timer by 1 (Data) block inside the third If/Then block. Change the number to 10 because you want to add 10 seconds each time the teacher grabs the clock.

9 Add a Delete This Clone (Control) block underneath the Change Timer by 10 block inside the third If/Then block.

The completed movement script in figure 13.40 states what will happen if the right arrow is pressed (the clock will move to the left), the clock reaches the end of the Stage (it will disappear), or if the teacher touches the clock (the timer will add 10 seconds, and the sprite will disappear).

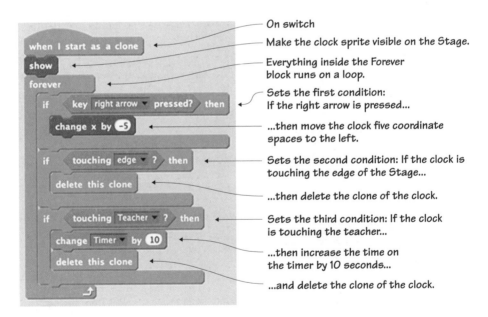

Figure 13.40   The completed movement script sets up three possible conditions for the clock.

Making a pause movement script

The clock will keep coming toward Ms. Finebean as long as the right arrow is pressed, but there's one situation when you don't want the clock to keep moving: when Ms. Finebean is leaning against a desk, as in figure 13.41.

This script stops the clock from moving when this situation happens so you can keep up the illusion that it is Ms. Finebean who is running forward rather than reality—all the objects are coming toward Ms. Finebean:

You want the clock to stop moving (even if the right arrow is pressed) when Ms. Finebean isn't moving because she is up against the desk.

Figure 13.41   The clock needs to stop moving when Ms. Finebean is against the desk.

1 Start with a When I Receive Move Back (Events) block. This script only runs if it receives the Move Back message that you broadcasted from the desk script.

2 Add a Change X by 10 (Motion) block underneath. Change the number to 5. Because the clock is normally moving 5 coordinates to the left (–5), you'll counter that with 5 coordinates to the right (5) to keep it in the same spot.

Figure 13.42 shows the whole script.

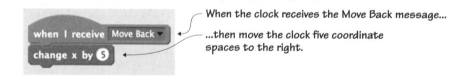

When the clock receives the Move Back message...

...then move the clock five coordinate spaces to the right.

Figure 13.42   The completed pause movement script stops the clock from moving.

Programming the door

The door is like the flagpole and castle at the end of each level of *Super Mario Bros.* It's the exit into the next level, though in this case, it's the end point for the game. There are two scripts that power the door: a cloning script and a game stopping script. Keep the blue box around the door sprite in the Sprite Zone for both scripts.

Making a cloning script

Like the kindergarteners, desks, and clocks, the door needs to appear at a certain time. The door in figure 13.43 signals the end of the game.

This script will tell Scratch to put the door on the screen at a certain time:

1. Start with a When Flag Clicked (Events) block.

2. Snap a Go to X/Y (Motion) block underneath the starter block. Don't worry if your values are slightly different. The block will show where you placed your door when you were setting up the Stage.

The door appears when the value of the scrollX variable equals 1,420.

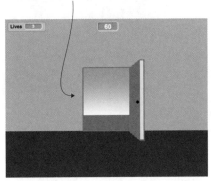

Figure 13.43   The door appears after Ms. Finebean has "run" the equivalent of 1,420 coordinates.

3. Add a Hide (Looks) block next to make the door invisible for the time being.

4. Place a Forever (Control) block at the bottom of the chain to create a loop.

5. Slide an If/Then (Control) block inside the Forever block to set a condition. Place a Square = Square (Operators) block inside the empty hexagonal space. Put the scrollX variable (Data) in the left square. Type 1420 in the right square. When the value of the scrollX variable equals 1420, something will happen.

6. Put a Create Clone of Myself (Control) block inside the If/Then block. This means the door will spawn when the scrollX variable reaches a value of 1420.

Check your work against figure 13.44.

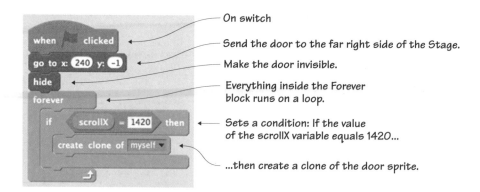

On switch

Send the door to the far right side of the Stage.

Make the door invisible.

Everything inside the Forever block runs on a loop.

Sets a condition: If the value of the scrollX variable equals 1420...

...then create a clone of the door sprite.

Figure 13.44   The completed cloning script tells the door when it should appear on the screen.

Creating a game stopping script

There are three ways for the game to end: run out of lives, run out of time, or reach the door, as in figure 13.45.

This script moves the door toward Ms. Finebean, but it also states what will happen when the teacher walks through the door.

The game ends when Ms. Finebean reaches the door and walks outside.

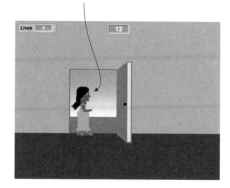

Figure 13.45   Ms. Finebean walks through the door and ends the game.

1   Start with a When I Start as a Clone (Control) block.

2   Snap a Show (Looks) block underneath to make the sprite visible on the Stage.

3   Add a Forever (Control) block to form a loop.

4   Stack two If/Then (Control) blocks inside the Forever block to set two conditions.

5   Add a Key Space Pressed (Sensing) block to the empty space on the first If/Then block. Change the option to Right Arrow using the drop-down menu. Add a Touching Mouse-Pointer (Sensing) block

to the empty space on the second If/Then block. Change the option to Teacher using the drop-down menu.

6 Put a Change X by 10 (Motion) block inside the first If/Then block. Change the number to –5 because you want the door to move 5 coordinates to the left.

7 Place a Stop All (Control) block inside the second If/Then block to end the game.

That's it! The last script in figure 13.46 officially ends the game.

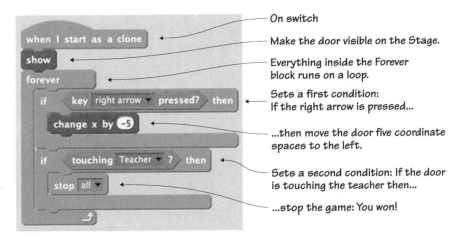

Figure 13.46   The game stopping script ends the game when the teacher reaches the door.

Troubleshooting the game

Try playing your version of School Escape. Ours worked perfectly on the first try, but you may run into some bugs with your game. Whenever you run into bugs, first check that your sprites are centered. Open each sprite in the Art Editor and center it using the tool in the top right corner of the canvas.

Next, make sure the teacher is on the top layer. She should be on the top layer because you coded it into the game, but it can't hurt to click the teacher on the Stage and move her a tiny bit to ensure she is the top sprite.

Learning in action

There are many variables in this game, including a few that create the illusion of movement by counting upward as the right arrow is pressed and using that value to stand in place of an X-coordinate. But there are also lists, which are similar to variables in the sense that they are tracking information, though in the case of lists, there are multiple items. Lists (also known as arrays) are an important part of programming—not only in Scratch but in every form of coding, from storing your friends list on a social media site to tracking a character's inventory in a game.

Play with the code

Single-screen platformers are already pretty complicated, but you can still kick it up a notch by trying out some of these challenges.

CHALLENGE The lists contain 30 (Kindergarteners) or 14 (Desk Positions) items. You can add more items to the list so that students or desks spawn more frequently. You can also lengthen the game by adding to the end of the list, though make sure you also tweak the value that spawns the door or the player will exit the game before they reach the later items.

CHALLENGE Play with the timer and the clocks, not only rewarding or removing different time amounts, but also creating other reasons to deduct time. If Ms. Finebean stands on a desk, should it remove a few seconds? If she jumps over a kindergartener, should it add a second back on the timer?

CHALLENGE Add new obstacles. What if she has to jump over lunch boxes or book bags? Use the code in the game to tweak it for additional sprites.

CHALLENGE What if the door leads to the next level just as the flagpole in Super Mario takes the player to another screen? How could you design multiple single-screen platformers to hook together into one game?

What did you learn?

Before you return to helping Ms. Finebean get to her brother's wedding, take a moment to reflect on which common computer science ideas from chapter 3 were used in this game:

- Using an on switch for every script in the game, including using receiver hat blocks to kick into gear when they get a broadcasted message
- Setting X- and Y-coordinates to make it look as if Ms. Finebean is moving toward the sprites
- Writing If/Then conditional statements to make things happen if Ms. Finebean is against the desk
- Creating loops to have a timer tick down
- Using variables to help you bring items from the original list to the duplicate list
- Creating Booleans with the mod block to have an action occur only if two conditions are true
- Cloning to create all the obstacles, platforms, and power-ups in the game
- Broadcasting messages to stop sprite movement whenever Ms. Finebean is against the desk

Another game that uses eight out of eight common programming ideas! Additionally, in School Escape you learned

- How to use lists to make the kindergarteners and desks spawn at the right moment
- How to use the mod block to add even more randomness into your game
- How to add a timer into a game
- How to simulate movement without having a sprite move

After you enjoy a few more rounds of jumping over kindergarteners, allow Ms. Finebean to get to her wedding and turn the page.

Congratulations! You are officially a game maker with five games under your belt. But wait! What if you want a little more practice before you finish off this book? Once again, we created a set of extra practice chapters that push these eight core coding concepts a little farther. In the racing game Mermaid Splash, you'll make the sprite's arms look as if they're swimming as she moves through the water, dodging jellyfish and turtles.

If you're reading the print version, this extra practice can be downloaded at the Manning site, or you can register your book and download a free e-book version that contains the extra practice. If you're reading the e-book version, this extra practice is at the back of the book.

But you may be ready to move on. You have internalized eight core concepts of computer science and can probably recite them in your sleep. The final chapter will help you take a leap into the Scratch community, design new games, and maybe even turn your eye to other coding languages.

14

Becoming a game maker

When you started this book, you were a Scratch novice. But look at you! You have five games under your belt, and you probably have dozens of ideas churning in your brain. You've also learned some of the basic building blocks of computer science, such as conditional statements, variables, loops, and Booleans, which means you're ready to branch out into other coding languages, too.

Now that you're officially a game maker, you're ready to dive into the greater Scratch community. This chapter will help you get your bearings as you set off to design your own games.

Sharing your work

Right now, you're the only person who can see your games. But you can push them live on Scratch and allow other people to find them and play them.

How to share your projects

Sharing your project means that it's visible to all Scratchers. They can play your game, remix your project (more on that below), and leave you comments. Sharing means you can send your friends and family a link to your game online.

There are two ways to share a project. If you're on the Inside Project view (where you've been making sprites and writing scripts) as in figure 14.1, the grey Share button is in the top right corner next to the blue See Project Page button. When you click the Share button, the screen automatically changes to the Project Page screen. If you accidentally share a project before you're ready, click your name at the top of the screen and go to the My Stuff menu. You'll see an unshare option listed with every shared project.

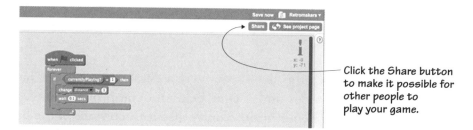

Click the Share button to make it possible for other people to play your game.

Figure 14.1   The Share button is in the top right corner of the Inside Project screen.

If you're on the Project Page screen, as in figure 14.2, the Share button is also in the top right corner. Clicking this button will push your game live, and the peach-colored bar across the top of the screen will turn green and show the words *Your project is now shared*.

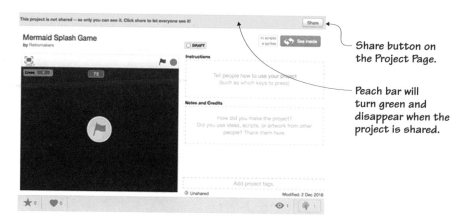

Share button on the Project Page.

Peach bar will turn green and disappear when the project is shared.

Figure 14.2   The Share button is also in the top right corner on the Project Page view.

Once shared, you can add a description of your game under Instructions (see figure 14.3). For instance, this is a good space for writing directions for playing the game, including the keys used for moving the sprites. There is additional space for Notes and Credits where you can tell players any stories behind the making of your game.

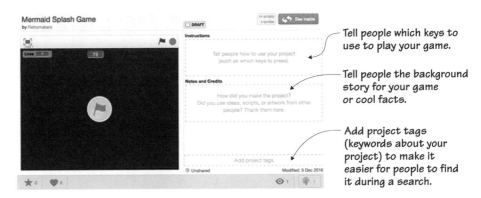

Figure 14.3   Add instructions, notes, and project tags on the Project Page screen for the game.

Finally, there are project tags that you can add to your project to make it easier for people to find your game (see figure 14.3). Think of project tags like hashtags on social media sites. People can use the search bar at the top of the Scratch page to look for their favorite things, like Harry Potter, bunnies, or retro games. Think of some keywords that apply to your game.

How to become a Scratcher

Everyone gets New Scratcher status when they first start out. This means that there are some limits put on your account for the first two weeks. Once you've published two projects and participated in some of the social aspects of Scratch, such as leaving comments or favoriting projects, you get bumped up to full Scratcher status. You don't need to do anything special to get this new status. The Scratch team will notify you when they've noticed that you've met their requirements for becoming a full Scratcher.

Once you receive a notification email of your full Scratcher status, you'll be able to build games with cloud data. *Cloud data* is an advanced programming feature that allows you to store variables on the server. For instance, you could keep track of high scores for everyone who plays your game. Or you could make a game that asks people to vote for their favorite sprite and use cloud data to store the vote. Full Scratchers only have a 60-second (as opposed to a 120-second) delay when posting comments or questions in the forum.

How to follow Scratchers

Following other Scratchers is a big part of learning new tricks and becoming a better programmer. Once you find a game you like, it's time to follow that Scratcher so you'll be able to see all of their future projects. Go to their profile by clicking their hyperlinked name under the game's title, as seen in figure 14.4.

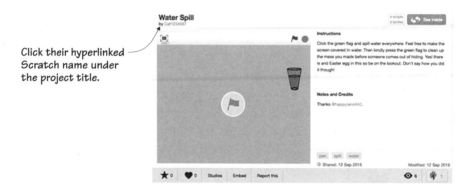

Click their hyperlinked Scratch name under the project title.

Figure 14.4   The hyperlinked name under the title will take you to the user's profile page.

When you're on their profile page, you'll see the Follow button in figure 14.5. Click that button and you'll see the button turn grey and now read Unfollow, which means you've successfully followed the person. Don't click it again (unless you want to unfollow them).

Figure 14.5   Click the Follow button to link your accounts together.

Any accounts you follow will be listed on your profile page. This means that you'll not only be able to find those games again, but the front page of Scratch will show you the user's new projects as they go live.

How to write comments

Once you start finding games you like, it's time to leave a few comments. Coderdojo, the free computer programming club that started in Ireland before spreading across the world, has a single rule for club members: be cool. This two-word rule applies to Scratch, too. It's not only easy to remember, but it will guide you in writing good comments.

Before you leave a comment, think about how you would feel if someone left those words on your project. Compliment people on their hard work whenever possible, and if you're offering feedback, make sure it's constructive and not hurtful. There are no private postings on Scratch, so your identity is always tied to your words. Think before you speak and you'll become a valuable member of the community. See table 14.1 for some suggestions.

Table 14.1   Uncool and cool comments for Scratch

Uncool comments	Cool comments
Your game is terrible!	Wow, this was a really hard game.
Your game doesn't work! It's junk!	I noticed the control keys are glitching. Can you check on your code and make sure you've added a delay?
This game is stupid!	This is an interesting concept.

How to create or join a studio

Once you start following people, you may notice that some people belong to studios. *Studios* are collections of projects, and you can think of them like a digital club whose members all want to make projects around the same idea, such as Harry Potter, bunnies, or retro games.

If you see a studio you want to join, leave a request under the comment tab shown in figure 14.6. Some studios will allow you to add projects without being a curator for the studio. Those studios have an Add Projects button at the top of the Projects tab. Our studio is called Hello Scratch Arcade. You can add your projects because it's an open studio, and meet other readers online.

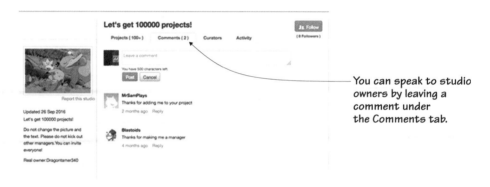

You can speak to studio owners by leaving a comment under the Comments tab.

Figure 14.6   Join a studio to find other people making projects similar to your projects.

You can also start your own studio. To create a studio, go to My Stuff and click the New Studio button, as in figure 14.7.

Start a new studio and invite others to join you.

Figure 14.7   Click the New Studio button to start a studio.

This will take you to the screen shown in figure 14.8. You can name the studio and write a description for your online club. You can decide whether you want anyone to be able to add a project or whether you only want group members (curators) to add projects. On the Curators tab, you'll find a button to invite other Scratchers you know to join your studio. You will need to know their username or, if you're already following them, their account will be listed as a choice you can select for sending invitations.

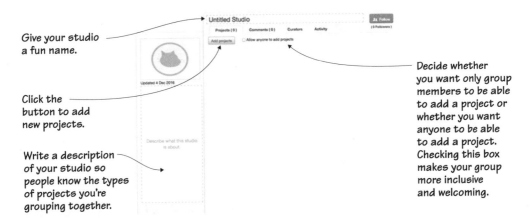

Give your studio a fun name.

Click the button to add new projects.

Write a description of your studio so people know the types of projects you're grouping together.

Decide whether you want only group members to be able to add a project or whether you want anyone to be able to add a project. Checking this box makes your group more inclusive and welcoming.

Figure 14.8   Make your own studio if you want to start your own online club.

The benefit of studios is that you can get more people to find your projects because often a studio is a collection of projects all on the same topic. That makes it easy for players to find similar games.

Remixing projects

An important part of the Scratch community is remixing projects. *Remixing* allows you to learn by not only seeing another person's code but being able to play with it to see how small changes can make a big difference in the game. It's against the spirit of Scratch to ask others *not* to remix your projects.

How to remix someone else's project

To remix someone else's project, go to the Inside Project view and navigate to the orange Remix button, shown in figure 14.9 in the top right corner.

Click the orange Remix button to make your own copy of the project.

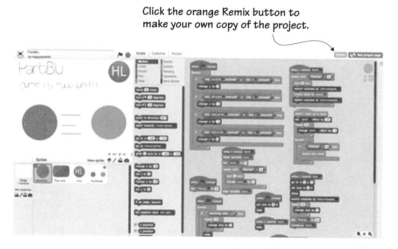

Figure 14.9   The Remix button on other people's projects lets you tweak their code.

Now play with the code and see what happens. What features can you add to their game? What changes can you make to learn how the blocks work together?

When you share your remix, give credit (on the project Notes and Credits section) and thanks to the original poster, explaining the changes you made. This not only helps other people learn from your changes, but it may even spark an idea for the original poster.

By the way, you *do* need to change something before you publish your project. If you publish someone else's project without making any changes, the remix may be reported and removed.

How to use your remix tree

You can also see how other people have changed *your* work. From the Project Page screen, navigate to the tree icon near the bottom right side of the screen (see figure 14.10).

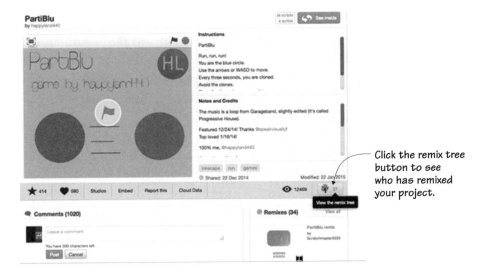

Click the remix tree button to see who has remixed your project.

Figure 14.10   Click the tree to see remixes of your projects.

This will take you to the remix tree, shown in figure 14.11. The main project is on the trunk, and each remix is a branch. Remixes of remixes are smaller branches off of the branches. Click any of the projects to see how your project was remixed.

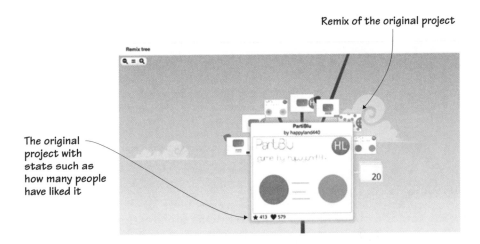

Remix of the original project

The original project with stats such as how many people have liked it

Figure 14.11   The remix tree helps you see how other people have changed the project.

Using the forums

You can leave us questions and comments on the Manning forum, but Scratch additionally has its own set of forums, and both forums are a great place to meet other Scratchers, get quick answers to questions, and talk about things that interest like-minded Scratchers.

How to read the forums

To read the Scratch forums, go to the blue tab at the top of the Project Page screen (or the opening screen of Scratch) and click Discuss. This will take you to the forums seen in figure 14.12. Click a subforum on the list, such as Help With Scripts, Show and Tell, or Project ideas, and then select a topic under the subforum. You can scroll down and read through the posts. Doing so can help you to know what is possible on Scratch.

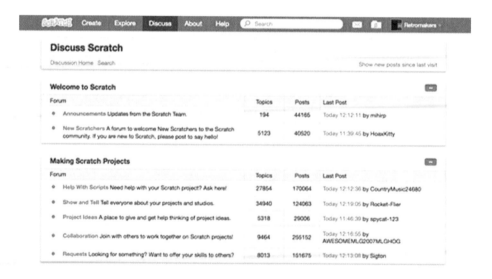

Figure 14.12   The forums are a great place to read questions and answers about Scratch.

How to post on the forums

You don't have to wait to jump into a conversation: everyone is welcome to join in. If you have a question, place it in the correct subforum. Just click the New Topic button (see Figure 14.13) to start a new thread.

Once you're in the correct subforum, click the
New Topic button to start a new conversation.

Discussion Forums » **Help With Scripts** 🔖

Help With Scripts

« previous 1 2 3 4 ... 1112 1113 1114 1115 next »

New topic

Topic	Replies	Views	Last Post
🔖 Sticky: List of Helpful Topics for Scripting by Paddle2See (New Posts)	628	52928	Today 12:20:35 by MM20160101
🔖 Sticky: [scratchblocks] OFFICIAL testing topic by Paddle2See (New Posts)	693	6709	Yesterday 07:40:28 by Eastereggs-BFDI
🔖 Sticky: >>>>>>>>>>IF YOU NEED HELP READ THIS<<<<<<<<<< by MathlyCat (New Posts)	57	4655	July 2, 2016 14:19:56 by MathlyCat
🔖 Sticky: How to make a better project. by dsaztur (New Posts)	162	23915	Oct. 17, 2014 18:12:28 by SzAmmi
● I'm new to scratch by leiabird (New Posts)	30	294	Today 12:10:19 by leiabird
● How to make notes and credits box bigger by Rxjxy (New Posts)	0	3	Today 12:02:06 by Rxjxy
● How to make a sprite fall faster over time? by OriginalName1 (New Posts)	9	63	Today 11:57:20 by eeyenicky

Figure 14.13   Start a new thread if you want to ask a question.

If you have an answer, give the person advice by leaving a comment under *their* thread. If you're a new Scratcher, you need to wait 120 seconds between publishing each comment. Full Scratchers only have a 60-second delay. This stops people from spamming the forums.

Jumping to other languages

This is a book about Scratch, but it's interesting to see how blocks in Scratch translate into other coding languages such as JavaScript, Python, or Ruby. When you start comparing languages, you see how much Scratch prepares you to become a professional coder down the road.

For instance, conditional statements exist in many computer languages. In Scratch, conditionals are set using one of the If/Then block options. The yellow blocks contain an empty hexagonal space where you set the condition, usually with the help of an Operator or Sensing block. Finally, after setting the condition, you slip the actions you want to occur inside the If/Then block.

In JavaScript, though it's written without a yellow block, it still follows the same general idea. For instance, this is what it would look like if you wanted to set up a condition where the game would show the message "You win!" on the screen when a score of 7 is reached, as in figure 14.14.

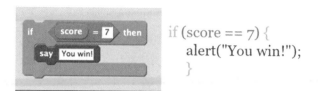

```javascript
if (score == 7) {
    alert("You win!");
}
```

Figure 14.14   Scratch on the left, JavaScript on the right

The If/Then block in Scratch begins with an *if*, and the code written in JavaScript begins with this word to start a conditional, too. It then contains the condition: if the score is equal to 7. Think of whatever appears in those parentheses as the equivalent to the empty hexagonal space in the If/Then block. It's the condition that needs to be true in order for the action to happen. That action is slipped inside the If/Then block in Scratch, but it appears inside the curly brackets in JavaScript. This conditional statement will run the words "You win!" if the condition is met.

It's not important to learn JavaScript (or Python or Ruby) to use Scratch, but you can see how Scratch is preparing you for other languages down the road.

Diving into game making

This is it! You're officially ready to design your own games. You have all the tools you need to make something fantastic, and if you ever get stuck, turn back to an earlier game and scavenge a bit of code—such as a movement script or the falling velocity script—to make part of your game.

You may want to start carrying around a programmer's journal—a place to jot down game ideas and sketch out future sprites. Having this tool with you at all times ensures that your good ideas don't get away. Who knows? You may become the next Atari, Intellivision, or Nintendo. (Or, more recently, the next Mojang or Activision.) Everyone needs to start somewhere, and you have definitely gotten started.

We can't wait to encounter your games as we're traveling through Scratch. Welcome to the game-making Scratch community.

Appendix

Scratch quick start guide

What it's called	What it looks like	Where it is	What it does
Scratch logo	SCRATCH	Grey Toolbar	Brings you back to the homepage
Duplicator tool		Grey Toolbar	Makes a copy of the sprite
Delete tool		Grey Toolbar	Removes a sprite
Grow tool		Grey Toolbar	Enlarges a sprite
Shrink tool		Grey Toolbar	Shrinks a sprite
New sprite	New sprite:	Sprite Zone	Paintbrush icon opens the Art Editor for a sprite
New backdrop	Stage 1 backdrop	Sprite Zone	Opens the Art Editor for a backdrop
Paintbrush tool		Art Editor	Makes dots and allows you to freehand draw

What it's called	What it looks like	Where it is	What it does
Line tool	\	Art Editor	Makes lines
Square tool	▬	Art Editor	Draws a square or rectangle
Circle tool	●	Art Editor	Draws a circle
Text tool	T	Art Editor	Adds words to the sprite
Paint Bucket tool	◆	Art Editor	Fills a contained area with color
Eraser tool	▱	Art Editor	Removes or erases parts of the drawing
Select tool	⌐🖐	Art Editor	Outlines a section of the drawing
Duplicate tool	⬇	Art Editor	Makes a copy of the selected section of the drawing
Zoom	🔍 = 🔍 100%	Color Toolbar	Makes the canvas larger or smaller
Line width	—— ─○──	Color Toolbar	Changes the thickness of the dot or line

Index